THE FOREST

Smoking

IN LONDON

Cycles
Cycles must not be left chained
or unattended on Railtrack
property. Any cycle so found
will be removed without war
Cycles must be left in the
cycles racks provided at
rear of Boots
In wet weather conditi
exercise care as th
and platforms bec
No Smoking
on Liverpool Stree
Fire precaution (Subsurface Railway

Liverpool Street station.

THE FOREST GUIDE TO
Smoking
IN LONDON

Promoting equal rights for smokers

Edited by James Leavey

Quiller Press
London

THANKS!

The Editor would like to thank the many organisations and people who have given their time, help, information and support, including:
BBC, British Airports Authority, British Rail, CAMRA, Daily Express, London Tourist Board, London Transport, Royal Institute of British Architects, Skoob Books, Madame Tussauds, House of Commons press office, Guy Smith, Desmond Sautter, Alfred Dunhill Ltd, Frank Dickens, Jerome Leavey, Justin Quillinan, Beverley Legge, Francesca Leavey, Tim Best, Christine Green, Jane Jones, Peterson of Dublin, Bob Barknay, Edward Sahakarian at Davidoff, Ray Bulman, Jon Franklin, Bill Williamson at Midweek magazine, Simon Chase at Hunters & Frankau, and Philip Shervington.

If you notice any mistakes or omissions please let me know, so that we can put them right for the next edition.

Many thanks.

City smoker.

Jan Olofsson was one of Sweden's first rock stars (known in the late Fifties as Rock-Ola) before he went to Hamburg, met the Beatles and came to London to work as a photographer in the Swinging Sixties. A selection of his photos of pop icons (Jimi Hendrix, Johnny Cash, the Beatles, Rolling Stones etc) was published by Taschen as *My Sixties*. He also produced for his own company, Young Blood Records, several hit records in the Seventies including one of Rod Stewart's early hits, *In a Broken Dream*, and the classic football anthem, *Nice One Cyril*.

James Leavey left BT in 1990 after a decade in international marketing and PR and has since written for a growing list of publications including the *European*, *Daily Express*, the *Independent*, *Daily Mirror*, *Radio Times* and *ES* magazine. He has also broadcast on BBC Radio 4's *Breakaway*, *Going Places* and *Pick of the Week* and worked as a stagehand with the English National Opera, been a West End cinema doorman, a coconut ice maker and trained as an actor and teacher. In 1995, he edited *Taylors Corporate Northern Ireland*, the first major independent business guide to the province and now edits *The Humidor*, a cigar newsletter published by JJ Fox (St James's) Ltd.

Tower Bridge, from Butlers Warf.

Copyright © FOREST 1996
First published 1996 by Quiller Press Ltd, 46 Lillie Road, London SW6 1TN

ISBN 1 899163 29 8

Designed by Jo Lee
Photographs by Jan Olofsson
Printed by Biddles Ltd

CONTENTS

FOREWORD

by Auberon Waugh

This volume may well be the world's first travel guide for smokers, but then this is the first time in human history that such a guide has been needed. I hope it will be complemented before very long by a World Guide for Smokers, advising us which areas are best to avoid. The London guide should be brought up to date every year as restaurants, bars and other places of public haunts, change hands.

The terrible example before all our eyes must be what has happened in New York and Los Angeles.

As I shook the dust of Los Angeles off my feet for the last time recently, I was aware that on January 1st 1997 a total ban on smoking in bars, clubs and casinos would come into force. This will complement the existing ban on smoking in work places and restaurants. The anti-smoking fanatics, whether or not influenced by the hideous pall of evil-smelling smog caused in part by traffic pollution, in part by the hamburger gases which add many tons of meat fat to the atmosphere every day, have finally made Los Angeles unbearable.

No doubt greed for money will continue to attract Europeans to this unhealthy city, whose vast office buildings now stand as temples of oppression. But we may wonder how long the money will be here. The film industry centred around Hollywood is now the biggest single foreign currency earner in the United States. Its rubbish pours out to pollute non-American minds all over the world. But as more and more cinemas ban smoking, their profits fall by the essential margin for survival and the film industry may soon be dead.

London is less extreme in its application of the Great Lie about the dangers of passive smoking, but we must all remain vigilant. There can be no conceivable reason why privatised railway companies are even more reluctant to allow smoking carriages than the former nationalised industry, unless the demented attitudes of the nanny state have somehow communicated themselves to private business. Why should railway companies care whether their passengers who voluntarily choose to smoke in a carriage set aside for the purpose, might damage their health?

Those who die younger, rather than older, are doing a great service to their country, in the geriatric explosion which threatens to cripple the economy. Railway companies, in particular, make smaller profits from concessionary old age pensioner fares. What are they playing at?

A great development from the persecution has been the spirit of solidarity which has arisen among smokers. Long may it prosper. If we are prepared to abandon our freedom of choice in this matter, we might as well accept direction on what we eat, drink, wear, say and think. Let us hope this book strikes a blow against the new control terrorists.

Earls Court.

by James Leavey

A lady friend asked why we needed a smokers' guide to London as people seem to be lighting up in Britain's capital everywhere she looked, unlike some parts of the USA. Good question. At least she was polite. The day before, a virulent anti-smoker who I'd just met for the first time told me that the very idea of a smokers' guide was 'bloody disgusting' and asked me to put my cigar out. I politely declined as we were in a smoking area at the time, and suggested that intolerance was much more of a social evil than smoking and that he would have got on very well with Adolf Hitler, another ardent anti-smoking fascist. I sat back as he stormed off, enjoying the rest of my cigar, even more convinced that a smokers' guide was essential if we are to avoid confrontations like this.

The first thing I must make clear is that this book is for the adult smoker, someone who has made a personal decision to smoke. You won't find a list of branded tobacco in the following pages, or specific details of where to buy it. But then you can purchase tobacco at any time of the day or night in London, in its 24 hour shops and garages, if you're desperate.

What you will discover, for the first time ever, are some of the places in London where smokers are still welcome, and a little on our most famous smoker, Sherlock Holmes.

As to why we need a guide like this...

Well, just in case you've been hiding in a cellar for the past ten years or so and haven't noticed, smokers have been added to the black list of late 20th century pariahs, alongside paedophiles, rapists, drug pushers, tax collectors, traffic wardens, TV gameshow hosts and National Health Service managers.

It's enough to make Sir Walter Raleigh spin in his grave. Or for the non-smoker to breathe in with a sigh of relief.

> **"Nobody comes whose talk is half as good to me as silence. I fly out of the way of everybody, and would much rather smoke a pipe of wholesome tobacco than talk to any one in London just now. Nay, their talk is often rather an offence to me, and I murmur to myself Why open one's lips for such a purpose?" (Thomas Carlisle, 'The Witching Weed, A Smokers' Anthology', 1890)**

Smokers are the largest (15-16 million) minority group in the UK. Despite growing opposition by the anti-smoking lobby to what they claim is a filthy, unhealthy, anti-social habit, about 27 per cent of London's adult population continues to smoke. To do so, we've had to learn to live under a low-tar cloud and be prepared to withstand scornful stares and comments - often from complete strangers.

The trouble is London's smokers are increasingly treated as second-class citizens, or mobile pollution zones. We're banished from all buses, most planes, coaches and trains, London Underground, some taxis, the auditoriums of theatres, cinemas and concert halls, shops, museums and art galleries, a few restaurants, too many offices and a growing number of hotel rooms.

Up to now, London's smokers have tolerated what are in most cases unofficial and often unenforceable (at least in the eyes of the law) bans. Confronted with yet another 'no smoking' sign we meekly extinguish whatever we're enjoying - anything for a quiet life.

> **"Some sigh for this and that, My wishes don't go far, The world may wag at will, So I have my cigar..."**
> **(Thomas Hood, 'The Cigar')**

But does it ever occur to non-smokers, and our more rabid critics, that smokers have rights too? And that some of us are fed up with being classified as social outcasts?

Many of London's businesses have grown to cater for our love of tobacco, whether it's in the form of cigarettes, cigars and snuff, loose and hand-rolled, stuffed in a pipe, or collectables such as lighters, cigarette cards, matchboxes, humidors and cigar cutters. For them, the puffer's pound still rules. How much longer this will last, is anybody's guess. The final decision is up to smokers, who should have the right to choose what to do with their life.

Oh, and if you're a non-smoker, maybe this guide is also good news for you. At least you can see the places to avoid.

We had thought of printing this book on cigarette paper, so you could rip out the pages and roll your own smokes, but decided against it. However you use the guide, I hope it helps to light up your life.

This book would not be possible without the help and encouragement of many people and organisations, most of them already listed elsewhere. I would particularly like to thank Marjorie Nicholson, Judith Hatton, Juliet and Jules Wallbridge, Madeleine Wood, Richard Stirling, Sean Gabb, Tony Boyd and all my other friends at FOREST, Jan Olofsson, Jeremy Greenwood, Robert Emery at JJ Fox, and my patient wife, Gwenda. Last but not least, a special thank you to Auberon Waugh and Jeffrey Bernard.

Etiquette of Smoking

Some people feel they can smoke anywhere and may prefer not to read on. But they can't, so you should.

Rightly or wrongly, public opinion tends to be on the side of the anti-smokers, despite their frequent lack of good manners. Which means we have to be twice as polite.

Old-fashioned courtesy is an essential quality for today's smoker, whether it's in a public place or seated at a private dinner. If you're looking for tolerance remember consideration works both ways. Every smoker is an ambassador for tobacco.

LITTER

There are still too many thoughtless smokers who ruin everything for the rest of us. It is not acceptable to discard matches, empty fag packets, cellophane, cigarette and cigar stubs, leaving a mess for other people to fume about. Even worse and all too common, there are still careless smokers who throw lit cigarettes out of car windows while driving.

Wherever you are in London you should watch your smoke, avoid creating litter, and be careful with your ashes. And never light up in 'no smoking' areas, unless you want to make a formal political statement in front of witnesses.

Although we don't like to encourage the habit of dropping cigarette butts in the street, we must admit that it can be reassuring to a smoker to see a number of them in say, a doorway, or on a railway platform. At least you know you're among friends. Just don't let your dog-ends join the pile under your feet.

If you can't take your smoker's litter with you, do at least ensure that it's fully extinguished before you discard it in a litter bin or ash tray, or drop it in the nearest gutter to be swept away.

EATING OUT

It's best to check with the restaurant if you can smoke there, or not. If not, look for somewhere else to eat - London now has one of the best and widest selection of restaurants in the world, and most of them are still smoker-friendly. Though how long they will remain so is another story.

If you are just wandering in off the street and you can't see a 'no smoking' sign, it's best to look through the windows first, to see if there are ashtrays

Passing a light in Brixton

on the tables, or if any diners are smoking. When you enter, try to sit next to a table where someone is already smoking, so if anyone starts a fuss there are two of you to deal with.

One of London's best known film critics, who is usually a sensible chap, recently boasted in print that he spits in the food of smokers at restaurants if they have the temerity to smoke near him while he is eating. If you are on the receiving end of such extreme and crass behaviour don't be tempted to pour the contents of your plate or glass over his head. Call the manager, or police, and refuse to pay the bill. Let them sort it out.

Tobacco smoke can spoil the taste of good food and wine for some people, so heavy smokers who light up during meals run the risk of causing offence. You should always ask permission of your host and other diners at your table, first. If the restaurant is cramped, also ask diners on nearby tables as an unexpected noseful of smoke may lead to unnecessary confrontation.

Going out of your way to upset non-smokers, such as blowing clouds of smoke in their direction, or trying to set fire to their hair and clothing, isn't acceptable either - at any time, no matter how tempting, or how much you have been provoked.

> "A fugitive Mafia convict gave his hideout away after police spotted his pile of cigarette butts outside his window... Police said Votano, 30, gave himself away by throwing hundreds of cigarette ends from a tiny window of his lair, which they said was otherwise virtually invisible from the street..." (Leicester Mercury, 6 July 1996).

If you have lit up on a smoking table and somebody complains, tell them to speak to the manager. In these cases, it should be the non-smoker who moves, not you. Of course, a bit of courtesy can go a long way. If someone asks you very nicely, especially if they're on their hands and knees, you could always do the decent thing and refrain from lighting up. It's your choice.

The smoking of cigars (and pipes, if they're allowed, which is becoming rarer every day) is best left until everyone on the table has finished eating, unless you're attending a cigar dinner, or among friends who really don't mind - although you should be aware that some people may be too polite to mention it.

Yes, we know there's no law that says you can't light up at any time, if you wish. Still, a good smoke is worth waiting for as it finishes off a meal, nicely.

Do wait until the host has given the signal before you light up a cigar, and make sure there's an ashtray handy to discard the match and ashes. It's polite to offer cigars from an open humidor or box to fellow smokers, and allow them to select. It really doesn't do to hint that the larger sizes are just for your own personal pleasure. You should only offer cigars if you can afford to give them away. Otherwise, don't bother.

As for the lucky recipient, it's downright rude to closely inspect your host's selection of cigars then decline and smoke one of your own. Take what's offered, try to enjoy it, and don't elucidate your criticisms. It is, however, perfectly acceptable for the husband, wife or friend of an absent cigar lover to ask if they can take a cigar on their behalf.

The act of sharing is one of the nicest things that smokers do. It's a good way to make friends.

DRINKING

Very few of London's pubs and bars have non-smoking areas. If the one you're supping in does, honour it. Do try not to blow smoke into fellow drinkers' faces (whether they smoke, or not) as this is very rude and in some countries could lead to blows. Remember at all times that smokers should tolerate the non-smoker, as well as vice-versa.

PARTY MANNERS

There are those who will not permit any smoking in their home. It is their prerogative but of course their smoking guests may consider this anti-social. It is very unkind to confront a heavy smoker in your home with the fact that he or she will have to suffer a smoke-free evening. Better to warn your guests when you invite them, so they can decide whether or not to turn down your invitation.

There are some hosts who don't like smoking but permit their guests to do so. Hosts are no longer obliged to provide cigarettes for guests (although we would argue that thoughtful people who can afford to do so will always keep spare tobacco for their friends and acquaintances) but should have a sufficient number of ashtrays, preferably too many rather than too few. All ashtrays should be emptied regularly, rather than left to overflow. And always ensure your stub is out, not still burning away.

Some hosts may even politely ask smoking guests to wait until after dinner, where they can go to a separate room or be ushered out of doors (in the

> **The Priestess of the Oracle at Delphi is said to have uttered her prophesies while drunk on the vapours that issued from a cleft in the rocks beneath her feet.**

Ashtray's in Gent's toilet, Embankment.

nicest possible way, and only in good weather) for a communal smoke. The polite guest will accept this suggestion, gracefully.

If this is your first visit and you've had no warning, look for the ashtrays, as this will give you some indication of whether you can light up, or not. Even if there are none it may be all right to light up but first you must ask permission. It's also polite to carry a little tin or, in smart company, a portable ashtray, in case the response to your request is: 'Oh, yes, of course, but I don't know if we've got an ashtray.' You can then reply: 'I've got one of my own!'

There's nothing to stop you carrying a small canister of air freshener (Neutradol is particularly effective, doesn't smell like a tart's boudoir and one squirt obliterates most known smells). This is also useful if the place you're visiting reeks of other things, which is all too often in these days of central heating, double-glazing and odd diets.

A non-smoker who allows you to light up in their home is doing you the biggest favour - they've got to live with the fumes long after you've gone. So be polite and don't take advantage of other people's generosity.

Most caring smokers go out into the garden or just outside the front door, or smoke next to an open window exhaling through it, out of courtesy. However, if your host is downright unpleasant and tells you not to smoke anywhere near the house, never mind inside it, the best response is to say nothing at all. Whether you return for a second visit, or not, is entirely up to you.

> **"Some live life as a poem. Others as a sentence."**
> **(Zino Davidoff, 'A Renaissance of Pleasure')**

If your host starts lecturing you on the subject of smoking you are permitted to use what has been defined as the rudest word in the English language: 'Really!'

Naturally, there's no reason why you shouldn't argue back, provided you remain calm, rational and can simply explain your point of view. If they still go on, it's probably best to make your apologies and leave at the first opportunity.

HOTELS

Always check when booking to ensure you are given a smoking room. If they change this at the last moment, without warning, either go to another hotel or ask for a refund or discount.

Fortunately, most of London's hotel rooms are still smoker-friendly, so the problem shouldn't occur too often. This may change in the next year or so which is another good reason for smokers to vote with their feet. Hotels, like restaurants and pubs, can't afford to turn business away and the puffer's pound still rules. Whatever you do, don't set fire to the bed.

TOILETS

It has to be said that some men have the disgusting habit of using discarded cigarette ends for target practice in public urinals. No, we won't explain the pros and cons, figure it out for yourself. And cigarettes have a nasty habit of swirling around in toilet bowls, remaining resolutely unflushed - so don't dump them there either.

Now there's nothing wrong with smoking in a toilet if you stub out the cigarette in an ashtray, but not if you discard it thoughtlessly, leaving it to some poor devil, who may also be a smoker, to clean the mess. So behave yourselves.

BUSINESS

Think before you smoke. Just because smoking is permitted in a business meeting, that does not give you the license to light up without asking permission of the most senior person present. If you're the chief executive of the company then we think you should do what you bloody well like - provided you also allow your employees the same privilege.

As for lighting up in offices or other work environments, this really depends on three factors: 1. safety (as in a factory or garage full of inflammable products), 2. hygiene (such as in food preparation areas, operating theatres and

Litter bins, Tobacco Dock.

THE ETIQUETTE OF SMOKING

doctor's surgeries) and, not least, 3. the prevailing wishes of co-workers, the majority of whom may prefer to work in a non-smoking environment.

Ideally, every business should set aside at least one smoking room or area for their employees if smoking restrictions are desired. The negative image of smokers forced to congregate outside buildings suggests that the people they work for don't take into consideration the needs of the entire workforce. And some of the world's most influential business people are also heavy smokers so do you really want to go out of your way to upset them?

One of the advantages of enforced communal smoking is that smokers are now forming impromptu networks, as everybody from the cleaner to the managing director can now meet, puffing in the doorway. So if you're forced outside, make the most of it. And always offer your colleagues, no matter what their status, a light, or a smoke, if you can spare it. Again, don't leave smokers' litter to carpet the company entrance as mountains of cigarette ends will only confirm to non-smokers what messy, undesirable people their smoking colleagues are.

OPEN SPACES

London has experienced long dry summers for the last few years and the grass in its parks, commons, heaths, squares, allotments and gardens has been tinder dry. Never discard a lit match, cigarette or cigar. The last thing we want is for smokers to be seen as a fire risk. Also, discarded tobacco litter is unsightly and spoils the view.

FINALLY

At all times you should try to avoid stoking the fuel of anti-smokers' hostility. It's really not worth it as most of them won't listen to reason, anyway. Hold your tongue, keep your temper and remember that you can always relax with a smoke. They can't.

> **Roget's Thesaurus lists the following variations of tobacco: nicotine, the weed, filthy weed, snuff, rappee, maccaboy, plug of tobacco, quid, fid, twist, flake, shag, cigar, cheroot, smoke, cigarette, coffin-nail, reefer, joint, tobacco pipe, churchwarden, briar, meerschaum, hubble-bubble, hookah, narghile, pipe of peace, calumet, smoker, tobacconist, snuff box, cigarette case, humidor, smokeroom, smoking compartment. So what happened to butt, gasper, cough and a drag, oily rag or stogie?**

4

TRAVEL

Airports

> I wish I could light up in a plane
> On a bus or a boat or a train
> But the PC bandidos
> Won't let me smoke weedos
> In my neck they give me a pain.
> (James Leavey)

In this day and age of smoking bans on flights, smokers need to know where they can have that last fag before taking to the skies, and the first one upon reaching the safety of terra firma.

Of the five airports serving London some exhibit greater degrees of smoker-friendliness than others. Terminals 1 and 4 at Heathrow are the most smoker-friendly to departing travellers, followed by Gatwick's South Terminal and Stansted, all of which make provision for smokers in the final departure lounge.

For those arriving in the UK, you are best advised to avoid Luton. Smoking is not allowed until you have collected your baggage, and passed through the customs check. You can, however, smoke in a toilet if you can find one!

DUTY FREE ALLOWANCES

The EC countries are: Austria, Belgium, Denmark, Finland, France, Germany, Greece, the Irish Republic, Italy, Luxembourg, the Netherlands, Portugal, Spain (but not the Canary Islands), Sweden, the UK (but not the Channel Islands).

DUTY FREE GOODS YOU BUY IN THE EC

Each time you travel to or from another EC country, you are entitled to buy 200 cigarettes; or 100 cigarillos; or 50 cigars; or 250 grms of tobacco from the duty free shop. The same applies for travellers arriving from outside the EC. If you try to import more than the above limits in duty free tobacco products you could find yourself forced to pay the excess duty and even prosecuted.

Under EC law, duty-free and tax-free shops cannot sell you more than these quantities each time you travel to another EC country. But you can buy them on each journey you make and bring them back to the UK as long as they are for your personal use.

DUTY PAID GOODS YOU BUY IN THE EC

You do not have to pay any more duty or tax on goods you have bought in ordinary shops within the EC for your personal use if you have already paid duty and tax on them. Personal use includes gifts, but it is an offence to sell duty-free or duty-paid goods that you have bought for personal use. If you are caught, the goods will be seized and you could get up to seven years in prison.

EC law sets out guidance levels. If you bring in more than these levels, you must be able to show, if you are asked, that the goods are for your personal use. If you can't, the goods may be seized. The guidance levels on tobacco goods bought in the EC for your personal use are: 800 cigarettes; or 400 cigarillos; or 200 cigars; or 1 kg smoking tobacco.

Heathrow | **Hounslow, Middlesex (0181 759 4321)**
Terminal 1 | **Departures** - *Check-in*: Designated smoking area. *Waiting areas*: Designated smoking areas. *Restaurants, bars, etc*: Designated smoking areas. All shops are non-smoking. *Departure lounge*: Designated smoking areas. *Walkways to piers/gates*: Smoking prohibited. *Piers/gates*: Designated smoking areas in gates 4, 5, 8, 38 and 48.

Arrivals - *Arrival lounge*: Smoking prohibited. *Walkways to Passport Control*: Smoking prohibited. *Luggage reclaim*: Designated smoking area. *Customs*: Smoking prohibited. *Toilets (Departures & Arrivals)*: Smoking prohibited. NB: Additional no smoking signs and free-standing smoking area signs to be installed.

Terminal 2 | **Departures** - *Check-in*: Designated smoking area. *Waiting areas*: Designated

Left: Entrance to Heathrow Airport. Right: Spotted a smoker inside!

smoking area on main concourse. *Restaurants, bars, etc*: Designated smoking areas. All shops are non-smoking. *Departure lounge*: Designated smoking area. *Walkways to piers/gates*: Smoking prohibited. *Piers/gates*: Smoking prohibited. **Arrivals** - *Arrival lounge*: Designated smoking area on main concourse. *Walkways to Passport Control*: Smoking prohibited. *Luggage reclaim*: Smoking prohibited. *Customs*: Smoking prohibited. *Other areas*: Smoking prohibited. *Toilets (Departures & Arrivals)*: Smoking prohibited. NB: Smoking areas are signposted. All other areas are non-smoking, some of which are signed.

Terminal 3 **Departures** - *Check-in*: Smoking prohibited. *Waiting areas*: Two designated smoking areas on first floor. *Restaurants, bars, etc*: Designated smoking areas. All shops are non-smoking. *Departure lounge*: Designated smoking areas. *Walkways to piers/gates*: Smoking prohibited. *Piers/gates*: Smoking prohibited. **Arrivals** - *Arrival lounge*: Designated smoking area on ground and first floors. *Walkways to Passport Control*: Smoking prohibited. *Luggage reclaim*: Smoking prohibited. *Customs*: Smoking prohibited. *Toilets (Departures & Arrivals)*: Smoking prohibited.

Terminal 4 **Departures** - *Check-in*: Designated smoking areas. *Waiting areas*: Designated smoking areas. *Restaurants, bars, etc*: Designated smoking areas in most catering outlets. Costas has no restrictions. *Departure lounge*: Designated smoking areas. *Walkways to piers/gates*: Smoking prohibited. *Piers/gates*: Designated smoking areas. **Arrivals** - *Arrival lounge*: Designated smoking areas on the concourse. *Walkways to Passport Control*: Smoking prohibited. *Luggage reclaim*: Smoking prohibited. *Customs*: Smoking prohibited. *Toilets (Departures & Arrivals)*: Smoking prohibited. NB: Smoking area signage is currently under review to ensure it is clear.ly understood.

Gatwick **Gatwick, West Sussex (01293 535353).**
Departures - *Check-in*: North Terminal - smoking area at entrance to check-in hall. South Terminal - smoking prohibited. *Waiting areas*: North and South Terminals have designated smoking areas. *Restaurants, bars, etc*: North and South Terminals have designated smoking areas within most individual facilities, except McDonald's which prohibits smoking, and within the general retail shopping area. *Departure lounge*: North and South Terminals have designated smoking areas. *Walkways to piers/gates*: Smoking prohibited. *Piers/gates*: North Terminal - typically prohibits smoking, South Terminal - 50% of gates/piers have designated smoking areas nearby.
Arrivals - *Arrival lounge*: North Terminal - smoking prohibited, South Terminal - designated smoking areas in some pier areas. *Walkways to Passport Control/ Immigration*: Smoking prohibited. *Luggage reclaim*: Smoking prohibited but there are designated smoking areas in the Buffer lounges prior to luggage reclaim. *Customs*: Smoking prohibited. *Other areas*: There are designated smoking areas in the Landside Arrivals areas. *Toilets*: Smoking prohibited.

London City **Silvertown, E16 (0171 474 5555).**

Departures - Check-in: Not prohibited. Ashtrays situated within area. *Waiting areas*: Not prohibited. Ashtrays situated within area. *Restaurants, bars, etc*: Generally one quarter to one third of each facility is available to smokers. *Departure lounge*: Approximately one quarter of the area is designated for smoking. *Walkways to piers/gates*: Smoking prohibited. *Piers/gates*: Smoking prohibited. *Arrivals - Arrival lounge*: Smoking prohibited. *Walkways to Passport Control*: Smoking prohibited. *Luggage reclaim*: Smoking not prohibited. *Customs*: Smoking prohibited. *Other areas*: Smoking allowed once in terminal building. *Toilets (departures & arrivals)*: Smoking not prohibited. NB: Areas where smoking is prohibited are indicated by signs. Designated smoking areas are indicated by signs and ashtrays.

Stansted **Stansted, Essex (01279 680500).**

Departures - Check-in: Two designated smoking areas. *Waiting areas*: Designated smoking areas. *Restaurants, bars, etc*: All offer designated smoking areas. *Departure lounge*: Domestic departure lounge has one designated smoking area, International departure lounge has two designated smoking areas. *Walkways to gates*: Smoking prohibited. *Gates*: Designated smoking area adjacent to each gate.

Arrivals - Arrivals concourse: Domestic and International arrivals concourses have designated smoking areas. *Walkways to Passport Control*: Smoking prohibited. *Luggage reclaim*: Domestic luggage reclaim has a small designated smoking area. International luggage reclaim has two designated smoking areas. *Customs*: Smoking prohibited. *Other areas*: Domestic arrivals - designated smoking areas available in landside area. International arrivals - large designated smoking area immediately after Customs. *Toilets (departures & arrivals)*: Smoking prohibited. NB: By October 1996 there will be signs on entry to all major waiting areas indicating the nearest smoking area.

London Luton **Luton, Bedfordshire (01582 405100).**

Departures - Check-in: Smoking prohibited. *Waiting areas*: Smoking prohibited. *Restaurants, bars, etc*: Designated smoking areas. *Departure lounge*: Designated smoking area. *Walkways to piers/gates*: Smoking prohibited. *Piers/gates*: Smoking prohibited.

Arrivals - Arrival lounge: Smoking prohibited. *Walkways to Passport Control*: Smoking prohibited. *Luggage reclaim*: Smoking prohibited. *Customs*: Smoking prohibited. *Other areas*: Designated smoking areas in catering and bar areas. *Toilets (departures & arrivals)*: Smoking not prohibited. NB: Non-smoking areas are well sign-posted and there are tannoy messages reminding people not to smoke. Although designated smoking areas are not particularly well sign-posted, staff are usually available to give directions.

The Thames and London's canals

London has over 40 miles of canal towpaths and umpteen miles of Embankment to walk along; a fine place for a smoke on a warm day or cool evening. Over the centuries the capital's smokers used to throw their clay pipes into the river after they'd finished with them. You can still find bits and pieces of the pipes washed up on the Thames's shores when the tide is out, but do be careful.

Most of the river and canal craft allow smoking, usually on deck in the open air.

THAMES RIVERBOATS

Catamaran Cruises

Charing Cross Pier and Victoria Embankment, WC2 (0171 987 1185). Embankment tube or Charing Cross tube/BR. Sightseeing between Charing Cross, Tower, Greenwich and the Thames Barrier. Sightseeing cruise every 30 mins, 1000-1700 hrs from Charing Cross Pier. Lunch cruise, 1215hrs from Temple Pier. Evening cruise, 1930hrs, from Temple Pier.

Smoking policy: Smoking allowed on the upper deck only.

City Cruises Cherry Garden Pier, Cherry Garden Street, Rotherhithe, SE16 (0171 237 5134). Rotherhithe tube. Modern fleet of luxury vessels with two spacious decks offering first class facilities and quality catering. Trip every 30 mins, 1000-1700 hrs, or on the hour, 1700-2100 hrs.

Smoking policy: No restrictions.

The London Showboat

Westminster Pier, SW1 (0171 237 5134). Westminster tube. Cruise from Westminster Pier to the Thames Barrier and back, with a "quality" four course meal, and cabaret. £39 per person. May to Sept cruises run Thur, Fri, Sat and Sun, leaving 1900 hrs and returning 2230 hrs.

Smoking policy: Smoking sections inside the boat. No restrictions on deck.

Red Fleet Office 5, Westminster Pier, Victoria Embankment, SW1 (0171 930 9033). Westminster/Tower Hill tube. Cruise past London's landmarks between Westminster and Tower Piers. Daily services all year round from Westminster and Tower Piers every 20-30 minutes from 1020 hrs.

Smoking policy: No restrictions on this open top boat.

Thames Leisure

Swan Pier, Swan Lane, London Bridge, EC4 (0171 623 1805). London Bridge tube/BR. Private hire for weddings, parties, corporate functions and a variety of other events. Ring for details.

Smoking policy: No restrictions.

Woolwich Ferry

New Ferry Approach, Woolwich, SE18. (0181 854 8888). Woolwich Arsenal BR. Free transport and foot passenger river ferry. Journey takes about three minutes. Times: Monday-Friday, 0600-2030 hrs. Saturdays, 0600 hrs from South Woolwich (closes at 19.40 hrs), or 0620 hrs from North Woolwich (closed at 2000 hrs). Sundays, 11.30-1930hrs.

Smoking policy: Foot passengers can smoke on the ferry, down below. You can do what you like inside your own vehicle.

CANALS

Jason's Trip Opposite 60 Blomfield Road, W9 (0171 286 3428). Warwick Avenue tube. Narrowboat cruise through Regent's Park to Camden Lock. The round trip lasts 90 minutes. Food is available but customers must pre order. Boats leave 1030, 1230 and 1430 hrs daily. 1630 hrs trip added at weekends.

Smoking policy: No restrictions.

The Jenny Wren

250 Camden High Street, NW1 (0171 485 4433). Camden Town tube. Sightseeing trip, Mar-Oct, Camden Lock to Little Venice and back by narrowboat. 90 minutes' round trip. Phone for details.

Smoking policy: Smoking allowed in this open-sided narrowboat.

My Fair Lady 250 Camden High Street, NW1 (0171 485 4433). Luxury/restaurant narrowboat cruise, Camden Lock to Little Venice and back. Open all year round. Lunch, 2 hour trip. Dinner, singer/guitarist, 3 hour trip. Phone for details.

Smoking policy: No restrictions.

London Waterbus Company

Camden Lock, NW1 and Little Venice, W2 (0171 482 2550). Narrowboat sightseeing tour from Camden Lock to Little Venice. The round trip lasts 110 minutes. Boats leave on the hour, 1000-1700 hrs, Apr-Oct (Nov-Mar weekends only).

Smoking policy: No restrictions.

The London Canal Museum

12/13 New Wharf Road, King's Cross, N1 (0171 713 0836). King's Cross/St Pancras tube/BR.

Smoking policy: Smoking prohibited.

Main railway stations

The trains may no longer puff and smoke but you can still light up in most of London's railway stations, although this may change in a year or so. There's some confusion at the top of the management chain so each station sets its own policy. Check the following list for details, otherwise if there isn't a 'no smoking' sign anywhere, light up until a member of the station staff tells you not to. NB: No smoking on escalators at any British Rail (BR) station.

Blackfriars Queen Victoria Street, EC4 (0171 928 5100).
Smoking policy: No restrictions on the concourse or platforms or in the ticket office. *Shopping*: Smoking not allowed in W H Smith.

Cannon Street
Cannon Street, EC4 (0171 928 5100).
Smoking policy: No restrictions on the concourse or platforms or in the ticket office or waiting rooms. *Food and drink*: No restrictions in Café Bar. *Shopping*: No restrictions in W H Smith.

Charing Cross
Strand and Cockspur Street, SW1 (0171 928 5100).
Smoking policy: Smoking not allowed on platforms or in public toilets. No restrictions on the concourse. *Food and drink*: Smoking not allowed in Burger King. No restrictions in Kent Tavern Bar. *Shopping*: Smoking not allowed in Sock Shop, Knickerbox or W H Smith.

Euston Eversholt Street, NW1 (0171 928 5100).
Smoking policy: Smoking not allowed in the ticket office, waiting room or customer reception. No restrictions on the concourse or platforms or in toilets. *Food and drink*: Smoking not allowed in the Croissant Shop, Quicksnack or Sweet Factory. No restrictions in Café Select. *Shopping*: Smoking not allowed in John Menzies, The Travel Centre, Tie Rack, The Tanning Shop, Boots, Sock Shop or Knickerbox.

Fenchurch Street
Fenchurch Street, EC3 (0171 928 5100).
Smoking policy: Smoking not allowed on concourses or in the ticket office. No restrictions on platforms. *Food and drink*: Smoking not allowed in Benny's Café. *Shopping*: Smoking not allowed in W H Smith.

No smoking on the Brighton line.

Gatwick Airport Station
Gatwick Airport (0171 928 5100).
Smoking policy: In covered areas, smoking is not allowed. However, this policy is under discussion. Meanwhile, where are the 'no smoking' signs?

King's Cross York Way, N1 (0171 928 5100).
Smoking policy: Smoking not allowed in the ticket office, waiting rooms or public toilets. No restrictions on the concourse or platforms. *Food and drink:* Smoking not allowed in Burger King. No restrictions in Café Select or Cooper's Pub. Half of Gingham's Café allocated to smokers. *Shopping:* Smoking not allowed in W H Smith.

King's Cross Thameslink
Pentonville Road/Saint Chad's Street, W1 (0171 928 5100).
Smoking policy: Smoking not permitted, anywhere.

Liverpool Street
Bishopsgate, EC2 (0171 928 5100).
Smoking policy: Smoking not permitted, anywhere.

London Bridge
Tooley Street/St Thomas's Street, SE1 (0171 928 5100).
Smoking policy: Smoking not allowed in the public toilets. No restrictions in the ticket office or waiting rooms or on the concourse or platforms. *Food and drink:* Smoking not allowed in Quicksnack. No restrictions in Oast House Pub, Garfunkel's or Costa Coffee. *Shopping:* Smoking not allowed in W H Smith, Whistlestop, Knicker box, Tie Rack, Sock Shop or Boots.

Marylebone Melcombe Street/Boston Place, NW1 (0171 928 5100).
Smoking policy: Smoking not allowed in the customer service centre. No restrictions in the ticket office, concourse or platforms. *Food and drink:* No restrictions in One Stop Shopper or Whistlestop Café. One third of BR Buffet Café allocated to smokers. *Shopping:* Smoking not allowed in W H Smith or Whistlestop.

Moorgate Moorfields, EC2 (0171 928 5100).
Smoking policy: No smoking anywhere, including the Thameslink and Northern Electric British Rail areas of the station, or Moorgate tube station.

Paddington Praed Street/Eastbourne Terrace, W2 (0171 928 5100).
Smoking policy: Smoking is not allowed in public toilets. No restrictions in the ticket office or waiting rooms, on the concourse or platforms. *Food and drink:* No restric-

tions in Gingham's Café or Cooper's Pub/Restaurant. *Shopping*: Smoking not allowed in Boots or John Menzies. No restrictions in the Off Licence.

St Pancras   St Pancras Street/Euston Road, W1 (0171 928 5100).
Smoking policy: No restrictions in the ticket office or public toilets, on the concourse or platforms. *Food and drink*: No restrictions in Shires Pub. Half of Coffee Shop allocated to smokers. *Shopping*: Smoking not allowed in Whistlestop. No restrictions in W H Smith.

Stratford   Station Street, E15 (0171 928 5100).
Smoking policy: Smoking not allowed on the concourse or in the ticket office as both of these areas are below ground. No restrictions in the waiting rooms or on the platforms. *Food and drink*: Smoking not allowed in Quicksnack.

Victoria   Buckingham Palace Road, SW1 (0171 928 5100).
Smoking policy: Smoking not allowed in the international ticket office, London Underground information office or tourist information centre. No restrictions on concourses or platforms. *Food and drink*: No smoking in Coffee Shop. No restrictions in Cooper's Pub or Victoria Tavern Pub. Half of Café Select allocated to smokers. *Shopping*: Smoking not allowed at the Bureau de Change in the station entrance or in Whistlestop, Our Price, Off Licence, Tie Rack, Sock Shop, Knickerbox, Boots or W H Smith. No restrictions in Bureau de Change on concourse.

> **"If I paid $10 for a cigar, first I'd make love to it, then I'd smoke it." (George Burns)**

Waterloo   York Road, SE1 (0171 928 5100).
Smoking policy: Smoking not allowed in public toilets. No restrictions in the ticket office or waiting rooms, on concourses or platforms. *Food and drink*: Smoking not allowed in Burger King. No restrictions in Balcony Bar or Bonapartes Bar. Half of Coffee Shop allocated to smokers. *Shopping*: Smoking not allowed in Our Price, Bags on Wheels, W H Smith or Paperchase. NB Smoking is not allowed on the bridge between Waterloo and Waterloo East stations.

Waterloo East
Waterloo Road, SE1 (0171 928 5100).
Smoking policy: No restrictions on platforms. *Food and drink*: No restrictions in Quicksnack or Cooper's Pub. *Shopping*: Smoking not allowed in W H Smith, Sock Shop or Knicker box.

Train services from London

The following information is the most definitive and up-to-date, although virtually all the railway companies we spoke to were unclear about where their passengers may, or may not, light up.

For smoking policies outside London it is best to check with the individual stations. Ask the ticket collector. Or better still, write and ask the railway companies what's going on.

0345 484950 is a new travel bureau information telephone number for nationwide rail enquiries. All calls to it will be charged at the local rate. Some companies may still be offering a local number (see below).

The 'other areas' information in the following list refers to the platforms, concourses, toilet facilities and waiting rooms of inter-route stations.

Anglia Railways Ltd

Customer Relations, Ipswich Station, Burrell Road, Ipswich, Suffolk IP2 8AL (01473 693383. Fare/Timetable Enquiries: 01473 693396/01603 765676/0345 484950). Main areas served: InterCity: Liverpool Street to Norwich, Harwich. Local: Norwich to Sheringham, Great Yarmouth, Lowestoft. Ipswich to Lowestoft, Felixstowe, Cambridge, Peterborough.

Smoking policy: Trains - Smoking allowed in designated areas and on selected routes. InterCity routes - Standard class has one smoking carriage (coach B, not near the buffet). First class has half a carriage (sic!) for smokers (coach K, near the buffet - there's also a food and drink trolley service if you're thirsty or hungry). Local routes - Two smoking carriages, one non-smoking carriage. Other areas - Smoking allowed on all platforms and concourses. Waiting rooms and toilets are non-smoking.

Central Trains Ltd

Customer Relations Manager, MP 533, P O Box 4323, Birmingham, West Midlands B1 1TH (0121 654 3833. Fare/Timetable Enquiries: 0345 484950). Main areas served: Local trains in a ten mile radius from Birmingham New Street, eg to Redditch, Malvern, Lichfield (connect from Euston by InterCity West Coast trains).

Smoking policy: Trains - No smoking. Other areas - Smoking allowed everywhere, except in Birmingham New Street station.

The Chiltern Railway Company

Customer Relations, 2nd Floor, Western House, 14 Richfords Hill, Aylesbury, Buckinghamshire HP20 2RX (01296 332113. Fare/Timetable Enquiries: 0990 165165). Main areas served: Marylebone to High Wycombe, Birmingham,

Amersham, Aylesbury.

Smoking policy: Trains - No smoking. Other areas: No restrictions.

CrossCountry Trains Ltd

Customer Relations, 3rd Floor West, Meridian, 35 Smallbrook Queensway, Birmingham, West Midlands B5 4HX (0121 654 7400. Fare/Timetable Enquiries: 0345 484950). Main areas served: Paddington (via Birmingham) to Scotland, North West, North East, Midlands, South West, South Coast.

Smoking policy: Trains - Smoking allowed in designated areas. Standard class has one smoking carriage (coach B). InterCity first class has half a carriage for smokers (coach H). Express trains are all non-smoking. Other areas - Platforms and concourses are non-smoking.

Eurostar

European Passenger Services, Customer Relations Department, Waterloo Station, EPS House, London SE1 8SE (0171 922 6071. Fare/Timetable Enquiries: 0345 881881). Main areas served: Waterloo, Ashford International (Kent) to Paris, Lille, Brussels, Calais-Frethum.

Smoking policy: Trains - Smoking allowed in designated areas. Standard class has two smoking and eight non-smoking carriages. First class has one smoking carriage and five non-smoking carriages. Smoking carriages are placed one-third and two-thirds down the train. Eurostar says it can accommodate special needs, ie increase smoking seats for a large number of smokers. Also, as no-one travels without a reservation, it is recommended that a smoking carriage is requested (subject to availability) when booking. Other areas - No smoking on Eurostar platforms and waiting areas, except for the waiting room in Paris and other mainland European cities. Ask, upon arrival.

> The Swiss once placed prohibition of tobacco among the Ten Commandments.

Gatwick Express Ltd

Customer Relations, The Plaza, Victoria Station, London SW1V 1JU (0171 922 9696/0990 301530. Fare/Timetable Enquiries: 0990 301530). Main areas served: Victoria to Gatwick non-stop.

Smoking policy: Trains - No smoking. Other areas - Smoking allowed on platforms and concourses.

Great Eastern Railways Ltd

Customer Relations Office, Hamilton House, 3 Appold Street, London EC2A 2AA (0171 922 4842. Fare/Timetable Enquiries: 01206 564777). Main areas served: Liverpool Street to Ipswich, Southend.

Smoking policy: Trains - No smoking. Other areas - No restrictions.

Liverpool Street Station.

Great Western Trains Operating Company

Customer Relations, Milford House, MH24, 1 Milford Street, Swindon, Wiltshire SN1 1HL (01793 49945. Fare/Timetable Enquiries: 0345 484950). Main areas served: Paddington to South West (Penzance, Taunton, Exeter), Avon (Bath, Bristol), South Wales (Cardiff), Cotswolds (Hereford, Worcester, Gloucester).

Smoking policy: Trains - Smoking allowed in designated areas. Standard class has one smoking carriage (coach B) and three or four non-smoking carriages. First class has half a carriage for smokers (coach H) and one-and-a-half non-smoking carriages. One smoking carriage is at the front, one at the rear of the train. Other areas - Smoking allowed on all stations except Birmingham New Street.

InterCity East Coast Ltd

Customer Relations, East Coast, Room M93, Main HQ, Station Road, York, North Yorkshire YO1 1HT (01904 522420. Fare/Timetable Enquiries: 0345 484950). Main areas served: King's Cross to Edinburgh, Inverness, Aberdeen, Glasgow, Leeds, Hull, Bradford, York, Newcastle.

Smoking policy: Trains - Smoking allowed in designated areas and on selected routes. Routes to Bradford, Hull, Inverness, Aberdeen (diesel trains) - standard class has one smoking carriage (coach B). First class has half a carriage for smokers (coach H). Other routes (electric 225 trains) - standard class has one smoking carriage (coach A). First class has half a carriage for smokers (coach M). One

"The train now standing on platform four..."

smoking carriage is at the front, one at the rear of the train. Other areas: Smoking allowed on most platforms and in some waiting rooms. No smoking in most toilet facilities and travel centres.

InterCity West Coast Ltd

Customer Relations, P O Box 713, Birmingham, West Midlands B1 1SR (0121 654 3210. Fare/Timetable Enquiries: 0345 484950). Main areas served: Euston to Preston, Manchester, Liverpool, West Midlands, North Wales, Carlisle, Glasgow.

Smoking policy: Trains - Smoking allowed in designated areas. Standard class has one smoking carriage (coach M). First class has one smoking carriage (coach A). One smoking carriage is placed at the front, one at the rear of the train. Other areas - Varies. Smoking is allowed on most platforms but not those below ground, e.g. Birmingham New Street. If there are two waiting rooms, one is smoking, one non-smoking. Toilet facilities are largely non-smoking.

London, Tilbury and South Rail Ltd

Customer Services, Central House, Upside Offices, Southend Central, Clifftown Road, Southend-on-Sea, Essex SS1 1AB (01702 357603. Fare/ Timetable Enquiries: 01702 611811/0345 484950). Main areas served: Fenchurch Street to Barking, Upminster, Purfleet, Canvey Island, Tilbury, Southend Central, Southend East, Shoeburyness.

Smoking policy: Trains - No smoking. Other areas - No restrictions outside at stations. All buildings, eg waiting rooms, are non-smoking.

Midland Main Line Ltd

Customer Relations, Room B109, Midland House, Nelson Street, Derby, Derbyshire DE1 2SA (01332 262010. Fare/Timetable Enquiries: 0345 484950). Main areas served: St Pancras to Luton, Bedford, Kettering, Milton Keynes, Wellingborough, Market Harborough, Leicester, Nottingham, Derby, Chesterfield, Sheffield, Doncaster, Loughborough, Westgate, Leeds.

Smoking policy: Trains - Smoking allowed in designated areas. Standard class has one smoking carriage and four non-smoking carriages. First class has half a carriage for smokers and one-and-a-half carriages for non-smokers. Neither smoking carriages are near the buffet coach. Other areas: No restrictions on platforms and concourses.

Network SouthCentral Ltd

Customer Relations, Floor 7, Stephenson House, 2 Cherry Orchard Road, Croydon, Surrey CR9 6JB (0181 667 2780. Fare/Timetable Enquiries: 01273 206755/0345 484950). Main areas served: Victoria, Charing Cross, Waterloo, London Bridge to Epsom, Dorking, Horsham, Gatwick Airport, Brighton, East Grinstead, Newhaven, Eastbourne, Hastings, Ashford International, Chichester, Portsmouth, Bournemouth.

Smoking policy: Trains - No smoking ("Network SouthCentral have a total non-smoking policy on all our trains"). Other areas - Smoking allowed on most platforms, but varies from one station to another.

North London Railways

Melton House, 65/67 Clarendon Road, Watford, Hertfordshire WD1 1DP (01923 207818. Fare/Timetable Enquiries: 0171 3877070/01923 245001/ 01908 370883/0345 484950). Main areas served: Euston via Watford, Milton Keynes to Birmingham. Richmond via Willesden Junction, Gospel Oak, Highbury & Islington to Woolwich, Gospel Oak to Barking, Willesden Junction to Clapham Junction. Bletchley to Bedford. Watford to St Albans.

Smoking policy: Trains - No smoking. Other areas - Platforms are non-smoking if owned by London Underground, or below ground. Most waiting rooms are non-smoking.

> If all the statisticians in the world were laid end to end they would not reach a conclusion, but it would be a great thing.

South Eastern Train Company

Passenger Liaison, CP43C Friarsbridge Court, 41-45 Blackfriars Road, London SE1 8NZ (0171 620 5555. Fare/Timetable Enquiries: 0345 484950). Main areas served: Victoria, Cannon Street, Blackfriars, London Bridge, Waterloo East, Charing Cross to Canterbury, Margate, Dover, Ashford, Hastings, East Sussex.

Smoking policy: Trains - No smoking. Other areas - Platforms are non-smoking if they're below ground. Waiting rooms and toilet facilities generally non-smoking.

South Wales and West Railway Ltd

Customer Services, Regional Railways, Western House, 1 Holbrook Way, Swindon, Wiltshire SN1 1BY (01793 515350. Fare/Timetable Enquiries: 0345 484950). Main areas served: Waterloo to Carmarthen, South Wales to Manchester, Liverpool, Birmingham, Brighton, Portsmouth, Penzance.

Smoking policy: Trains - Smoking allowed in designated areas and on selected routes. Inter-urban routes (class 158 trains, eg London to Carmarthen, Cardiff to Manchester) have one smoking carriage and one non-smoking carriage. All other routes (shorter journeys) are non-smoking. Other areas - Varies from station to station.

> **Victorian epithet:** Fill the bowl, you jolly soul,
> And burn all sorrow to a coal.

South West Trains

Customer Relations, 41-45 Blackfriars Road, London SE1 8NZ (0171 902 3732. Fare/Timetable Enquiries: 0345 484950). Main areas served: Waterloo to Richmond, Wimbledon, Clapham Junction, Woking, Guildford, Portsmouth, Exeter, Weymouth, Bournemouth.

Smoking policy: Trains - Smoking allowed in designated areas and on selected routes. For longer journeys, eg Waterloo to Woking and Guildford (although this varies according to number of carriages), standard class has ten percent of its seats allocated for smokers. First class has one smoking compartment of six seats and three or four non-smoking compartments. All smoking seats are near the buffet coach. Shorter journeys on local trains are completely non-smoking. No First class smoking seats available on journeys from Waterloo via Salisbury to Exeter. Other areas - No restrictions on platforms. Most waiting rooms are non-smoking but in larger stations where there are two, one waiting room is smoking, one is non-smoking.

Thames Trains Ltd

Customer Services, Venture House, 37-43 Blagrave Street, Reading, Berkshire RG1 1PZ (01734 579453. Fare/Timetable Enquiries: 0345 484950). Main areas served: Paddington to Hereford, Stratford-upon-Avon, Oxford, Worcester, Newbury, Bedwyn, Bicester. Reading to Basingstoke, Gatwick Airport.

Old train, new sign.

Smoking policy: Trains - No smoking. Other areas - No restrictions on most platforms. No smoking where station is below ground.

Thameslink Rail

Customer Relation, Floor 1, Friarsbridge Court, 41-45 Blackfriars Road, London SE1 8NZ (0171 620 5760. Fare/Timetable Enquiries: 0171 928 5100/0345 484950). Main areas served: Blackfriars, Farringdon, King's Cross Thameslink, City Thameslink, London Bridge to Bedford, St Albans, Brighton, Wimbledon.

Smoking policy: Trains - No smoking. Other areas - No restrictions on most platforms. No smoking in booking halls and most enclosed areas. No smoking in waiting rooms but if there are two, one is smoking, one non-smoking.

West Anglia Great Northern Railways Ltd

Customer Relations, Station Road, Canterbury, Kent CB1 2JW (01223 453613/0345 818919. Fare/Timetable Enquiries: 0345 484950). Main areas served: King's Cross, Liverpool Street, Moorgate to King's Lynn, Peterborough, Cambridge, Hertford North.

Smoking policy: Trains - No smoking. Other areas - No restrictions on platforms. Some waiting rooms and toilet facilities are non-smoking.

London Underground 'The Tube'

If you're on the underground platform at Waterloo or Piccadilly Circus and hear that famous recorded automated warning, "Mind the gap, please!" this is not a signal for you to fill yours, with a fag.

You can't smoke anywhere in London Underground, including the trains, platforms, booking halls, escalators or anywhere else. This includes those

No bloody trains again at Waterloo!

Left: News vendor, Right: Platform A, Southbound.

sections of the Tube when you leave the tunnels for the open air, including the open air platforms found at some stations.

The average travelling time between London's tube stations is two minutes so you can always get off and head for the exit, if you can't stand the strain any longer.

Relaxing on the Tube?

Buses & Coaches

Once upon a time you could smoke on the top deck of London's famous red buses and trams. Now there's a heavy fine for anybody who lights up anywhere on London's buses, so don't bother. What is particularly galling is that most of the drivers and remaining bus conductors still smoke on their vehicles during their rest periods.

You can smoke while you're waiting at the bus stop and in most of the bus stations. Some covered waiting areas are non-smoking, look for the signs.

Some coaches have become non-smoking so it is best to check when you're booking tickets, to save disappointment later.

COACHES

Victoria Coach Station

164 Buckingham Palace Road, SW1 (0171 730 3466). Victoria tube/BR and five minute's walk.

Smoking policy: The majority of the station is non-smoking. The only areas where smoking is allowed are by gates 1 and 21 and the section by gate 11 (which includes one

Lighting up at Liverpool Street bus stop.

of the departure information areas). Smoking is prohibited at gates 2-10 and 12-20, in ticket hall, departure information, VCS World Travel, Quicksnack, continental check-in and public toilets.

> Nobody knows who first introduced tobacco to England but there are a few British mariners who share the credit, or the blame, among them Sir Richard Grenville (1542-1591), a cousin of Sir Walter Raleigh, and Sir Francis Drake (1541-1596), the first sea captain to sail around the world...

Blueline Intercity Express Ltd
71 Pancras Road, NW1 (0171 278 3266). Euston/King's Cross tube/BR. Routes: King's Cross to Milton Keynes, Leeds, Bradford and other Yorkshire destinations, Teesside, Tyneside and other North East destinations.

Smoking policy: Smoking allowed on the upper deck of double-decker coaches and at the rear of single-decker coaches on most journeys.

Transpak Coach Agency
71 Pancras Road, NW1 (0171 833 4472). Euston/King's Cross tube/BR. Routes: King's Cross to Milton Keynes, Leeds, Bradford and other Yorkshire destinations, Teesside, Tyneside and other North East destinations.

Smoking policy: Seats allocated to smokers on most journeys.

Eurolines (UK) Ltd
52 Grosvenor Gardens, SW1 (0171 730 8235). Victoria tube/BR. Routes: Victoria to various Western and Eastern European destinations.

Smoking policy: Varies according to legislation within the country travelled through. Seats will be available for smokers on some journeys but smoking is generally prohibited from 2200 to 0600 hrs. There are breaks roughly every four hours. Smoking policy should be confirmed when booking.

> ...the most likely contender is Sir John Hawkins (1532-1595), the first English slave trader, who made three expeditions from Africa to the Caribbean in the 1560s.

SIGHTSEEING BUS TOURS

The Original London Sightseeing Tour

(Ring for more details and advance bookings: 0181 877 1722; otherwise tickets are available from pick up points or on the bus). The usual traditional sights of London from an open top bus. Available all year round. Hop-on hop-off service with recorded commentary in eight different languages, or by a live travel guide, in English. Times: Buses leave every 6 minutes between 1000-1700 hrs. The two hour tour costs £10 for adults and £5 for under 14s. Pick up points: Haymarket, Victoria, Marble Arch, Embankment and Baker Street.

Smoking policy: Smoking allowed on the upper deck on all buses.

London Pride Sightseeing

(Information: 01708 631122. Tickets available on the bus, or from London Tourist Board and London Transport information centres, selected hotels and agents). Traditional sights of London all year round from an open top bus. Hop-on hop-off service with full commentary. Times: Daily, from Piccadilly Circus. Every 5 minutes, 0900-2100 hrs, in Summer. Every 15 minutes, 0900-1800 hrs, in Winter. Pick up points: Over 60 stops. Ring for details.

Smoking policy: Smoking allowed on top deck. If there's bad weather a closed top bus is made available and smoking not permitted.

The Big Bus Company

(Information: 0181 944 7922. Tickets on the bus, from a London Tourist Board information centre, hotels or from Victoria Coach Station). Same old famous sights from an open top bus. Hop-on hop-off service with live commentary. Times: One or two hour tours, daily. Leave every 5-15 minutes, 0845-1900 hrs, in Summer. Every 15-30 minutes, 0845-1600 hrs, in Winter. Pick up points: 31, starting from Marble Arch. Ring for details.

Smoking policy: Smoking is allowed on the top, open deck.

> **Despite what is commonly believed, Sir Walter Raleigh (1552-1618) did not introduce tobacco to England although he did popularise it in the court of Elizabeth I. He was just a teenager at the time the first shipment reached Britain around 1565 and had not even been to sea.**

Taxis and Minicabs

Legally, no taxi or minicab driver can stop you from smoking in the back of their vehicle. However, many of London's taxi and minicab drivers now display 'no smoking' stickers, but you often won't see them until you get inside. The nicest sign we have ever seen in the back of a black taxi said: "If you wish to smoke, please open the window first."

When you're ordering a cab by phone always ask if they will provide a smoker-friendly vehicle. If they can't or won't, there are lots more companies to choose from in the Yellow Pages telephone directory.

Please do not smoke inside my taxi...

If you're hailing a black taxi from the street always ask the driver if you can smoke in his cab. If he prefers not, look for another one.

If you are picking up a black taxi from a taxi rank, look through the windows to see if there is a 'no smoking' sign on the glass partition between the driver and the back of the cab. If there is, move on to the next taxi and do the same, and so on down the rank until you find one without a 'no smoking' sign. As soon as you get in the smoker-friendly cab, the driver at the head of the rank will have caught up with you. Calmly explain that, being a smoker and having seen a 'no smoking' sign, you respect his wishes and will find a dri-

> King James I (1566-1625), in his treatise, 'A Counterblaste to Tobacco', described the plant as "...an invention of Satan" and banned tobacco from London's ale-houses. Later he had a change of heart, and 'nationalised' the burgeoning tobacco industry in England and even reduced tobacco taxes.

ver who doesn't mind smokers. The driver will probably say that he doesn't really mind smoking, and that you can smoke in his taxi. Politely decline, saying that you could not possibly allow him to compromise his principles, and get in the smoker-friendly taxi.

A situation may arise where you cannot find a taxi on the rank that does not have a 'no smoking' sign. Then, it is acceptable to ask the driver if he minds if you smoke. If he does, go to the next taxi and ask that driver. How long you are prepared to do this (and risk rebuttals from every driver) will depend on how quickly you need to reach your destination.

Sometimes you won't see another vehicle for hire (usually when it's raining) and may end up in a non-smoking taxi or minicab. Respect his or her choice and don't light up. You can always ask the driver to stop for a moment, while you get out and have a quick puff. You're paying for the time, anyway. If there's a fuss about this, don't give the miserable bleeder a tip!

A number of taxi firms and private hire companies offer a chauffeur-driven service, for tours or business, and some can even provide bilingual drivers. Again, always insist on a smoker-friendly vehicle. These services and limos cost enough!

Self-drive hire

All the main rental companies we have spoken to, including Alamo, Avis, Europcar, Eurodollar, Hertz and Kenning currently hire vehicles to smokers. We understand that some of their counterparts in the USA, don't, so it's only a matter of time before some keen British marketing manager introduces a non-smoking car rental service.

There are umpteen companies in London that rent or lease vehicles and so we can't see a problem in the near future. Prevention is better than a cure, as they say, so make sure you empty the ashtrays (not on the pavement, find a litter bin) and open the windows before you return your rental vehicle.

> 17th century Eton schoolboys smoked a pipe every morning to ward off the bubonic plague.

HOTELS 5

and B&B's

Most of London's hotels welcome guests who smoke. If it's not otherwise stated, apart from your room, you can usually smoke in the bar and lobby. Some restaurants have non-smoking areas.

If you have not booked ahead, London Tourist Board information centres will help - a small fee is charged and a deposit for reservations.

Also, the London Tourist Board (0171 824 8844) credit card accommodation booking service operates during normal office hours, ie 0930-1730 hrs, Monday-Friday. Bookings can be made using Visa and Mastercard only.

If you have a complaint about your London Hotel or B&B, you should inform the management at the time of the incident.

In some circumstances, Sheena Gibson at London Tourist Board, 26 Grosvenor Gardens, Victoria, SW1W 0DU (0171 730 3450) may look into the matter. It's best to write to her.

Chauffeur waiting outside London Hilton, Park Lane.

HOTELS AND BED AND BREAKFAST

HOTELS - LUXURY

Berkeley   Wilton Place, SW1 (0171 235 6000). Hyde Park Corner tube.
Smoking policy: One floor reserved for non-smokers. No other restrictions.

Berkshire   350 Oxford Street, W1 (0171 629 7474). Bond Street tube.
Smoking policy: Two floors reserved for non-smokers. No other restrictions.

Best Western
(0181 541 0050).
Smoking policy: This chain of hotels is run as a marketing consortium. Each hotel sets its own smoking policy. Ring for details.

Bloomsbury Park
126 Southampton Row, WC1 (0171 430 0434). Holborn tube.
Smoking policy: 50% of rooms allocated to smokers. No other restrictions. Other hotels in the chain follow the same policy.

Claridge's   Brook Street, W1 (0171 629 8860). Bond Street tube.
Smoking policy: Smoking and non-smoking rooms. Smoking not allowed on the terrace at breakfast.

Connaught   Carlos Place, W1 (0171 499 7070). Bond Street tube.
Smoking policy: Smoking and non-smoking rooms. Smoking and non-smoking areas in the restaurant.

Dorchester   53 Park Lane, W1 (0171 629 8888). Hyde Park Corner tube.
Smoking policy: Smoking and non-smoking rooms. No other restrictions.

Duke's   35 St James's Place, SW1 (0171 491 4840). Green Park tube.
Smoking policy: Smoking and non-smoking rooms. Smoking and non-smoking areas in the restaurant.

Forte/Meridian
(0171 301 2000).
Smoking policy: All hotels in this chain allocate about 50% of their rooms to smokers. Smoking not allowed in around 90% of the hotel restaurants. If there are leisure facilities such as a swimming pool or gym, smoking is not allowed in these areas.

Four Seasons Hamilton Place, W1 (0171 499 0888). Hyde Park Corner tube.
Smoking policy: Five of its eight floors allocated to smokers. The restaurant has smoking and non-smoking sections. Smoking not permitted in the conservatory or 24 hour fitness room.

46

Grafton   130 Tottenham Court Road, W1 (0171 388 4131). Warren Street/Goodge Street tube.
Smoking policy: Three floors reserved for non-smokers. Smoking and non-smoking areas in the restaurant.

Hampshire   31-36 Leicester Square, WC2 (0171 839 9399). Leicester Square tube.
Smoking policy: Two floors reserved for non-smokers. Smoking and non-smoking areas in the restaurant. No restrictions in the lounge.

London Hilton
                Park Lane, W1 (0171 493 8000). Hyde Park Corner tube.
Smoking policy: Over half of its floors are reserved for smokers. Smoking and non-smoking areas in all the restaurants. No restrictions in the lounge and bar. Pipe smokers only in the bar or lounge.

Holiday Inn (0800 897 121).
Smoking policy: All hotels in this chain have allocated around 50% of their rooms to smokers. All restaurants have smoking and non-smoking sections. If there are leisure facilities such as a swimming pool or gym, smoking is not allowed in these areas.

Pipemen of the Year, organised by the Pipesmokers Council

1964 Rupert Davies (the original tv 'Maigret')	1982 Dave Lee Travis
1965 Sir Harold Wilson	1983 Patrick Moore
1966 Andrew Cruickshank (the original 'Dr Finlay')	1984 Henry Cooper
1967 Warren Mitchell	1985 Jimmy Greaves
1968 Peter Cushing	1986 David Bryant
1969 Jack Hargeaves	1987 Barry Norman
1970 Eric Morecambe	1988 Ian Botham
1971 The Rt Hon The Lord Shinwell	1989 Jeremy Brett (probably the best tv 'Sherlock Holmes')
1973 Frank Muir	1990 Laurence Marks
1974 Fred Trueman	1991 Sir John Harvey-Jones
1975 Sir Campbell Adamson	1992 Tony Benn
1976 Sir Harold Wilson	1993 Rod Hull
1979 J B Priestley	1994 Sir Ranulph Fiennes
1980 Edward Fox	1995 Jethro
1981 James Galway	1996 Sir Colin Davis
	Pipeman of the Century: Lord Shinwell

Holiday Inn   3 Berkeley Street, W1 (0171 493 8282). Green Park tube.
Smoking policy: Three floors reserved for non-smokers. Smoking and non-smoking areas in the restaurant.

Holiday Inn   2 Bridge Place, SW1 (0171 834 8123). Victoria tube/BR.
Smoking policy: Three of the nine floors reserved for smokers. Smoking and non-smoking areas in the restaurant.

Holiday Inn   100 Cromwell Road, SW7 (0171 373 2222). Gloucester Road tube.
Smoking policy: Two floors reserved for non-smokers. Smoking not allowed in the restaurant at breakfast or lunch, however a section is reserved for smokers during dinner. Smoking areas in the bars and lounge.

Holiday Inn   1 King's Cross Road, WC1 (0171 833 3900). King's Cross tube/BR.
Smoking policy: Two floors reserved for non-smokers. Smoking and non-smoking areas in the restaurant.

Holiday Inn, Heathrow
Stockley Road, West Drayton, Middlesex (01895 445555). Heathrow tube/West Drayton BR.
Smoking policy: One floor reserved for non-smokers. Smoking not allowed in the fine dining restaurant. Smoking and non-smoking areas in the main restaurant.

Hospitality Inn Piccadilly
39 Coventry Street, W1 (0171 930 4033). Piccadilly Circus tube.
Smoking policy: Four floors reserved for non-smokers. Smoking not allowed in the restaurant. Smoking and non-smoking areas in the lounge.

Hyatt Carlton Tower
2 Cadogan Place, SW1 (0171 235 1234). Sloane Square tube.
Smoking policy: One floor reserved for smokers. No other restrictions.

Hyde Park   66 Knightsbridge, SW1 (0171 235 2000). Knightsbridge tube.
Smoking policy: Smoking and non-smoking rooms. Smoking and non-smoking areas in the bar, lounge and restaurant.

Kenilworth   97 Great Russell Street, WC1 (0171 637 3477). Tottenham Court Road tube.
Smoking policy: Smoking and non smoking rooms. Smoking not allowed in the restaurant.

Kensington Park
16-32 De Vere Gardens, W8 (0171 937 8080). Gloucester Road/High Street Kensington tube.
Smoking policy: One floor reserved for smokers. Smoking not allowed in the restaurant.

> **"If your wife doesn't like the aroma of your cigar - change your wife." (Zino Davidoff)**

London Marriot Hotel
Grosvenor Square, W1 (0171 493 1232). Bond Street tube.
Smoking policy: Three of the six floors are allocated to smokers. Smoking and non-smoking areas in the restaurants. Smoking is not allowed in the fitness room.

Lowndes
21 Lowndes Street, SW1 (0171 823 1234). Hyde Park Corner tube.
Smoking policy: Two floors reserved for non-smokers. No other restrictions.

Lighting up!

> **During the Past Overseer's Society of St Margaret and St John, Westminster's 285th annual dinner at the Reform Club in November 1995, a unique tobacco-box was handed over to its new custodians with the traditional warning that "When next it is produced it shall contain three pipes of tobacco at least under penalty of six bottles of claret, and that it is restored to the society with some additional ornament under penalty of 200 guineas."**

Meridien London

21 Piccadilly, W1 (0171 734 8000). Green Park tube.

Smoking policy: Seven of the nine floors allocated to smokers. Smoking and non-smoking areas in the restaurant. Smoking not allowed in the fitness centre or beauty salon.

Mount Royal (Thistle)

Bryanstone Street, W1 (0171 629 8040). Marble Arch tube.

Smoking policy: Smoking and non-smoking rooms. Smoking and non-smoking areas in the bar, lounge and restaurant.

Radisson Edwardian, Heathrow

140 Bath Road, Hayes, Middlesex (0181 759 6311). Heathrow tube/West Drayton BR.

Smoking policy: Second floor reserved for non-smokers. Smoking and non-smoking areas in both restaurants.

Ritz

Piccadilly, W1 (0171 493 8181). Green Park tube.

Smoking policy: Six floors for smokers. 20% of restaurant tables reserved for non-smokers. Smoking not allowed in Palm Court between 1400-1800 hrs.

Royal Horseguards (Thistle)

Whitehall Court, SW1 (0800 181716). Embankment tube/Charing Cross tube/BR.

Smoking policy: 50% of rooms reserved for non-smokers. Smoking and non-smoking areas in the restaurant. Smoking not allowed in the foyer/lobby.

Royal Trafalgar (Thistle)

Whitcombe Street, WC2 (0171 930 4477). Leicester Square tube.

Smoking policy: One floor reserved for non-smokers. Smoking and non-smoking areas in the restaurant.

Royal Westminster (Thistle)
49-75 Buckingham Palace Road, SW1 (0171 834 1821). Victoria tube/BR.
Smoking policy: One of the two floors reserved for non-smokers. Smoking and non-smoking areas in the restaurant.

St James's Court Hotel (Taj)
45 Buckingham Gate, SW1 (0171 834 6655). St James's Park tube.
Smoking policy: No smoking on fifth floor. Smoking and non-smoking areas in the restaurant.

Savoy   Strand, WC2 (0171 836 4343). Charing Cross tube/BR or Embankment tube.
Smoking policy: Smoking and non-smoking rooms. No other restrictions.

Selfridge (Thistle)
Orchard Street, W1 (0171 408 2080). Bond Street/Marble Arch tube.
Smoking policy: Smoking and non-smoking rooms. Smoking not allowed in the breakfast room. You can smoke in the bar.

Waldorf Restaurant, Aldwych.

Sheraton Belgravia

20 Chesham Place, SW1 (0171 235 6040). Hyde Park Corner/Knightsbridge tube.

Smoking policy: 25 rooms reserved for non-smokers. Two floors reserved for smokers. Smoking and non-smoking areas in the restaurant.

Tower (Thistle)

St Katharine's Way, E1 (0171 481 2575). Tower Hill tube.

Smoking policy: Three floors reserved for smokers. Smoking and non-smoking areas in both restaurants. You can smoke in the bar.

> "Sublime tobacco! which from east to west
> Cheers the tar's labour or the Turkman's rest;
> Which on the Moslem's ottoman divides
> His hours, and rivals opium and his brides;
> Magnificent in Stamboul, but less grand,
> Though not less loved, in Wapping or the Strand.
> Divine in hookas, glorious in a pipe,
> When tipped with amber, mellow, rich and ripe;
> Yet they lovers more admire by far
> Thy naked beauties — Give me a cigar!"
> (Lord Byron, 'The Island')

Whites (Thistle)

90/92 Lancaster Gate, W2 (0171 262 2711). Lancaster Gate/Queensway tube.

Smoking policy: One floor reserved for non smokers. OK to smoke in the lobby.

HOTELS - MID-RANGE

Charing Cross (Mount Charlotte)

Strand, WC2 (0171 839 7282). Charing Cross tube/BR.

Smoking policy: 50% of rooms reserved for non-smokers. Smoking and non-smoking areas in the bar, lounge, foyer and restaurant.

Charles Dickens (Mount Charlotte)

66 Lancaster Gate, W2 (0171 262 5090). Lancaster Gate/Queensway tube.

Smoking policy: Smoking and non-smoking rooms. Smoking and non-smoking areas in the bar, lounge and restaurant.

Franklin Hotel

28 Egerton Gardens, SW3 (0171 584 5533). South Kensington tube.

Smoking policy: Smoking and non-smoking rooms. No smoking in the restaurant during breakfast. No other restrictions.

Heathrow Park (Mount Charlotte)
Bath Road, Longford, West Drayton, Middlesex (0181 759 2400). Heathrow tube/West Drayton BR.
Smoking policy: Smoking and non-smoking rooms. Smoking and non-smoking areas in the bar, lounge and restaurant.

Henry VIII (Vienna)
19 Leinster Gardens, W2 (0171 262 0117). Paddington tube/BR, Queensway tube.
Smoking policy: Smoking and non-smoking areas in the restaurant. No other restrictions.

Hospitality Inn (Mount Charlotte)
104 Bayswater Road, W2 (0171 262 4461). Queensway tube.
Smoking policy: Smoking and non-smoking rooms.

Kennedy (Mount Charlotte)
43-48 Cardington Street, NW1 (0171 387 4400). Euston tube/BR.
Smoking policy: Smoking and non-smoking rooms. Smoking and non-smoking areas in the bar, lounge and restaurant.

Kensington Palace (Thistle)
De Vere Gardens, W8 (0171 937 8121). Gloucester Road/High Street Kensington tube.
Smoking policy: Smoking and non-smoking rooms. Smoking and non-smoking areas in the bar and restaurant.

Cartoon characters who enjoyed a smoke include Andy Capp (the permanent fag in the corner of his mouth was recently quietly removed by the Daily Mirror), The Dandy's Desperate Dan, James Bond, Popeye (a pipe permanently in his mouth), Captain Haddock in Herge's Tintin, the Thing in Marvel's Fantastic Four (he can get a light from fellow hero, the Torch), Belgium's cowboy, Lucky Luke, Modesty Blaise's sidekick, Willie Garvin, Granpaw and Paw in The Broons, Our Ernie's Pa (in the British 1950s comic, Knockout), Howard the Duck, Weary Willie and Tired Tim - one of the longest- lived (1896-1952) of British comic strips, Uncle Scrooge, and Clark (Superman) Kent's editor, Perry White.

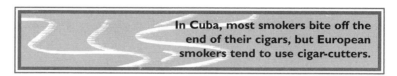

In Cuba, most smokers bite off the end of their cigars, but European smokers tend to use cigar-cutters.

Kingsley (Thistle)

Bloomsbury Way, WC1 (0171 242 5881). Holborn tube.

Smoking policy: Two floors reserved for non-smokers. Smoking and non-smoking areas in the restaurant.

London House (Vienna)

81 Kensington Gardens Square, W2 (0171 727 0696, reservations: 0171 221 1400). Bayswater tube.

Smoking policy: No restrictions.

London Marriott

Grosvenor Square, W1 (0171 493 1232). Bond Street tube.

Smoking policy: Three of the five floors reserved for smokers. Smoking and non-smoking areas in the bar, lounge and restaurant.

London Ryan (Mount Charlotte)

Gwynne Place, 10-42 King's Cross Road, WC1 (0171 278 2480). King's Cross tube/BR.

Smoking policy: Smoking and non-smoking rooms. Smoking and non-smoking areas in the bar, lounge and restaurant.

New Atlantic (Vienna)

1 Queens Gardens, W2 (0171 262 4471, reservations: 0171 221 1400). Paddington tube/BR, Queensway tube.

Smoking policy: No restrictions.

New Barbican (Mount Charlotte)

Central Street, EC1 (0171 251 1565). Barbican/Old Street tube.

Smoking policy: Smoking and non-smoking rooms. Smoking and non-smoking areas in the bar, lounge and restaurant.

New Linden (Vienna)

59 Leinster Square, W2 (0171 221 4321, reservations: 0171 221 1400). Bayswater/Notting Hill Gate tube.

Smoking policy: No restrictions.

Park Court (Mount Charlotte)
>75 Lancaster Gate, W2 (0171 402 4272). Lancaster Gate/Queensway tube.

Smoking policy: Smoking and non-smoking rooms. Smoking and non-smoking areas in the bar, lounge and restaurant.

Pavilion (Vienna)
>37 Leinster Gardens, W2 (0171 258 0269, reservations: 0171 221 1400). Paddington tube/BR, Bayswater tube.

Smoking policy: Smoking and non-smoking areas in the restaurant.

Porchester (Vienna)
>33 Princes Square, W2 (0171 221 2101, reservations: (0171 221 1400). Bayswater tube.

Smoking policy: Smoking not allowed in one of the two common rooms.

Royal Norfolk
>25 London Street, W2 (0171 723 0044). Paddington tube/BR.

Smoking policy: No restrictions.

Royal Scott (Mount Charlotte)
>100 King's Cross Road, WC1 (0171 278 2434). King's Cross tube/BR.

Smoking policy: Smoking and non-smoking rooms. Smoking and non-smoking areas in the bar, lounge and restaurant.

Vanderbilt   68-86 Cromwell Road, SW7 (0171 589 2424). Gloucester Road tube.
Smoking policy: No restrictions.

Westminster (Vienna)
>16 Leinster Square, W2 (0171 221 9131, reservations: 0171 221 1400). Bayswater/Notting Hill Gate tube.

Smoking policy: No current policy. Non-smoking rooms are to be introduced in Autumn 1996.

> **"I was yesterday in a Coffee-House not far from the Royal Exchange,"** said Joseph Addison in The Spectator, July 16 1714, **"where I observed three persons in close conference over a pipe of tobacco; upon which, having filled one for my own use, I lighted it at the little wax candle that stood before them; and after having thrown in two or three whiffs amongst them, sat down and made myself one of the company. I need not tell the reader, that lighting a man's pipe at the same candle, is looked upon among brother-smokers as an overture to conversation and friendship.**

Putting on the Ritz, Piccadilly.

BED AND BREAKFAST

Brewers Inn 147 East Hill, SW18 (0181 874 4128). Wandsworth Town BR. Rooms: 4 Singles, 10 double, 2 family. Price: Single weekday £70, weekend £50, double weekday £80, weekend £60 (including breakfast).
Smoking policy: The restaurant has two floors, one of which is available for smokers. No restrictions in bar/restaurant. Half of its rooms are non-smoking.

Clarence Hotel
Park Road, Teddington, Middlesex (0181 977 8025). Teddington BR. Rooms: 16 double. Price: Single £48.50, double £59.50 (including breakfast).
Smoking policy: All rooms available for smokers. No restrictions in bar or restaurant.

Coach and Horses
8 Kew Green, Richmond, Surrey (0181 940 1208). Richmond tube, Mortlake BR. Rooms: 1 single, 4 doubles, 1 family. Price: Single £35, double £48 (including breakfast).
Smoking policy: All rooms available to smokers. Smoking permitted in all areas of bar and restaurant.

Kew Gardens Hotel
292 Sandycombe Road, Kew, Richmond, Surrey (0181 940 2220). Kew Gardens tube. Rooms: 18 Double. Price: Single £65, double £85 (excluding breakfast).
Smoking policy: No current policy. In autumn 1996 50% of rooms will become non-smoking. Smoking sections in bar and restaurant.

Mitre 130 Mitcham Road, SW17 (0181 672 5771). Tooting tube. Rooms: 9 singles, 6 doubles, 1 family. Price: £28 (including breakfast), £25 (excluding breakfast).
Smoking policy: All rooms available to smokers. No restrictions in bar or restaurant.

Olde Windmill
Clapham Common Southside, SW4 (0181 673 4578). Clapham Common/ Clapham South tube. Rooms: 26 doubles. Price: Single weekday £80, weekend £60, double weekday £90, weekend £68 (including breakfast).
Smoking policy: 10 rooms available for smokers. Smoking sections in bar and restaurant.

Plough 42 Christ Church Road, SW14 (0181 876 7833). Mortlake BR. Rooms: 6 doubles, 1 family. Price: Single £50, double £65 (including breakfast).
Smoking policy: All rooms available for smokers. Smoking permitted in all areas of bar and restaurant.

6

& Cafés

A small but growing number of London's restaurants now have non-smoking tables or areas. Many ban smokers of pipes and cigars completely. The problem is that far too many restaurants try to cram in as many punters as possible, ignoring their comfort, and you end up with tables that are too close for a private conversation, never mind a quiet smoke. The frequent lack of good ventilation also doesn't help.

We suggest that when booking you always check with the restaurant of your choice on whether you may smoke there, or not. If not, then perhaps you should consider eating at one of the places listed in this guide as at least you'll be sure of a welcome.

See our chapter on etiquette, for the finer details of lighting up when you're eating out.

H Forman & Son (Queen's Yard, White Post Lane, Stratford, E9. 0181 985 0378), one of the capital's oldest established salmon curers claim that smoked salmon originated in the East End via Eastern European Jewish immigrants. You can buy it in most non-smoking deli's and supermarkets, and the food halls at Harrods, Selfridges, Fortnum and Mason. Perhaps it should have a health warning, too.

APPH = average price per head (for a three course meal, excluding drinks and service unless otherwise stated)

> **"Tobacco smoke is the one element in which, by our European manners, men can sit silent together without embarrassment, and where no man is bound to speak one word more than he has actually and veritably got to say...and sedatitive, gently clarifying tobacco smoke (if the room were well ventilated, open at top, and the air kept good), with the obligation to a minimum of speech, surely gives human intellect and insight the best chance they can have."**
> **(Thomas Carlisle)**

AMERICAN/BURGERS

Christopher's

18 Wellington Street, WC2 (0171 240 4222). Covent Garden tube. Open: 1130-midnight, Mon-Sun. Seating: 110 - restaurant, 60 - café. Specialities: Steak, lobster and crab cakes. APPH: £25.

Smoking policy: No restrictions in the bar or restaurant. Free matches.

Ed's Easy Diner

12 Moor Street, W1 (0171 439 1955). Leicester Square tube. Open: 1130-midnight, Mon-Sun. Seating: 21. Specialities: Burgers. APPH: £10.

Smoking policy: No formal restrictions but pipes and cigars are not encouraged. Free matches.

Fat Sam's

489 Fulham Broadway, SW6 (0171 386 7577). Fulham Broadway tube. Open: 1200-2330 hrs, Sun-Wed. 1200-0130 hrs, Thur-Sat. Seating: 100. Specialities: Steaks, ribs, Fajitas. APPH: £15-£20.

Smoking policy: Smoking and non-smoking sections in the restaurant.

Fatboy's Diner

21/22 Maiden Lane, WC2 (0171 240 1902). Covent Garden tube. Open: 1030-2300 hrs, Mon-Fri. 1030-midnight, Sat/Sun. Seating: 65. Specialities: American style decor. The Fatburger, chicken, and veggie burgers. APPH: £8.

Smoking policy: 50% of restaurant allocated to smokers. No restrictions around the soft drinks bar.

Hard Rock Café

150 Old Park Lane, W1 (0171 629 0382). Green Park/Hyde Park Corner tube. Open: 1130-0100 hrs, Mon-Sun. Seating: 220. Specialities: Decades of pop/rock memorabilia. The Pig Sandwich. APPH: £20.

Smoking policy: 60% of restaurant allocated to smokers, no restrictions in the bar. Free matches.

Joe Allen

13 Exeter Street, WC2 (0171 836 0651). Covent Garden tube . Open: 1200-0100 hrs, Mon-Sun. Seating: 180. Specialities: Californian-style food, seafood and salads. APPH: £25-£30.

Smoking policy: 50% of the restaurant allocated to smokers. No restrictions in the bar. Free matches.

Maxwell's

8/9 James Street, WC2 (0171 240 3562). Covent Garden tube. Open: 0930-midnight, Mon-Sun. Seating: 250. Specialities: Tex-Mex, Fajitas, Cajun-style food. APPH: £15-£20.

Smoking policy: Two thirds of the restaurant allocated to smokers. No restrictions in the bar. Free matches.

P J's Grill   30 Wellington Street, WC2 (0171 240 7529). Covent Garden tube. Open: 1200-midnight, Mon-Sat. 1200-1700 hrs, Sun. Seating: 120. Specialities: Soft shell crabs, crab cakes and steak. Claims to serve the cheapest champagne in London (Louis Daumont £15.95). APPH: £12.
Smoking policy: Pipe and cigar smokers must use the bar area. Free matches.

Planet Hollywood
13 Coventry Street, W1 (0171 287 1000). Piccadilly Circus tube. Open: 1130-midnight, Mon-Sun. Seating: 450. Specialities: Californian cuisine and stacks of movie memorabilia. APPH: £25.
Smoking policy: 50% of the restaurant allocated to smokers. No pipes or cigars allowed in the bar or restaurant. (So where does Arnold Schwarzenegger, one of its famous owners and a well-known cigar aficionado, light up his Havanas when he's in town?) Free matches.

Rock Island Diner
London Pavilion, Piccadilly Circus, W1 (0171 287 5500). Piccadilly Circus tube. Open: 1200-2330 hrs, Mon-Sun. Seating: 165 - restaurant, 150 - bar. Specialities: Live DJ and American style menu. APPH: £12-£14.
Smoking policy: Pipes and cigars allowed in the bar only. Free matches.

Smollensky's on the Strand
105 Strand, WC2 (0171 497 2101). Embankment tube/Charing Cross tube/BR. Open: 1200-0030 hrs, Mon-Sun. Seating: 250. Specialities: Live jazz, modern American food. APPH: £20-£25.
Smoking policy: 50% of the restaurant allocated to smokers, no restrictions in the bar. Free matches.

Sticky Fingers
1a Phillimore Gardens, W8 (0171-938-5338). High Street Kensington tube. Open: 1200-2330 hrs, Mon-Sun. Seating: 120. Specialities: Bill Wyman-owned shrine to the Rolling Stones, packed with memorabilia. He smokes cigarettes. APPH: £15-£20.
Smoking policy: Pipes and cigars allowed in the bar only. Free matches.

> "...I promised myself that if I ever had some money that I would savour a cigar each day after lunch and dinner. This is the only resolution of my youth that I have kept, and the only realised ambition which has not brought disillusion."
> (W Somerset Maugham, 'Summing Up')

Ladies smoke them too.

TGI Friday's Matrix House, 2 North 4th Street, Milton Keynes, Buckinghamshire (01908 669911).
Smoking policy: The vast majority of their restaurants have both smoking and non-smoking sections. The actual number of smoker-friendly tables is left to the discretion of the branch manager. Free matches. Phone for details of nearest restaurant.

Village Soho 81 Wardour Street, W1 (0171 434 2124). Tottenham Court Road tube. Open: 1200-2300 hrs, Mon-Sat. 1200-2230 hrs, Sun. Seating: 30. Specialities: Vegetarian harvest pie, grilled duck breast. APPH: Set menu £5.95. A la carte £13.
Smoking policy: No pipes. Cigars can be smoked only at the discretion of the management. Well-ventilated bar.

BARBECUE

Blades Barbecue Restaurant
94 Lower Richmond Road, SW15 (0181 789 0869). Putney Bridge tube. Open: 1200-1500 hrs and 1800-2330 hrs, Tues-Sun. Seating: 70. APPH: Lunch £5.75, dinner £12.
Smoking policy: 50% of restaurant allocated to smokers. No smoking in reception.

BRAZILIAN

Amazona's 75 Westbourne Grove, W2 (0171 243 0090). Bayswater/Queensway tube. Open: 1900-2300 hrs, Mon-Fri. 1200-1500 hrs and 1900-2300 hrs, Sat/Sun. Seating: 40. APPH: £16.
Smoking policy: No pipes.

BRITISH: TRADITIONAL

Aberdeen/Angus Steak House

Aberdeen Steak Houses Group Plc, 124/126 Brompton Road, SW3 (0171 589 0782).

Smoking policy: No restrictions in any of its restaurants. Phone for details of nearest restaurant.

The Atrium

4 Millbank, Westminster, SW1 (0171 223 0032). Westminster tube. Open: 0815-1500 hrs and 1800-2300 hrs, Mon-Sun. Seating: 90. APPH: £20.

Smoking policy: 50% of restaurant allocated to smokers. No restrictions at the bar. Free matches.

Bumbles Restaurant

16 Buckingham Palace Road, SW1 (0171 823 2903). Victoria tube/BR. Open: 1200-1415 and 1800-2245 hrs, Mon-Fri. 1800-2245 hrs, Sat. Seating: 70. Specialities: English and international dishes. APPH: £25.

Smoking policy: No restrictions in restaurant or bar.

Butlers Wharf Chop House

36e Shad Thames, SE1 (0171 403 3403). London Bridge tube/BR. Open: 1200-1500 hrs and 1800-2300 hrs, Mon-Sun. Seating: 115 restaurant, 35 bar, 50 terrace. Specialities: Steak and kidney pudding, roast beef. APPH: £25-£30

Smoking policy: No restrictions in restaurant or bar. Free matches.

Garlic and Shots, Soho.

Dorchester Grill Room

The Dorchester, 54 Park Lane, WI (0171 317 6336). Hyde Park Corner tube. Open: 0700-2300 hrs, Mon-Sun. Seating: 80. Specialities: Wild smoked salmon, roast Angus beef, game. APPH: £25-£30.
Smoking policy: Ask for a table where you can smoke, there's plenty of them. Pipe smokers must remain at the bar. Free matches.

Fountain

Ground Floor, Fortnum & Mason, 181 Piccadilly, WI (0171 734 8040). Green Park/Piccadilly Circus tube. Open: 0900-2000 hrs, Mon-Sun. Seating: 120. Specialities: Mixed grill breakfast. APPH: Two courses £12-£15
Smoking policy: One-third of tables available for smokers. Free matches.

The Goring Hotel

15 Beeston Place, SWI (0171 396 9000). Victoria tube/BR. Open: 0700-1000 hrs, 1230-1430 hrs and 1800-2200 hrs, Mon-Sun (closed Sat lunch). Seating: 60. Specialities: Wide selection of wines. APPH: £40-£50.
Smoking policy: Plenty of smoker-friendly tables if you like cigarettes and cigars. Pipe smokers must remain at the bar. Free matches.

Greenhouse

27a Hays Mews, WI (0171 499 3331). Green Park/Hyde Park Corner tube. Open: 1200-1500 hrs and 1900-2300 hrs, Mon-Sun. Seating: 95. Specialities: Smoked haddock, Welsh rarebit. APPH: £35-£40.
Smoking policy: Pipe smokers must remain at the bar, otherwise smoker-friendly. Free matches.

Jack's Place

12 York Road, SWII (0171 228 8519). Clapham Junction BR. Open: 1200-2300 hrs, Mon-Sun. Seating: 60. Specialities: Scotch beef, Dover sole. APPH: £15.
Smoking policy: No restrictions in restaurant or bar. Free matches.

Langan's Brasserie

Stratton House, Stratton Street, WI (0171 493 6437). Green Park tube. Open: 1215-2345 hrs, Mon-Fri. 2000-0045 hrs, Sat. Seating: 300. Specialities: Spinach soufflé, rack of lamb. APPH: £35.
Smoking policy: Pipe and cigar smokers must remain at the bar. Where does one of its celebrated owners, Michael Caine, smoke his cigars? Cigarettes at table are OK. Ask for a smoker-friendly table. Free matches.

Porter's

17 Henrietta Street, WC2 (0171 836 6466). Covent Garden tube. Open: 1200-2330 hrs, Mon-Sun. Seating: 200. APPH: £15.
Smoking policy: No restrictions in restaurant or bar.

Quality Chop House

94 Farringdon Road, EC1 (0171 837 5093). Farringdon tube/BR. Open: 1200-1500 hrs and 1830-2330 hrs, Mon-Sun (closed Sat lunch and Sun evening). Seating: 40. Specialities: Salmon fishcakes, and chops. APPH: £40.

Smoking policy: Smoker-friendly but no pipes.

Rules

35 Maiden Lane, WC2 (0171 836 5314). Covent Garden tube. Open: 1200-midnight, Mon-Sun. Seating: 225. Specialities: Game. APPH: £20-£25.

Smoking policy: Smoker-friendly but no pipes. Free matches.

The Savoy Grill

Strand, WC2 (0171 836 4343). Embankment tube, Charing Cross tube/BR. Open: 1200-1500 hrs and 1800-2300 hrs, Mon-Fri. 1800-2300 hrs, Sat. Seating: 85. Specialities: Arnold Bennett omelette (recipe includes smoked haddock). APPH: £45.

Smoking policy: Pipe smokers must remain at the bar. Cigars and fags are OK just about anywhere. Free matches.

> **Persian proverb: Coffee without tobacco is like meat without salt.**

Shepherd's

Marsham Court, Marsham Street, SW1 (0171 834 9552). Westminster tube. Open: 1230-1445 hrs and 1830-2330 hrs, Mon-Fri. Seating: 70 restaurant, 32 private room. Specialities: Roast beef and Yorkshire pudding. APPH: £20.

Smoking policy: No restrictions in restaurant or bar. Free matches.

Simpson's of Lloyd's Avenue

Marlow House, Lloyd's Avenue, EC3 (0171 481 1168). Tower Hill tube. Open: 1100-2300 hrs, Mon-Fri. Seating: 120. APPH: £12-£15.

Smoking policy: No restrictions in restaurant or bar. Free matches.

Simpson's in the Strand

100 Strand, WC2 (0171 836 9112). Charing Cross tube/BR. Open: 0700-2300 hrs, Mon-Fri. 1200-2300 hrs, Sat. 1200-2100 hrs, Sun. Seating: 350. Specialities: Roast Beef. London's original cigar divan first opened in 1828. Charles Dickens smoked and ate here. APPH: £30.

Smoking policy: You can smoke cigars or fags on any table but pipesmokers must remain at the bar. Free matches.

Turner's

87/89 Walton Street, SW3 (0171 584 6711). Knightsbridge tube. Open: 1230-1430 hrs and 1930-2300 hrs, Mon-Sun (closed Sat lunch). Seating: 55. Specialities: Rack of English lamb. APPH: Lunch £15-£20, dinner £40-£45.

Smoking policy: No restrictions but consideration expected from customers. Free matches.

Wilson's 236 Blythe Road, W14 (0171 603 7267). Goldhawk Road/Shepherds Bush tube. Open: 1230-1400 hrs and 1930-2200 hrs, Mon-Fri. 1930-2200 hrs, Sat. 1230-1400 hrs, Sun. Seating: 45. Specialities: Finnan haddock pudding with spinach and bacon salad. Rack of lamb with haggis crust. APPH: £15-£20.
Smoking policy: No restrictions. Pipes and cigars not encouraged.

BRITISH - MODERN

Alastair Little
49 Frith Street, W1 (0171 734 5183). Leicester Square/Tottenham Court Road tube. Open: 1200-1500 and 1800-2300 hrs, Mon-Fri. 1800-2300 hrs, Sat. Seating: 38 restaurant, 18 bar. Specialities: Modern British dishes. APPH: £25.
Smoking policy: No restrictions in restaurant or bar. Free matches.

Atelier 41 Beak Street, W1 (0171 287 2057). Oxford Circus tube. Open: 1200-1430 hrs and 1800-2245 hrs, Mon-Fri. 1800-2245 hrs, Sat. Seating: 45 restaurant, 16 private room. Specialities: Raymond Blanc-trained chef. APPH: Before 2000 hrs £15, after 2000 hrs £30-£35.
Smoking policy: No restrictions in restaurant or bar but consideration for non-smokers is expected.

The Belvedere
Holland House, off Abbotsbury Road, W8 (0171 602 1238). High Street Kensington/Holland Park tube. Open: 1200-1500 and 1900-2300 hrs, Mon-Sun. Seating: 150. Specialities: Grilled calf's liver, peppered sirloin. APPH: £23.
Smoking policy: No restrictions in restaurant or bar. Free matches.

Bibendum Michelin House, 81 Fulham Road, SW3 (0171 581 5817). South Kensington tube. Open: 1230-1430 hrs and 1900-2300 hrs, Mon-Sun. Seating: 100. Specialities: Roast halibut with broad bean and truffle butter puré. APPH: £50-£60.
Smoking policy: No restrictions in restaurant or bars. Free matches.

Blue Print Café
Design Museum, Butlers Wharf, SE1 (0171 378 7031). London Bridge tube/BR. Open: 1200-1500 hrs and 1800-2300 hrs, Mon-Sat. 1200-1530 hrs, Sun. Seating: 88 restaurant, 70 balcony. Specialities: Deep fried plaice and chips, kedgeree. APPH: £35.
Smoking policy: No restrictions. Free matches.

Boisdale 15 Eccleston Street, SW1 (0171 730 6922). Victoria tube/BR. Open: Orders between 1200-1430 hrs and 1900-2230 hrs, Mon-Sun (closed Sat lunch).

Seating: 42. Specialities: Scottish mussels, fish cakes. Extensive wine list. APPH: £20-25.

Smoking policy: No restrictions but pipe smokers allowed in bar area only. Free matches.

Le Caprice   Arlington House, Arlington Street, SW1 (0171 629 2239). Green Park tube. Open: 1200-1500 hrs and 1800-midnight, Mon-Sun. Seating: 75. Specialities: Griddled scallops with bacon and sorrel. APPH: £35.

Smoking policy: No restrictions in restaurant or bar. Free matches.

Detroit   35 Earlham Street, WC2 (0171 240 2662). Leicester Square/Covent Garden tube. Open: 1200-1500 hrs and 1800-2300 hrs, Mon-Fri. 1800-midnight, Sat. Seating: 80. Specialities: Contemporary European menu. New world wine. APPH: £20.

Smoking policy: 50% of restaurant allocated to smokers. Pipes and cigars preferred at the bar only. Free matches.

The Fifth Floor

Harvey Nichols, Knightsbridge, SW1 (0171 235 5250). Knightsbridge tube. Open: 1200-1500 hrs and 1830-2330 hrs, Mon-Sat. 1200-1500 hrs, Sun. Seating: 110. APPH: Lunch £22.50, dinner £35-£45.

Smoking policy: No restrictions but pipes at the bar only. Free matches.

Hubble and Co

55 Charterhouse Street, EC1 (0171 253 1612). Farringdon tube/BR. Open: 1100-1500 hrs, Mon-Sun. Seating: 150. APPH: £15-£20.

Smoking policy: No restrictions in restaurant or bars. Free matches.

Kensington Place

201 Kensington Church Street, W8 (0171 727 3184). Notting Hill Gate tube. Open: 1200-1500 hrs and 1830-2345 hrs, Mon-Sat. 1830-2215 hrs, Sun. Seating: 140. Specialities: Chicken and goat's cheese mousse. Griddled foie gras with sweetcorn pancake. APPH: £25-£30.

Smoking policy: No restrictions in restaurant or bar. Free matches.

Mezzo and Mezzonine

100 Wardour Street, W1 (0171 314 4000). Tottenham Court Road tube. Open: 1200-1430 hrs and 1730-1130 hrs, Mon-Thur. 1200-1430 and 1730-0030 hrs, Fri/Sat. Bar open all day. Seating 700. Specialities: Chicken with black olive salad, potato and thyme rosti, oysters, rack of lamb. Live Jazz. APPH: £15-£20.

Smoking policy: Smoking and non-smoking in restaurant, no restrictions in the bars. Premium cigars can be purchased from one of London's last remaining cigarette girls.

Have a cigar at The Avenue, St James's Street.

Nicole's   158 New Bond Street, W1 (0171 499 8408). Green Park tube. Open: 1000-2245 hrs, Mon-Sun. Seating: 65 restaurant, 28 bar. Specialities: Grilled meat and seafood dishes. APPH: Lunch £20, dinner £40.

Smoking policy: One-third of restaurant allocated to smokers. Pipes and cigars at bar only. Free matches. Ashtrays can be purchased.

Premier at Selfridges

3rd Floor, Selfridges, Oxford Street, W1 (0171 318 3155). Bond Street tube. Open: 1000-1800 hrs, Mon-Sat. Seating: 68 restaurant, 50 bar. APPH: £15-£20.

Smoking policy: No restrictions but pipe smokers must remain at the bar. Free matches.

Quaglino's   16 Bury Street, SW1 (0171 930 6767). Green Park/Piccadilly Circus tube. Open: 1200-1500 hrs and 1800-0230 hrs, Mon-Sun. Last food orders midnight. Seating: 300. Specialities: Seafood, modern British and French cuisine. APPH: £35-£40.

Smoking policy: No restrictions in restaurant or bar. Free matches.

> **Tobacco is one man's blessing and another man's bane.**

St James's   4th Floor, Fortnum & Mason, 181 Piccadilly, W1 (0171 734 8040). Green Park/Piccadilly Circus tube. Open: 0900-2000 hrs, Mon-Sat. Seating: 120. APPH: £15-£20.

Smoking policy: One-third of restaurant allocated to smokers. No pipes. Free matches.

Tabac   46 Goldborne Road, W10 (0181 960 2433). Ladbroke Grove tube. Open: 1230-1530 hrs and 1930-2300 hrs, Mon-Sun (closed Mon lunch). Seating: 40 restaurant, 30 private room. Specialities: The Chef is from River Café. The entire menu changes every month. APPH: £15-£20.

Smoking policy: No restrictions in restaurant or bar. Free matches.

The Tate Gallery Restaurant

Millbank, SW1 (0171 887 8877). Pimlico tube. Open: 1200-1500 hrs, Mon-Sat. Seating: 100. Specialities: Extensive wine List. APPH: £20-£25.

Smoking policy: 25% of restaurant allocated to smokers. Pipes not encouraged. You can't smoke anywhere else in the gallery.

Union Café and Restaurant

96 Marylebone Lane, W1 (0171 486 4860). Bond Street tube. Open: 0930-2230 hrs, Mon-Fri. Seating: 70. Specialities: Different menu every day and frequently changing wine list. APPH: £20.

Smoking policy: No restrictions but consideration is expected. Free matches.

Walton's   121 Walton Street, SW3 (0171 584 0204). Knightsbridge/South Kensington tube. Open: 1230-1430 hrs and 1930-2330 hrs, Mon-Sat, 1230-1400 hrs and 1900-2200 hrs, Sun. Seating: 65 restaurant, 25 private room. Specialities: Traditional British fare. Over 200 wines. APPH: £30-35.

Smoking policy: No restrictions, except for pipes. Free matches.

BRITISH - FISH AND CHIPS

Sea Shell   49/51 Lisson Grove, NW1 (0171 723 8703). Marylebone tube/BR. Open: 1200-1400 hrs and 1715-2230 hrs, Mon-Fri. 1200-2230 hrs, Sat. 1200-1430 hrs, Sun. Seating: 160. Specialities: Daily specials. Wine of the month. APPH: £10.50.

Smoking policy: No restrictions. Free matches.

Sea Shell   Gutter Lane, Gresham Street, EC2 (0171 606 6961). St Paul's tube. Open: 1145-2045 hrs, Mon-Fri. Seating: 93. APPH: £20.

Smoking policy: No restrictions. Free matches.

Upper Street Fish Shop (unlicensed, customers can bring own alcohol)
    324 Upper Street, N1 (0171 359 1401). Angel tube. Open: 1200-1415 hrs and 0600-1015 hrs, Mon-Sat (closed Mon lunch). Seating: 50. Specialities: Fish lasagna. Home-made British puddings. APPH: £9.

Smoking policy: No pipes or cigars in restaurant but fags are allowed.

BRITISH - PIE AND MASH

A H Cooke   48 Goldhawk Road, W12 (0181 743 7630). Goldhawk Road tube. Open: 1030-1700 hrs, Mon-Fri. Seating: 70. Specialities: Eels. APPH: One course £4. (unlicensed)

Smoking policy: No restrictions.

> **"I couldn't help it. I can resist anything except temptation."**
> **(Oscar Wilde, 'Lady Windermere's Fan')**

F Cooke   150 Hoxton Street, N1 (0171 729 7718). 22A, 22B, 48, 55, 149, 243 bus. Open: 1000-1900 hrs, Mon-Thur. 0930-2000 hrs, Fri/Sat. Seating: 50. Specialities: Veggie pie. Delivers to the City. Sawdust floor (originally for customers to spit out their eel bones) so don't drop lit matches or fag-ends on it. Price: One course £2.

Smoking policy: Smoking and non-smoking sections.

Harringtons   3 Selkirk Road, SW17 (0181 672 1877). Tooting Broadway tube. Open: 1100-2100 hrs, Tues, Thur and Fri. 1100-1400 hrs, Wed. 1100-1930 hrs, Sat. Seating: 50. APPH: One course £1.20.

Smoking policy: No restrictions.

G F Kelly   414 Bethnal Green Road, E2 (0171 739 3603). Bethnal Green tube. Open: 1000-1500 hrs, Mon-Thur. 1000-1830 hrs, Fri. 0930-1630 hrs, Sat. Seating: 40-50. Specialities: Pie and mash only. Signed photo of customer, Charlie Magri (former flyweight champion of the world) on the wall. APPH: One course, £1.25.

Smoking policy: No restrictions.

CHINESE

There aren't many Chinese restaurants where you can't smoke...

China City   White Bear Yard, WC2 (0171 734 3388). Leicester Square tube. Open: 1200-2345 hrs, Mon-Sun. Seating: 500. Specialities: Cantonese food. APPH: £20.

Smoking policy: 50% of restaurant allocated to smokers, no restrictions in bar.

Fung Shing   15 Lisle Street, WC2 (0171-437-1539). Leicester Square/Piccadilly Circus tube. Open: 1200-2330 hrs, Mon-Sun. Seating: 110. Specialities: Cantonese food. APPH: £20.

Smoking policy: No restrictions.

Golden Dragon

28/29 Gerrard Street, W1 (0171 734 2763/1073). Leicester Square/Piccadilly Circus tube. Open: 1200-2330 hrs, Mon-Sun. Seating: 400. Specialities: Dim Sum, wedding and VIP parties. APPH: £10.

Smoking policy: No restrictions.

Harbour City

46 Gerrard Street, W1 (0171 439 7859). Leicester Square/Piccadilly Circus tube. Open: 1200-midnight, Mon-Sun. Seating: 180. Specialities: Traditional Peking dishes. APPH: £12.50.

Smoking policy: No restrictions. Free matches.

CUBAN

Cuba   11/13 Kensington High Street, W8 (0171 938 4137). High Street Kensington tube. Open: 1200-0200 hrs, Mon-Sun. Seating: 55. Specialities: Full menu and tapas. Dancing in basement club to a mixture of Salsa and modern dance music. APPH: £25.

Smoking policy: No restrictions in restaurant or bar. Free matches.

Cuba Libre   72 Upper Street, N1 (0171 354 9998). Angel tube. Open: 1200-0200 hrs, Mon-Sun. Seating: 90. APPH: £18-£20.

Smoking policy: No formal restrictions but pipes preferred at bar only. Free matches. Good place to light up a Havana.

FISH

Bentley's   11-15 Swallow Street, W1 (0171 734 4756). Piccadilly Circus tube. Open: 1200-1430 hrs and 1800-2315 hrs, Mon-Sat. Seating: 75. Specialities: Spaghetti with lobster and tomato. APPH: Lunch £19.50, dinner £25.
Smoking policy: No restrictions.

Caviar House

61 Piccadilly, W1 (0171 409 0445). Green Park tube. Open: 1230-1430 hrs and 1900-2245 hrs, Mon-Sat. Seating: 55. Specialities: Suvruga caviar with butter sauce. Fillet of sea bass with fresh leeks. APPH: Lunch £17.50, dinner £21.50.
Smoking policy: No restrictions.

Green's Restaurant and Oyster Bar

36 Duke Street, SW1 (0171 930 4566). Green Park/Piccadilly Circus tube. Open: 1230-1500 hrs and 1730-2300 hrs, Mon-Sun. Closed on Sun during summer. Seating: 70 restaurant, 25 bar. APPH: £35.
Smoking policy: No restrictions.

Lobster Trading Company

31 Broadgate Circle, EC2 (0171 256 5045). Liverpool Street tube/BR. Open: 1130-1530 hrs and 1700 hrs-Close, Mon-Sun. Seating: 78. Specialities: Shellfish. English wines. APPH: £15.
Smoking policy: No restrictions in bar or restaurant. Free matches.

Manzi's   1/2 Leicester Street, WC2 (0171 734 0224). Leicester Square tube. Open: 1200-1445 hrs and 1730-2345 hrs, Mon-Sat. 1800-2245 hrs, Sun. Seating: 70 restaurant, 65 private room. Specialities: Seafood. Average price: £25.
Smoking policy: No restrictions in the bar or restaurant, except for pipe smokers. Free matches.

L'Oranger   5 St James's Street, SW1 (0171 839 3774). Green Park tube. Open: 1200-1500 hrs and 1830-2315 hrs, Mon-Fri. Seating: 60. Specialities: Wide range of seafood. APPH: £22.
Smoking policy: No pipes or cigars in bar or restaurant.

> **"When all things were made, none was made better than this:**
> **To be a lone man's companion, A bachelor's friend,**
> **A hungry man's food, A sad man's cordial,**
> **A wakeful man's sleep, And a chilly man's fire, sir."**
> **(Charles Kingsley)**

Scott's   20 Mount Street, W1 (0171 629 5248). Green Park/Hyde Park Corner tube. Open: 1200-1500 hrs and 1800-2300 hrs, Mon-Fri. 1800-2300 hrs, Sat. Seating: 90. Specialities: Dover sole, fish cakes. Features London's only Gent's toilet tiled with the Montecristo cigar logo. APPH: £40.

Smoking policy: 50% of restaurant allocated to smokers. No restrictions in bar. Free matches.

Sheekey's Josef Brasserie
28-32 St Martin's Court, WC2 (0171 240 2565). Leicester Square tube. Opening times: 1200-1500 hrs and 1730-2330 hrs, Mon-Sun. Seating: 120-140. Specialities: Seafood platter. APPH: £40.

Smoking policy: 75% of restaurant allocated to smokers. No restrictions in bar. Free matches.

Sweetings   39 Queen Victoria Street, EC4 (0171 248 3062). Cannon Street tube/BR. Open: 1130-1500 hrs, Mon-Fri. Seating: 65. Specialities: Seafood. APPH: £20-£25.

Smoking policy: No restrictions.

Wheelers   19 Old Compton Street, W1 (0171 437 2706). Leicester Square tube. Opening times: 1230-1415 hrs and 1800-2315 hrs, Mon-Sun. Seating: 120. Specialities: One of London's oldest fish restaurants. Average price: £25-£30.

Smoking policy: Fags are OK but no pipes or cigars in the restaurant. No pipes in the bar. Free matches.

FRENCH

The Canteen Unit 4G, Harbour Yard, Chelsea Harbour, SW10 (0171 351 7330). Fulham Broadway tube, Earl's Court tube, then 3 bus. Open: 1200-1500 hrs and 1830-2300 hrs, Mon-Fri. 1830-2300 hrs, Sat. 1200-1500 hrs, Sun. Seating: 130. Specialities: "French-based modern European" food such as tranche of salmon with parsley. Occasional sightings of owner, Michael Caine. He gets around, doesn't he! APPH: £25.

Smoking policy: No pipes in restaurant. No restrictions in bar. Free matches. Fags and cigars are OK.

Chez Max   168 Ifield Road, SW10 (0171 835 0874). Earls Court tube. Open: 1930-2230 hrs, Mon-Sat. Seating: 60. Specialities: Traditional French cuisine. APPH: £24.50.

Smoking policy: No pipes or cigars. Fags are OK.

Chez Nico at Ninety Park Lane
90 Park Lane, W1 (0171 409 1290). Hyde Park Corner tube. Open: 1200-1400 hrs and 1900-2300 hrs, Mon-Fri. 1900-2300 hrs, Sat. Seating: 80. Specialities: Traditional French cuisine. APPH: £100.

Smoking policy: Cigars and fags are OK but not pipes.

La Dordogne 5 Devonshire Road, W4 (0181 747 1836). Turnham Green tube. Open: 1200-1430 hrs and 1900-2300 hrs, Mon-Fri. 1900-2300 hrs, Sat/Sun. Seating: 80. Specialities: Lobster, oysters. APPH: £25.
Smoking policy: No pipes or cigars in the bar or restaurant but fags are OK. Free matches.

Elena's L'Etoile
30 Charlotte Street, W1 (0171 636 7189). Goodge Street/Tottenham Court Road tube. Open: 1200-1430 hrs and 1800-2300 hrs, Mon-Sun. Seating: 70. Specialities: Salmon and leek fish cakes. APPH: £25.
Smoking policy: No restrictions.

L'Escargot 48 Greek Street, W1 (0171 437 2679). Leicester Square/Tottenham Court Road tube. Open: 1000-0015 hrs, Mon-Sat. 1800-2315 hrs, Sun. Seating: 90 restaurant, 45 private room. Specialities: Traditional French cuisine. APPH: £20-25, set menu £17.
Smoking policy: Pipe and cigar smokers must remain at bar. Fags are OK. Free matches.

Francofill 1 Old Brompton Street, SW7 (0171 584 0087). South Kensington tube. Open: 1100-2300 hrs, Mon-Sun. Seating: 100. Specialities: Quail, duck breast. APPH: £40.
Smoking policy: 50% of restaurant allocated to smokers. No restrictions in bar.

Mon Plasir 21 Monmouth Street, WC2 (0171 836 7243). Covent Garden/Leicester Square tube. Open: 1200-1415 hrs and 1750-2315 hrs, Mon-Fri. 1750-2315 hrs, Sat. Seating: 96. APPH: £20-£25.
Smoking policy: No restrictions. Free matches.

Le Muscadet 25 Paddington Street, W1 (0171 935 2883). Baker Street tube. Open: 1230-1445 and 1930-2245 hrs, Mon-Fri. 1930-2245 hrs, Sat. Seating: 35. Specialities: Hot foie gras with apples and Madeira sauce. APPH: £26.
Smoking policy: No restrictions. Free matches.

La Poule au Pot
231 Ebury Street, SW1 (0171 730 7763). Sloane Square tube, Victoria tube/BR. Open: 1230-1430 and 1900-2315 hrs, Mon-Sun. Seating: 80. Specialities: Traditional French food and wines. APPH: Lunch £13.75, dinner £25-£30.
Smoking policy: No restrictions.

The Room at the Halcyon
129 Holland Park Avenue, W11 (0171 221 5411). Holland Park tube. Open: 1200-1430 hrs and 1900-2230 hrs, Mon-Sun (closed Sat lunch). Seating: 60. Specialities: Traditional French cuisine. APPH: Lunch £40, dinner £50-£60.
Smoking policy: Pipes at the bar only; cigars and ciggies, everywhere. Free matches.

La Tante Claire

68 Royal Hospital Road, SW3 (0171 352 6045). Sloane Square tube. Open: 1230-1400 hrs and 1900-2300 hrs, Mon-Fri. Seating: 33. Specialities: Scallops, pigs trotters. Extensive wine list. APPH: £65.

Smoking policy: No restrictions in restaurant or bar. Free matches.

Le Gavroche 43 Upper Brook Street, W1 (0171 408 0881). Marble Arch tube. Open: 1200-1400 hrs and 1900-2300 hrs Mon-Fri. Seating: 60 restaurant, 20 private room. Specialities: Fine French food. APPH: Lunch £38, dinner £85.

Smoking policy: Cigarettes and cigars in lounge only, not at table.

GREEK

Daphne

83 Bayham Street, NW1 (0171 267 7322). Camden Town tube. Open: 1200-1430 hrs and 1800-2330 hrs, Mon-Sat. Seating: 85 restaurant, 25 roof terrace. Specialities: Fish and vegetarian. APPH: Set menu £9, à la carte £15.

Smoking policy: No restrictions in restaurant or bar. Free matches.

White Tower 1 Percy Street, W1 (0171 636 8141). Goodge Street/Tottenham Court Road tube. Open: 1230-1430 hrs 1830-2300 hrs, Mon-Fri. 1830-2300 hrs, Sun. Seating: 60-70. Specialities: Roast duckling. APPH: £20-£25.

Smoking policy: No restrictions. Free matches.

HOTEL RESTAURANTS

Claridge's

Brook Street, W1 (0171 629 8860). Bond Street tube. Open: Breakfast 0700-1030 hrs, lunch 1230-1515 hrs and dinner 1900-2315 hrs Mon-Sun. Seating: 120. Specialities: Classic French and British dishes. APPH: Lunch £29, dinner £38.

Smoking policy: Pipes and cigars not allowed during breakfast but cigarettes are OK. Free matches.

The Four Seasons

Four Seasons Hotel, Hamilton Place, W1 (0171 499 0888 ext 3172). Green Park/Hyde Park Corner tube. Open: 1230-1500 hrs and 1900-2230 hrs Mon-Sun. Seating: 50-80. Specialities: French cuisine, very good wines. APPH: Lunch £25, dinner £60.

Smoking policy: Smoking and non-smoking sections in restaurant, no pipes allowed in the restaurant or bar.

The Grill Room

Café Royal, 69 Regent Street, W1 (0171 437 9090 ext 296). Piccadilly Circus tube. Open: 0700-2300 hrs Mon-Sun. Seating: 1,000. Specialities: One of the largest wine cellars in London. APPH: £16.50.

Smoking policy: Smoking and non-smoking areas in restaurant and bar, no smoking in reception area.

Mezzo's bar, Wardour Street.

Halkin   5/6 Halkin Street, SW1 (0171 333 1100). Hyde Park Corner tube. Open: 1230-1430 hrs and 1930-2300 hrs Mon-Sun. Seating: 40. Specialities: Fine Indian dishes. APPH: Lunch £18, dinner £40-£45.

Smoking policy: Cigar and pipe smokers must remain at the bar. Cigarette smokers get to eat at the tables.

The Heights St George's Hotel, Langham Place, W1 (0171 636 1939). Oxford Circus tube. Open: 1200-1400 hrs and 1900-2200 hrs Mon-Fri. 1900-2200 hrs Sat. Seating: 85. Specialities: "All our food is special". APPH: Lunch £23, main course £40.

Smoking policy: Well ventilated, accommodates smokers and non-smokers.

Lanesborough

I Lanesborough Place, SWI (0171 259 5599). Hyde Park Corner tube. Open: 0700-midnight Mon-Sun. Seating: 106. Specialities: European and Asian cuisine. APPH: £24.50.

Smoking policy: Pipes and cigars not allowed during breakfast. Ciggies are OK. Free matches.

Ritz

Piccadilly, WI (0171 493 8181). Green Park/Piccadilly Circus tube. Open: 0700-1030 hrs, 1230-1445 hrs and 1800-2315 hrs Mon-Sat, 0730-1100 hrs and 1830-2230 hrs Sun. Seating: 110. Specialities: The live band and four course dinner is £49 Fri/Sat. APPH: £28.

Smoking policy: Cigars and cigarettes are OK but not pipes. Free matches.

Savoy

Strand, WC2 (0171 836 4343). Charing Cross tube/BR. Open: 0700-1030 hrs, 1230-1430 hrs and 1930-2330 hrs Mon-Sat 0800-1030 hrs, 1200-1430 hrs and 1930-2230 hrs Sun. Seating: 150. Specialities: French cuisine and dinner dance. APPH: £40.

Smoking policy: No restrictions in reception, restaurant or bar. Free matches.

Waldorf

Aldwych, WC2 (0171 836 2400). Covent Garden/Temple tube. Open: 1230-1400 and 1800-2300 hrs Mon-Sun. Seating: 60. Specialities: special City lunch. APPH: £20.

Smoking policy: No restrictions. Free matches.

INDIAN

Bombay Brasserie

Courtfield Close, Courtfield Road, SWI (0171 370 4040). Gloucester Road tube. Open: 1230-1500 hrs and 1930-2330 hrs, Mon-Sun. Seating: 180. Specialities: Indian food. APPH: Lunch £14.95, dinner £25.

Smoking policy: Smoking and non-smoking areas.

India Club

2nd Floor, Strand Continental Hotel, 143 Strand, WC2 (0171 836 0650). Charing Cross tube/BR or Temple tube. Open: 1200-1430 hrs, Mon-Sat. 1800-2200 hrs, Sun. Seating: 60. Specialities: South Indian dishes. APPH: £8.

Smoking policy: No restrictions.

Veeraswamy

99/101 Regent Street, WI (0171 734 1401). Piccadilly Circus tube. Open: 1200-1430 hrs and 1800-2330 hrs, Mon-Sat. Seating: 95-110. Specialities: Traditional dishes in London's oldest Indian restaurant. APPH: Lunch £13.75, dinner £25.

Smoking policy: 60% of restaurant allocated to smokers. Pipe and cigar smokers must remain at the bar. Free matches.

Viceroy of India

3/5 Glenworth Street, NW1 (0171 486 3515). Baker Street tube. Open: 1200-1500 hrs and 1800-2330 hrs, Mon-Sun. Seating: 150. Specialities: North Indian. APPH: £20.

Smoking policy: 50% of restaurant allocated to smokers.

IRISH

Mulligan's of Mayfair

13/14 Cork Street, Piccadilly Circus, W1 (0171 409 1370). Piccadilly Circus tube. Open: 1100-2300 hrs, Mon-Sat. Seating: 60. Specialities: Oysters. APPH: £26.50.

Smoking policy: No restrictions.

ITALIAN

Amalfi 29/31 Old Compton Street, W1 (0171 437 7284). Leicester Square/ Tottenham Court Road tube. Open: 0900-2315 hrs, Mon-Fri. Seating: 120. APPH: £13.

Smoking policy: No pipes or cigars.

Arts Theatre Café

6/7 Great Newport Street, WC2 (0171 497 8014). Leicester Square tube. Open: 1200-2300 hrs, Mon-Fri. 1700-2300 hrs, Sat. Seating: 35. APPH: £12.50

Smoking policy: No pipes or cigars allowed in bar or restaurant but fags are OK.

The Attic Wine Bar, W5.

Bella Pasta   Brightreasons Group, Bakers House, 25 Bakers Road, Uxbridge, Middlesex
(01895 811911).
Smoking policy: All of their restaurants have smoking and non-smoking areas. Phone for
details of nearest restaurant.

Bertorelli's   44a Floral Street, WC2 (0171 836 3969). Covent Garden tube. Open: 1200-
1500 hrs and 1730-2330 hrs, Mon-Sat. Seating: 90 main restaurant, 50 bistro.
APPH: Restaurant £25, bistro £15.
Smoking policy: 50% of restaurant allocated to smokers. No restrictions in reception or bar.
Free matches.

Buona Sera   22 Northcote Road, SW11 (0171 228 9925). Clapham Junction BR. Open:
1230-1430 hrs and 1830-midnight, Mon-Sun. Seating: 95. APPH: £12-£14.
Smoking policy: No pipes or cigars but ciggies are OK.

Centro 50   150 Notting Hill Gate, W11 (0171 221 2442). Notting Hill Gate tube. Open:
1200-2330, Mon-Sat. 1200-2230, Sun. Seating: 225. Specialities: excellent
pizza. APPH: £25.
Smoking policy: No restrictions - you can smoke anywhere except the kitchen!

Leoni's Quo Vadis
26-29 Dean Street, W1 (0171 437 4809). Leicester Square/Tottenham Court
Road tube. Open: 1200-1430 hrs and 1800-2300 hrs, Mon-Fri. 1800-2300
hrs, Sat. 1900-2200 hrs, Sun. Seating: 85. APPH: £25.
Smoking policy: No restrictions in bar or restaurant. Free matches.

Neal Street Restaurant
26 Neal Street, WC2 (0171 836 8368). Covent Garden tube. Open: 1230-
1430 hrs and 1800-2300 hrs, Mon-Sat. Seating: 65. Specialities: Wild mush-
rooms and truffles. APPH: £40.
Policy: No restrictions. Free matches.

Orso   27 Wellington Street, WC2 (0171 240 5269). Covent Garden tube. Open:
1200-midnight, Mon-Sat. Seating: 130. APPH: £30.
Smoking policy: Smoking and non-smoking sections. Free matches.

The River Café
Thames Wharf, Rainville Road, W6 (0171 381 8824). Hammersmith tube.
Open: 1230-1445 hrs and 1930-2300 hrs, Mon-Sun. Last reservation 2130
hrs. Seating: 90. Specialities: Organic menu, changed twice a day. Award-win-
ning wines. APPH: £30.
Smoking policy: Smoking and non-smoking sections. Free matches.

JAPANESE

Abeno   Yaohan Plaza, 399 Edgware Road, NW9 (0181 205 1131). Colindale tube.
Open: 1200-1500 hrs, Wed-Fri. 1800-2300 hrs, Mon and Fri. 1200-2300 hrs,
Sat/Sun. Seating: 48. APPH: £10-£15.
Smoking policy: Smoking is not encouraged but ashtrays will be provided if requested.

Ikkyu   61 Tottenham Court Road, W1 (0171 636 9280). Goodge Street tube. Open:
1200-1430 hrs and 1800-2145 hrs, Mon-Fri. 1830-2130 hrs, Sat. Seating: 50.
APPH: £12.
Smoking policy: No restrictions in the bar or restaurant. Free matches.

Mitsukoshi   Dorland House, 14-20 Lower Regent Street, SW1 (0171 930 0317). Piccadilly
Circus tube. Open: 1800-2130 hrs, Mon-Sat. 1200-1400 hrs, Sun. Seating:
150. APPH: £30-£40.
Smoking policy: No restrictions in the foyer, bar or restaurant. Free matches.

Noto Ramen House
7 Bread Street, EC4 (0171 329 8056, no reservations). Bank/Mansion House
tube. Open: 1130-2100 hrs, Mon-Fri. 1130-1800 hrs, Sat. Seating: 32.
Specialities: Noodles. APPH: £10.
Smoking policy: Fags are OK but not pipes or cigars.

Suntory   72/73 St James's Street, SW1 (0171 409 0201). Green Park tube. Open: 1200-
1400 hrs and 1800-2200 hrs, Mon-Sun. Seating: 130. Specialities: Shabu shabu,
suki yaki, sushi and sashimi. APPH: £10.
Smoking policy: No restrictions in reception, bar or restaurant. Free matches.

Yaohan Plaza Food Court
399 Edgware Road, NW9 (0181 200 0009). Colindale tube. Open: 1000-
1900 hrs, Mon-Sun. Seating: 250. Specialities: Dim sum, udon noodles, Korean,
Chinese, Thai and Malaysian food. APPH: £10.
Smoking policy: Smoking and non-smoking areas adapted according to bookings. Lots of ashtrays for Nipponese smokers, especially at weekends when they watch the
Sumo wrestling on the tv in the centre of the food court, while slurping up
noodles.

JEWISH

Dizenhoff   118 Golders Green Road, NW11 (0181 458 7003). Golders Green tube.
Open: 1200-midnight, Mon-Sun. Seating: 60. Specialities: Kosher nosh. APPH:
£15.
Smoking policy: No pipes or cigars but cigarettes are OK. Free matches.

Solly's   148 Golders Green Road, NW11 (0181 455 0004/2121). Golders Green tube. Open: Upstairs 1800-2330 hrs, downstairs 1100-2300 hrs, Mon-Fri. Seating: 180. Specialities: Fresh bread baked on the premises. APPH: £15.

Smoking policy: Smoking permitted in the upstairs restaurant.

KOREAN

Arirang   31/32 Poland Street, W1 (0171 437 9662). Oxford Circus/Tottenham Court Road tube. Open: 1200-1500 hrs and 1800-2300 hrs, Mon-Sun. Seating: 25 downstairs, 36 upstairs. APPH: £15.

Smoking policy: No restrictions in the bar or restaurant. Free matches.

Kangnam   178 Upper Richmond Road West, SW14 (0181 876 9063). Mortlake BR. Open: 1200-1500 hrs and 1800-2300 hrs, Mon-Sat. 1800-2300 hrs, Sun. Seating: 55. APPH: £25.

Smoking policy: Smoking and non-smoking sections in the restaurant. No restrictions in the bar.

MEXICAN

Si Senor   86 Dean Street, W1 (0171 494 4632). Oxford Circus/Tottenham Court Road tube. Open: 1200-midnight, Mon-Fri. 1800-midnight, Sat/Sun. Seating: 160. APPH: Lunch £6.50, dinner £15.

Smoking policy: 75% of the restaurant is allocated to smokers. No restrictions at bar. Free matches.

MIDDLE EASTERN

Fakhreldine   85 Piccadilly, W1 (0171 493 3424). Green Park tube. Open: 1200-0100 hrs, Mon-Sun. Seating: 180. Specialities: Different dish every day. APPH: £25.

Smoking policy: No restrictions in the reception, bar or restaurant. Free matches.

NEPALESE

Great Nepalese

48 Eversholt Street, NW1 (0171 388 6737). Euston tube/BR. Open: 1200-1430 hrs and 1800-2330 hrs, Mon-Sun. Seating: 48. Specialities: Nepalese mixed grill and Phutuwa chicken. APPH: £10-£12.

Smoking policy: No restrictions. Free matches.

PIZZERIA

Deep Pan Pizza Company

City Centre Restaurants (UK) Ltd, 531 High Road, Wembley, Middlesex (0181 900 0955). Phone for details of nearest restaurant.

Smoking policy: Approximately one-third of their restaurants have designated smoking areas.

Eco   162 Clapham High Street, SW4 (0171 978 1108). Clapham Common tube.

Open: 1130-1530 hrs and 1830-2300 hrs, Mon-Fri. 1130-1630 hrs and 1830-2300 hrs, Sat. 1200-1700 hrs and 1830-2230 hrs, Sun. Seating:70. APPH: £12.

Smoking policy: No restrictions in bar, restaurant or reception. Pipes and cigars at discretion of management.

Kettners 29 Romney Street, W1 (0171 734 6112). Leicester Square/Tottenham Court Road tube. Open: 1200-midnight Mon-Fri. Seating: 300. Specialities: Champagne bar. Live music. APPH: £15-£17.

Smoking policy: Smoking and non-smoking sections in reception, bar and restaurant. Free matches.

Pizza Express

30 Coptic Street, WC1 (0171 636 3232). Tottenham Court Road tube. Open: 1130-midnight, Mon-Sat. 1200-2330 hrs, Sun. Seating: 110. Specialities: Four Seasons pizza (one of best traditional italian pizzarias in London). APPH: £12.

Smoking policy: 60% of restaurant allocated to smokers. Free matches.

Pizza Express

Pizza Express PLC, Unit 7, McKay Trading Estate, Kensal Road, W10 (0181 960 8238). Phone for details of nearest restaurant.

Smoking policy: No fixed non-smoking areas. The chain's restaurant director operates what he calls a "moving line" in relation to smoking and non-smoking seating. Free matches.

Pizza Hut Pizza Hut (UK) Ltd, 1 Imperial Place, Elstree Way, Borehamwood. Hertfordshire (0181 732 9000). Phone for details of nearest restaurant.

Smoking policy: The vast majority of these restaurants have smoking and non-smoking areas. The balance of smoking/non-smoking tables in each restaurant is left to the discretion of the manager.

POLISH

Lowiczanka 238-246 King Street, W6 (0181 741 3225). Ravenscourt Park tube. Open: 1200-1500 hrs and 1800-2300 hrs, Mon-Fri. 1800-2300 hrs, Sat/Sun. Seating: 150. APPH: Lunch £6, dinner £10.

Smoking policy: Fags are OK but not pipes or cigars. Probability of further restrictions.

Wodka 12 St Alban's Grove, W8 (0171 937 6513). Gloucester Road tube. Open: 1230-1430 hrs and 1900-2300 hrs, Mon-Fri. 1900-2300 hrs, Sat/Sun. Seating: 60. APPH: Lunch £12.50, dinner £25.

Smoking policy: No restrictions.

PORTUGUESE

O Fado 49/50 Beauchamp Place, SW3 (0171 589 3002). Knightsbridge/South

Kensington tube. Open: 1200-1500 hrs and 1830-0100 hrs, Mon-Sun. Seating: 80. Specialities: Seafood. APPH: £15.

Smoking policy: No restrictions in reception or bar area. No cigars in the restaurant. Free matches.

RUSSIAN

Nikita's 65 Ifield Road, SW10 (0171 352 6326). Earls Court tube. Open: 1930-2330 hrs, Mon-Sat. Seating: 70. Specialities: Caviar, smoked fish. Claims to serve the largest selection of vodkas in London. APPH: £25-£30.

Smoking policy: Pipes and cigars allowed in the bar and private room only. Cigarettes are OK.

SCANDINAVIAN

Anna's Place 90 Mildmay Park, N1 (0171 249 9379). Canonbury BR. Open: 1215-1415 hrs and 1900-2300 hrs, Mon-Sun. Seating: 30 inside, 20 garden. APPH: £20.

Smoking policy: Fags are OK but pipes and cigars only at the manager's discretion. Free matches.

The Causerie Claridge's Hotel, Brook Street, W1 (0171 629 8860). Bond Street tube. Open: 1200-1500 hrs and 1730-2300 hrs, Mon-Sun. Seating: 42. APPH: £28.

Smoking policy: No restrictions in reception, restaurant or bar. Free matches.

Garbo's 42 Crawford Street, W1 (0171 262 6582). Baker Street/Edgware Road tube. Open: 1200-1430hrs and 1800-2330 hrs, Mon-Fri. 1800-2330 hrs, Sat. 1200-1500 hrs, Sun. Specialities: Excellent Swedish food. APPH: Set lunch smorgasbord, £8.95. Dinner, £18.

Smoking policy: No pipes but cigars and cigarettes are OK.

Ake, owner of Garbo's Restaurant - he welcomes smokers.

Garlic and Shots

> 4 Frith Street, W1 (0171 734 9505). Tottenham Court Road/Leicester Square tube. Open: 1730-0130 hrs, Mon-Sun (last food order 0015 hrs). Seating: 50. Specialities: Transylvanian garlic steak. Mind you, just about every dish has garlic in it. APPH: £20-£25.

Smoking policy: No restrictions. Free matches. You can drink at the bar, even if you're not eating.

Scandinavian

> 14/15 Little Chester Street, SW1 (0171 245 1224). Hyde Park Corner tube, Victoria tube/BR. Open: 1200-1500 hrs and 1800-2230 hrs Mon-Sat. Seating: 50. Specialities: Swedish beers and schnapps. APPH: £20-£25.

Smoking policy: No restrictions in reception, restaurant or bar. Free matches.

SPANISH

The Gallery 76 Parry Street, Broadway, SW8 (0171 820 9857). Vauxhall tube/BR. Open: 1200-2300 hrs, Mon-Thur. 1200-1400 hrs, Fri. 1900-0200 hrs, Sat. Seating: 180. APPH: £15.

Smoking policy: No restrictions in restaurant or bar. Free matches.

Leadenhall Wine Bar

> 27 Leadenhall Market, EC3 (0171 623 1818). Bank/Monument tube. Open: 1130-2300 hrs, Mon-Fri. Seating: 130. Specialities: Paella. APPH: £15.

Smoking policy: No restrictions. Free matches.

Seville Mia 22 Hanway Street, W1 (0171 637 3756). Tottenham Court Road tube. Open: 1800-0100 hrs, Mon-Sat. 1900-midnight, Sun. Seating: 35. APPH: Tapas £2.50 each.

Smoking policy: No restrictions in restaurant or bar.

SRI LANKAN

Chithaara 18 The Avenue, W13 (0181 810 6606). Ealing Common tube, West Ealing BR. Open: 1200-1500 hrs and 1800-2330 hrs, Tues-Sun. Seating: 100. APPH: Lunch £4.95, dinner £7.95.

Smoking policy: Smoking and non-smoking areas in bar and restaurant.

SWISS

Marché Swiss Centre, Leicester Square, WC2 (0171 494 0498). Leicester Square tube. Open: 0800-midnight, Mon-Sat. 0900-midnight, Sun. Seating: 350. Specialities: Fondue. APPH: £10.

Smoking policy: 50% of restaurant allocated to smokers.

THAI

Khun Akorn 136 Brompton Road, SW3 (0171 225 2688). Knightsbridge tube. Open: 1200-1500 hrs and 1830-2300 hrs, Mon-Sun. Seating: 80. Specialities: Noodles. APPH: £25.

Smoking policy: No restrictions in the reception, bar or restaurant. Free matches.

TURKISH

Café Sofra 10 Shepherd Street, W1 (0171 495 3434). Green Park/Hyde Park Corner tube. Open: 1200-midnight, Mon-Sun. Seating: 30. APPH: £10.

Smoking policy: No pipes or cigars but fags are OK.

That Turkish Place
29/31 Lewisham Way, SE14 (0181 692 6357). New Cross/New Cross Gate BR/tube. Open: 1200-midnight, Mon-Wed. 1200-0100 hrs, Thur. 1200-0200 hrs, Fri. 1700-0200 hrs, Sat. 1700-midnight, Sun. Seating: 90. APPH: Four course meal £12.

Smoking policy: No restrictions.

BRASSERIES

Bar Central The Tower, 11 Bridge Street, Richmond, Surrey (0181 332 2524). Richmond tube/BR. Open: 1200-1600 hrs and 1800-2300 hrs, Mon-Sun. Seating: 90 restaurant, 160 garden. Specialities: Sea bass poached in ginger, marinated chicken. APPH: £15-£20.

Smoking policy: No restrictions in bar or restaurant.

La Brasserie 272 Brompton Road, SW3 (0171 584 1668). South Kensington tube. Open: 0800-midnight, Mon-Sat. 0900-midnight, Sun. Seating: 140. Specialities: Crépes. APPH: £15.

Smoking policy: No pipes or cigars in restaurant or bar. Ciggies are OK. Free matches.

Brasserie du Marché aux Puces
349 Portobello Road, W10 (0181 968 5828). Ladbroke Grove tube. Open: 1000-2330 hrs, Mon-Sun. Seating: 40 restaurant, 25 garden. Specialities: French food and wines. APPH: £15-£20.

Smoking policy: No pipes or cigars in restaurant or bar. Ciggies are OK.

Café Delancy 3 Delancy Street, NW1 (0171 387 1985). Camden Town tube. Open: 0800-midnight, Mon-Sun. Seating: 200. Specialities: Fish, meat and vegetarian. APPH: £15-£20.

Smoking policy: No restrictions in bar or restaurant. Free matches.

> **The man who smokes, thinks like a sage and acts like a Samaritan. (Bulwer Lytton, 1803-1873)**

Café Pelican 45 St Martin's Lane, WC2 (0171 379 0309). Leicester Square tube, Charing Cross tube/BR. Open: 1100-2330 hrs, Mon-Fri. 1100-0030 hrs, Sat. 1200-2230 hrs, Sun. Seating: 200. Specialities: French food and wines. APPH: £18-£20.

Smoking policy: No restrictions in bar or restaurant. Free matches.

Café Rouge 2 Lancer Square, off Kensington Church Street, W8 (0171 938 4200). High Street Kensington tube. Open: 1000-2300 hrs, Mon-Sat. 1000-2230 hrs, Sun. Seating: 50. Specialities: Vegetarian dishes. APPH: £15.

Smoking policy: No pipes or cigars in bar or restaurant. Fags are OK. Free matches.

Christoph's 7 Park Walk, off Fulham Road, SW3 (0171 349 8866). South Kensington tube, then 14 bus. Open: 1230-1430 and 1930-2300 hrs, Mon-Sun. 1230-1430 hrs, Sun. Seating: 65. Specialities: Roast lamb, fish cakes, duck breast. APPH: Set lunch £14, dinner £20-£25.

Smoking policy: No restrictions in bar or restaurant.

The Dome 58-62 Heath Street, NW3 (0171 431 0399). Hampstead tube. Open: 0800-2300 hrs, Mon-Fri. 0900-midnight, Sat. 0900-2230 hrs Sun. Seating: 170. Specialities: 23 blends of coffee. French food, chargrilled salmon. Happy hour cocktails. APPH: £13.

Smoking policy: Smoking and non-smoking sections in the restaurant.

Just Around the Corner
446 Finchley, NW2 (0171 431 3300). Golders Green/Finchley Road tube. Open: 1830-2330 hrs, Mon-Sat. 1200-1500 hrs and 1830-2330 hrs, Sun. Seating: 150. Specialities: Chef special every night. APPH: No fixed charge. You pay what you believe the meal is worth.

Smoking policy: 50% of restaurant allocated to smokers. Free matches.

The Oratory 232 Brompton Road, SW3 (0171 584 3493). Knightsbridge/South Kensington tube. Open: 1100-2300 hrs, Mon-Sat. Seating: 40. Specialities: Traditional British two course set menu. APPH: £12-£14.

Smoking policy: No restrictions in bar or restaurant. Free matches.

> **83% of restaurants say smokers are important to their business according to a survey by the Restaurateurs Association in October 1995.**

Pelican Group PLC, (Amalfi, Café Rouge, Café Uno, The Dome)
78 Wardour Street, W1 (0171 478 8000).
Smoking policy: No common policy for the group but every restaurant tries to accommodate both smokers and non-smokers. Free matches.

Soho Soho 11 Frith Street, W1 (0171 494 3491). Leicester Square/Tottenham Court Road tube. Open: 1200-1445 hrs, Mon-Fri. 1800-2345 hrs, Sat. 1200-2230 hrs, Sun. Seating: 60. Specialities: French Provençale. Sautéd pork and tiger prawns in peanut sauce. APPH: Restaurant £20-£25, rôtisserie £15.
Smoking policy: No smoking in reception area. No pipes or cigars in bar or restaurant but fags are fine. Free matches.

Vic Naylor 38/40 St John Street, EC1 (0171 608 2181). Farringdon tube/BR. Open: 1200-midnight, Mon-Fri. Seating: 84. Specialities: Dish of the day. APPH: £17-£18.
Smoking policy: No restrictions in bar or restaurant. Free matches.

CAFES

Aroma 36a St Martin's Lane, WC2 (0171 836 5110, no reservations). Leicester Square tube, Charing Cross tube/BR. Open: 0800-2300 hrs, Mon-Sat. 1200-2000 hrs, Sun. Seating: 70. Price: £4. (unlicensed)
Smoking policy: Smoking and non-smoking sections in restaurant and bar.

Cyberia Cyber Café
39 Whitfield Street, W1 (0171 209 0982). Warren Street/Goodge Street tube. Open: 1100-2200 hrs, Mon-Fri. 1000-2100 hrs, Sat/Sun. Seating: 50. Specialities: Internet site. Price £4-£5.
Smoking policy: No restrictions. Light up the ether.

Fifth Floor Café
Harvey Nichols, Knightsbridge, SW1 (0171 235 5000). Knightsbridge tube. Open: 1000-2230 hrs, Mon-Sat. 1200-1800 hrs, Sun. Seating: 140 restaurant, 35 garden. APPH: £15.
Smoking policy: No restrictions in bar or restaurant. Patrons are expected to be considerate when smoking pipes or cigars. Free matches.

Fortnum and Mason's St James's Restaurant
181 Piccadilly, W1 (0171 734 8040). Green Park/Piccadilly Circus tube. Open: 0930-1715 hrs, Mon-Sat. Seating: 150. Specialities: Traditional British menu. Average price: £18.50.
Smoking policy: No restrictions. Free matches.

Patisserie Valerie
44 Old Compton Street, W1 (0171 437 3466). Piccadilly Circus tube. Open:

0800-2000 hrs, Mon-Sun. Seating: 43. Specialities: Continental breakfast. Great cakes. Average price: £16.50.

Smoking policy: No restrictions.

The Place Café

17 Dukes Road, WCI (0171 383 5469). Euston tube/BR. Open: 0900-2000 hrs, Mon-Sat. Seating: 80. Specialities: Vegetarian dishes. Price: £5.

Smoking policy: No restrictions in reception area, bar or restaurant.

PARK CAFES

Clissold Park Café

Stoke Newington Church Street, N16 (0171 249 0672). 73/141 bus. Open: 1000 hrs-close, Mon-Sun (closing depends on the time of year and weather). Seating: 30 inside, 24 outside under cover, 100 on lawn. Specialities: Vegetarian food only. APPH: Main course £5.

Smoking policy: No pipes or cigars but fags are fine.

Lauderdale Restaurant

Lauderdale House, Waterlow Park, Highgate Hill, N6 (0181 341 4807). Archway tube. Open: 0800-1900 hrs, Tues-Sun. Seating: 30 inside, 50 outside. APPH: £10.

Smoking policy: No pipes or cigars in restaurant or bar but fags are fine.

FAST FOOD

Burger King Burger King Ltd, Cambridge House, Highbridge Industrial Estate, Oxford Road, Uxbridge, Middlesex (01895 206000).

Smoking policy: All branches have a non-smoking area and some outside London are totally non-smoking. If in doubt, ask.

Kentucky Fried Chicken

Pepsico Restaurants International, 32 Goldsworth Road, Woking, Surrey (01483 717000).

Smoking policy: You can usually smoke in their eateries. If in doubt, ask.

McDonald's McDonald's Restaurants Ltd, 11-49 High Road, East Finchley, N2 (0181 700 7000).

Smoking policy: Operates as a franchise so every branch has its own policy. If in doubt, ask.

Wendy's Wendy's Ltd, 4th Floor, Congress House, Lyon Road. Harrow, Middlesex (0181 424 9411).

Smoking policy: Most branches have both smoking and non-smoking areas. If in doubt, ask.

Wimpy   Wimpy International Ltd, 2 The Listons, Liston Road, Marlow, Bucking-
               hamshire (01628 891655).

Smoking policy: Operates as a franchise so each branch sets its own smoking policy. Head
               office advises each branch to set aside a non-smoking area. If in doubt, ask.
               Believed to be named after Popeye the sailorman's hamburger-loving sidekick,
               Wimpy. Popeye has a pipe permanently stuck in his mouth, at least in the
               older cartoons and comics.

Burger King, Piccadilly Circus.

Wine & Cocktail bars

If you can smoke nowhere else in the capital, there's always the pub or nearest bar, most of which are still smoker friendly. Those who have tried to ban smoking have usually ended up reversing their policy once they've counted the takings. The puffer's pound still rules.

> We have it on good authority that a number of London's leading wine critics smoke during tastings but it doesn't seem to adversely affect their palate. Indeed, some are so used to combining the two pleasures that if they quit smoking tomorrow, they would have to give up their job!

Sections:	Each pub is placed alphabetically in its relevant postcode area, i.e. a pub in Victoria, SW1, will be found under 'South West'.
APPH:	Average price per head for a 3-course meal excluding drinks and service, unless otherwise stated.
DLR:	Dockland Light Railway.
Entertainment:	Mostly live music (this varies - what's stated is an example, only), quizzes and karaoke nights - check with the pub for more up-to-date information.
Food:	Pubs sometimes have a separate area for food, including restaurants.
Times:	Refers to the availability of food. London's pubs are legally allowed to stay open for up to 12 hours a day, ie 11am-11pm. Some close between 3pm-6pm, usually on Sundays, when they also shut at 10.30pm. Some pubs in the City of London do not open on Sundays, so do check.
Information:	Correct at time of going to press, but subject to change. Do check, for the latest details.

CENTRAL

Audley   41-43 Mount Street, W1 (0171 499 1843). Green Park/Marble Arch tube. Bars: 2 (main and wine bar/function room in cellar). Food: 2 areas. Restaurant (separate room upstairs) - traditional English cuisine, Mon-Sun, 1200-1415, 1730-2115. APPH: £12.95. At bar - pub snacks, Mon-Sun, 1100-2115. APPH: £2-£7 per main course. Entertainment: None. Specialities: Wine bar in cellar. 4 tables out side. Grand Victorian pub attached to hotel. Chandeliered, it cuts a dash in Mayfair. 4 real ales.

Smoking policy: No restrictions.

Lost in thought, Waterloo station.

Overheard in a London pub: "Every time I light up a fag in public some intolerant git comes out with the usual unimaginative comment, 'You smoke, I choke.' And I always answer: 'Sounds like a good idea to me.'"

Bloomsbury Tavern

236 Shaftesbury Avenue, WC2 (0171 836 5065). Tottenham Court Road/Holborn tube. Bars: 1. Food: Pub grub, Mon-Sat, 1200-1430. APPH: £3.95 per main course. Entertainment: None. Specialities: Ideal for pre-theatre (and intervals) imbibing. A tiny pub with wooden partitions. 6 real ales.

Smoking policy: No restrictions.

Chandos

29 St Martin's Lane, WC2 (0171 836 1401). Charing Cross tube/BR. Bars: 2 (main and Opera Room). Food: 2 areas, Mon-Sun. Opera Room - pub grub, 0900-1030, 1100-1430, 1730-2100; salad bar, afternoons. APPH: £4-£10 per main course. At main bar - pub snacks, 1100-1430, 1730-2100. APPH: £1.25-£3.95 per main course. Entertainment: None. Specialities: Located next to the Coliseum, this is not only a good stopping place for *entr'acte drinks*, but also for food. The leather banquettes in the Opera Room upstairs are much sought after by the after-work crowd. 1 real ale.

Smoking policy: No restrictions.

Coach & Horses

29 Greek Street, W1 (0171 437 5920). Leicester Square tube. Bars: 1. Food: Bar snacks - sandwiches. Mon-Sat, 1100-2300; Sun, 1100-2230. APPH: £2 per sandwich. Entertainment: None. Specialities: Bustling home to employees of the long-running satirical magazine, Private Eye, designers, artists and the like. Used to be Jeffrey Bernard's favourite watering hole. The landlord claims to be London's rudest, a belief left undisputed by one and all. 4 real ales.

Smoking policy: Designated non-smoking area, otherwise no restrictions.

Coal Hole

91 Strand, WC1 (0171 836 7503). Charing Cross tube/BR or Embankment tube. Bars: 2 (mezzanine bar and cellar wine bar [open evenings only]). Food: Pub grub, Mon-Sat, 1130-1430. APPH: £2.25-£5 per main course. Entertainment: None. Specialities: Young crowd at weekends replaces the business clientele of weekdays. Edmund Kean used to frequent this handsome old pub. 6 real ales.

Smoking policy: No restrictions.

Devereux   20 Devereux Court, Essex Street, WC2 (0171 583 4562). Covent Garden/Leicester Square tube. Bars: 1, 1 function room. Food: 2 areas, Mon-Fri, 1200-1430. Restaurant (45 seats) - English restaurant cuisine. APPH: £10-£15. At bar - pub grub. APPH: £4.50 per main course. Entertainment: None. Specialities: Elegant pub in a quiet courtyard, frequented by barristers and clerks from nearby Temple Inn. 5 real ales.
Smoking policy: No restrictions.

Fitzroy Tavern
16 Charlotte Street, W1 (0171 580 3714). Goodge Street/Tottenham Court Road tube. Bars: 2 (cellar and main). Food: Home-cooked pub grub, 1200-1500, 1830-2230. APPH: £4.25 per main course. Entertainment: None. Specialities: Lively with a tradition of visits by writers and artists - Richard Attenborough, George Orwell and Dylan Thomas among them. 2 real ales.
Smoking policy: No restrictions.

Flyman & Firkin
166-170 Shaftesbury Avenue, WC2 (0171 240 7109). Tottenham Court Road/Leicester Square tube. Bars: 1. Food: Pub grub. APPH: £4.50 per main course. Entertainment: Live music (covers of hits of 1960s-1980s), Thur & Sat. Specialities: Typical Firkin pub with young, lively clientele. Real ale.
Smoking policy: No restrictions.

French House
49 Dean Street, W1 (0171 437 2799). Leicester Square tube. Bars: 1. Food: 2 areas . French House Dining Room restaurant (30 seats), Mon-Sat, 1230-1500, 1830-2300. APPH: £23. At bar - pub snacks, Mon-Sat, 1230-1500, 1830-2230. APPH: £3 per main course. Entertainment: None. Specialities: Strong Gallic history to this watering hole which has been frequented by Maurice Chevalier, Francis Bacon, Lucien Freud among other famous celebrities. No real ale. 15 wines.
Smoking policy: No restrictions.

Fulmar & Firkin
51 Parker Street, WC2 (0171 405 0590). Holborn tube. Bars: 1. Food: Pub grub, 1200-2230. APPH: £4.95 per main course. Entertainment: Live comedy, Sat. Specialities: Bare floorboards. Popular with students and tutors from London School of Economics. Busy at weekends, especially Saturday with its free comedy night. Real ale.
Smoking policy: No restrictions.

Glassblower   42 Glasshouse Street, W1 (0171 734 8547). Piccadilly Circus tube. Bars: 2. Food: Pub grub. Mon-Thur, 1100-2100; Fri & Sat, 1100-1700; Sun 1200-2100.

APPH: £5 per main course. Entertainment: None. Specialities: Real ale. Traditional pub.

Smoking policy: No restrictions.

> **Less is more, even in smoking. Make it a philosophy. Make it a delightful celebration. (Zino Davidoff, 'A Renaissance of Pleasure')**

Grafton Arms

72 Grafton Way, W1 (0171 387 7923). Warren Street/Goodge Street tube. Bars: 2. Food: Pub grub. APPH: £3.50 per main course. Summer barbecue, Mon-Fri, 1830-2030. APPH: £1.50 per burger. Specialities: Roof garden provides an excellent sun-trap.

Smoking policy: No restrictions.

Guinea

30 Bruton Place, W1 (0171 409 1728). Green Park/Bond Street tube. Bars: 1. Food: 2 areas. Restaurant (40-60 seats). APPH: £25.00. At bar - pub grub. APPH: £5 per main course. Entertainment: None. Specialities: Dates back to 1423. Famous for its steaks and those who have enjoyed them - including Liz Taylor, Richard Burton, Frank Sinatra, King Hussein of Jordan and Princess Margaret. Even its steak and kidney pie and grilled sandwiches have won prizes. Real ale.

Smoking policy: No restrictions.

Hope

15 Tottenham Street, W1 (0171 637 0896). Goodge Street tube. Bars: 1, 1 function room. Food: 2 areas (table service in function room or self-service. counter at bar), lunchtime. Pub grub and tasty meals, range of sausages. APPH: £3-£5 per main course. Entertainment: None. Specialities: A 'local' hidden away in the West End. Tables outside. Real ale.

Smoking policy: No restrictions

Lamb & Flag

33 Rose Street, WC2 (0171 497 9504). Covent Garden tube. Bars: 2. Food: Pub grub, lunchtime. APPH: £3-£4 per main course. Entertainment: Live jazz, Sun. Specialities: Tiny pub in a side alley. Real ale.

Smoking policy: No restrictions.

Lyceum Tavern

354 Strand, WC2 (0171 836 7155). Covent Garden tube. Bars: 2. Food: Home-cooked pub grub. APPH: £4.25 per main course. Entertainment: None. Specialities: The old Lyceum Theatre next door is currently under renovation, promising the Tavern a rejuvenation of its original reputation as a haunt for theatricals. Real ale.

Smoking policy: No restrictions.

Marquess of Granby

51-52 Chandos Place, WC2 (0171 836 7657). Charing Cross tube/BR. Bars: 2. Food: 2 areas (40-seat dining room and bar area). Home-cooked pub grub. Mon-Sat, 1100-2100; Sun, 1200-1830. APPH: £4.50 per main course. Entertainment: None. Specialities: Handy drinking parlour for opera fans, at the back of the London Coliseum. 4 real ales. Sky Sport on the tv. Brews its own beer.

Smoking policy: No restrictions.

Moon and Sixpence

181-185 Wardour Street, W1 (0171 734 0037). Tottenham Court Road/Leicester Square tube. Bars: 1. Food: A la carte English restaurant cuisine, 1100-2200. APPH: £10. Entertainment: None. Specialities: As with all J. D. Wetherspoon pubs, no music. Board games available and popular. Real ale.

Smoking policy: All Wetherspoon pubs have a large non-smoking section - approx. 30 per cent (as in this pub), depending on the size of the building.

Moon under the Water

28 Leicester Square, WC2 (0171 839 2837). Leicester Square tube. Bars: 1. Food: Pub grub. Mon-Fri, 1100-2200; Sun, 1200-2130. APPH: £4.50 per main course. Entertainment: None. Specialities: If you can get in it's a good place to forget a bad film. Real ale.

Smoking policy: Designated non-smoking area (25% of pub).

Museum Tavern

49 Great Russell Street, WC1 (0171 242 8987). Tottenham Court Road tube. Bars: 1. Food: Pub grub. Mon-Sat, 1100-2200; Sun, 1200-2100. APPH: £4.99 per main course. Entertainment: None. Specialities: Once a haunt of Karl Marx, a student at the nearby British Museum, it still retains its scholarly charm. Real ale.

Smoking policy: No restrictions.

Newman Arms

23 Rathbone Street, W1 (0171 636 1127). Tottenham Court Road/Goodge Street tube. Bars: 1. Food: Pies, 30-seat restaurant upstairs. APPH: £5.95 per pie including veg. Entertainment: None. Specialities: Serves one of the best ranges of traditional pies and puddings in London. Real ale.

Smoking policy: No restrictions.

Old Crown

33 New Oxford Street, WC1 (0171 836 9121). Tottenham Court Road tube. Bars: 1, 1 function room. Food: Lunchtimes - steak sandwich, triple-decker and fries. Evenings - continental menu. APPH: £5 per main course. Entertainment: None. Specialities: Lively in the evening. Real ale.

Smoking policy: No restrictions.

Half a pint of beer and a fag, Covent Garden.

O'Neill's   4 Conway Street, WI (0171 631 5300). Warren Street tube. Bars: 2 (main and first floor/function room). Food: Irish pub grub. APPH: £4-£6 per main course. Entertainment: Live traditional Irish music. Specialities: Real ale. Whisky bar. Good craic.
Smoking policy: No restrictions.

Princess Louise
208 High Holborn, WCI (0171 405 8816). Holborn tube. Bars: 2 (main and wine bar/buffet area upstairs). Food: Pub snacks, lunchtime and evening. Thai food upstairs, lunchtime. APPH: £5 per main course. Entertainment: None. Specialities: Grade II listed Victorian building with beautiful ornate interior. Real ales.
Smoking policy: No restrictions.

Punch & Judy
40 The Market, Covent Garden, WC2 (0171 379 0923). Covent Garden tube. Bars: 2. Food: Home-cooked pub grub. Mon-Fri, 1130-1700; Sat, 1130-1500; Sun, 1200-1500. APPH: £4.95 per main course. Entertainment: None. Specialities: Real ale. Set in the heart of Covent Garden with a balcony over-looking the Piazza and excellent views of street entertainers.
Smoking policy: Non-smoking section in cellar food area, otherwise no restrictions.

Queen Mary Victoria Embankment, WC2 (0171 240 9404). Embankment tube or Charing Cross tube/BR. Bars: 3 (1 on deck, 2 inside). Food: Restaurant (92 seats). Weekdays: restaurant, lunches and evenings. APPH: £10.95 3-course set price; or à la carte. Weekends: carvery, Sat lunch and evening, Sun all day. APPH: £12.95 per two courses. Entertainment: Disco, Fri, 1900-1100. Specialities: Old pleasure steamer turned into an on-river pub with a free weekend disco. Great for summer drinking. No real ale as they can't store it on board, but plenty of other tipples.

Smoking policy: No restrictions.

> ## "If I cannot smoke in heaven, then I shall not go."
> ### (Mark Twain)

Sherlock Holmes

10 Northumberland Street, WC2 (0171 930 2644). Embankment tube or Charing Cross tube/BR. Bars: 1. Food: 2 areas. Restaurant (36-seat room on first floor) - à la carte English cuisine. APPH: £15-£20. At bar - pub grub. APPH: £4-£5 per main course. Entertainment: None. Specialities: Homage to the most famous smoker in the world with one room set up as an exact replica of Holmes's study. Tables outside. 6 real ales.

Smoking policy: Designated non-smoking section in restaurant, otherwise no restrictions.

Windmill Mill Street, W1 (0171 491 8050). Oxford Circus tube. Bars: 2. Food: Pub grub, lunchtime and evening. APPH: £4.95 per main course. Entertainment: None. Specialities: No background music. Comfortable old pub ideal for conversation. Real ale.

Smoking policy: Designated non-smoking section in food area at lunchtime, otherwise no restrictions.

Ye Grapes 16 Shepherd Market, W1 (0171 499 1563). Green Park tube. Bars: 1. Food: 2 areas (served at bar or in 40-seat dining area upstairs). Pub grub. Mon-Sat, 1200-1500, 1800-2200; Sun, 1200-1500, 1800-2100. APPH: £4-£4.75 per main course. Entertainment: None. Specialities: Walls adorned with horned beasts, guns and glass cased objects True real ale pub with 8 varieties.

Smoking policy: No restrictions.

> **Two smokers overheard in a pub:**
> **Q: "What do you think of the the two main candidates for the next election, who both want to ban smoking in public?"**
> **A: "I'm glad that only one of them can get in."**

Artillery Arms

102 Bunhill Row, EC1 (0171 253 4683). Moorgate/Barbican tube/BR. Bars: 1. Food: Pub grub APPH: £2-£5 per main course. Entertainment: None. Specialities: Traditional, popular pub. Upstairs function room overlooks Bunhill cemetery where Daniel Defoe is buried. Real ale.

Smoking policy: No restrictions.

Betsy Trotwood

56 Farringdon Road, EC1 (0171 253 4285). Farringdon tube/BR. Bars: 2 (main and cellar). Food: 3 areas (at main bar, in seating area upstairs, in cellar wine bar). Pub grub, lunchtime. APPH: £3.95 per main course. Entertainment: None. Specialities: Popular with staff from the nearby offices of the *Guardian* and the *Observer*. Real ale.

Smoking policy: No restrictions.

Bishops Finger

9-10 West Smithfield Street, EC1 (0171 248 2341). Barbican/Farringdon/St Paul's tube. Bars: 2. Food: Pub grub. APPH: £2-£4 per main course. Entertainment: None. Specialities: 4 real ales. 2 outside tables - only pub in City licensed to have these. Relaxed, what landlord calls 'attitude-friendly' pub.

Smoking policy: No restrictions.

Blackfriar

174 Queen Victoria Street, EC4 (0171 236 5650). Blackfriars tube/BR. Bars: 1. Food: Pub grub, lunchtime APPH: £3.95 per main course. Entertainment: None. Specialities: On the site of an old Dominican monastery, this renovated Victorian pub has a unique art nouveau aspect with its marbled fascia and interior of panels depicting monks at play. Real ale.

Smoking policy: No restrictions.

Cartoonist

76 Shoe Lane, EC4 (0171 353 2828). Chancery Lane, Blackfriars tube/BR. Bars: 2. Food: Bistro cuisine. APPH: £4-£12 per main course. Entertainment: None. Specialities: Walls covered in original cartoon drawings, this is a popular meeting place for newspaper cartoonists and their victims - Margaret Thatcher, Frank Bruno, Enoch Powell, Ken Livingstone and Jeffrey Archer among others. Real ale.

Smoking policy: No restrictions.

> **"Little tube of mighty power, Charmer of an idle hour."**
> **(Isaac Hawkins Browne, 'A Pipe of Tobacco')**

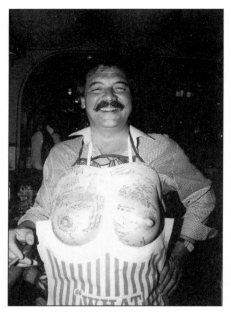

Left: Bill Bebb's birthday party at EFES restaurant. Right: Game of snooker in St Pancras pub

Eagle   159 Farringdon Road, EC1 (0171 837 1353). Farringdon tube/BR. Bars: 1.
Food: Spanish/South American cuisine, lunchtime and evening. APPH: £10-
£15. Entertainment: None. Specialities: Very lively atmosphere. Egon Ronay
liked the food here. Art gallery upstairs, open Thurs & Fri, 1100-1800; Sat &
Sun, 1100-1600. Admission free. Real ale.

Smoking policy: No restrictions.

Fox & Anchor
        115 Charterhouse Street, EC1 (0171 253 4838). Farringdon/Barbican
tube/BR. Bars: 1, 1 function room. Food: 2 areas (served in function room
and at bar). Traditional English cuisine, breakfast and lunchtime. APPH: English
breakfast: £6.50. Lunch: £8-£10. Entertainment: None. Specialities: Close to
Smithfield meat market (vegetarian menu available). Well known for its mas-
sive breakfasts and gourmet steaks. Real ale.

Smoking policy: No restrictions.

Golden Fleece
        8-9 Queen Street, EC4 (0171 236 1433). Bank, Mansion House tube. Bars: 1.
Food: 2 areas. Cellar restaurant - English & continental menu. APPH: £8 per
two courses. At bar - home-cooked pub grub. APPH: £4 per main course.

Entertainment: None. Specialities: Real ale.
Smoking policy: No restrictions.

Hand and Shears

1 Middle Street, EC1 (0171 600 0257). Barbican tube/BR. Bars: 1, 1 function room. Food: 2 areas. Dining area (30 seats, upstairs) - pub grub. APPH: £4.95 per main course. At bar - pub snacks. APPH: £2-£3 per main course. Entertainment: None. Specialities: Former customers include John Betjeman. who lived nearby, Winston Churchill and Stanley Baldwin.
Smoking policy: No restrictions.

Hoop and Grapes

47 Aldgate High Street, EC3 (0171 480 5739). Aldgate tube. Bars: 1. Food: International cuisine (100 seats within bar area), Mon-Sat, 1200-1500. APPH: £5 per main course. Entertainment: None. Specialities: Claims to be the only pub to survive the Great Fire that swept through the City in 1666. There's at least another City pub that makes the same claim. Real ale.
Smoking policy: No restrictions.

Lamb Tavern 10-12 Leadenhall Market, EC3 (0171 626 2454). Bank tube. Bars: 3 (main, upstairs, Dive Bar in cellar), 1 function room. Food: 3 areas. Restaurant (dining area on top floor), lunchtimes. APPH: £6.50 per main course. Dive Bar bar snacks. APPH: £2-£3 per snack. Ground floor bar pub grub. APPH: £4 per main course. Entertainment: None. Specialities: Spacious Victorian pub with a mezzanine bar and balcony overlooking Leadenhall Market. Real ale.
Smoking policy: Top bar/restaurant is non-smoking, otherwise no restrictions.

Magpie and Stump

18 Old Bailey, EC4 (0171 248 5085). Holborn Central BR, St Paul's tube. Bars: 2. Food: Pub snacks, 1200-1400. APPH: £2-£3 per main course. Entertainment: Disco, Thur. Specialities: Once opposite the dreaded Newgate Jail this pub is now completely rebuilt. Spot the barristers. Real ale.
Smoking policy: No restrictions.

O'Hanlons 8 Tysoe Street, EC1 (0171 837 4112). Farringdon tube/BR. Bars: 1. Food: Irish restaurant cuisine, APPH: £5.50 per main course. Entertainment: None. Specialities: Open Mon-Fri only. Serves a range of Irish and other tipples as well as own-brewed beer. 25-seat patio.
Smoking policy: No restrictions.

> **There is no mention of cigars in Graham Greene's novel,
> Our Man in Havana.**

Fountain's Abbey

109 Praed Street, W2 (0171 723 2364). Paddington tube/BR. Bars: 1, 1 function room. Food: Pub grub. Mon-Sat, 1100-2300; Sun, 1200-2230. APPH: £4.50 per main course. Entertainment: None. Specialities: Traditional pub serving real ale. Famous for being the place where Alexander Fleming, popping in from his laboratory opposite, is said to have found the mould that led to the invention of Penicillin.

Smoking policy: No restrictions.

Old Bell Tavern

95 Fleet Street, EC4 (0171 583 0070). Blackfriars tube/BR. Bars: 1. Food: Pub snacks, Mon-Fri, 1200-1500. APPH: £2 per main course. Entertainment: None. Specialities: Built in 1678 as a home for his masons by Sir Christopher Wren while he was rebuilding St Bride's, the journalists' church in Bride Lane. Listed building. Real ale.

Smoking policy: No restrictions.

Old King Lud

78 Ludgate Hill, EC4 (0171 329 8517). Blackfriars tube/BR. Bars: 1. Food: Pub grub, 1200-1500, 1700-2000. APPH: £4 per main course. Entertainment: None. Specialities: Real ale.

Smoking policy: Designated non-smoking section at lunchtime, otherwise no restrictions.

Ye Olde Cheshire Cheese

Wine Office Court, 145 Fleet Street, EC4 (0171 353 6170). Chancery Lane, Blackfriars tube/BR. Bars: 6, 1 function room on first floor. Food: 4 areas, Ground floor - traditional English pub grub. APPH: £6-£10. Ground floor - bar snacks. Second floor - English restaurant cuisine. APPH: £15. Cellar bar - sandwiches and snacks (mind your head). Entertainment: None. Specialities: Busy. Caters for tourists, solicitors and businessmen alike. Good range of filling food. Charles Dickens used to frequent this ancient tavern, as did Dr Samuel Johnson who used to eat and talk here. He didn't smoke or drink but gave money to the poor and didn't mind if they spent it on tobacco or gin. Real ale.

Smoking policy: No restrictions.

Ye Olde Mitre Tavern

1 Ely Court, EC1 (0171 405 4751). Chancery Lane tube. Bars: 2. Food: Sandwiches, 1100-2200. APPH: £1 per sandwich. Entertainment: None. Specialities: First opened in 1546, this Elizabethan building tucked down an alley is one of the oldest pubs in London. No juke box or fruit machines, thank God. Popular at lunchtimes and in evenings. Real ale.

Smoking policy: No restrictions.

Ye Olde Wine Shades

6 Martin Lane, EC4 (0171 626 6303). Cannon Street tube/BR. Bars: 2. Food: 3 areas. Restaurant (40-seat waitress service area, 30-seat self-service area) - pub grub, 1130-1500. APPH: £13-£15. At bar - pub snacks. APPH: £4 per main course. Entertainment: None. Specialities: Excellent range of wines at this pub which - like the Hoop and Grapes - claims to be the only building to survive the Great Fire of London (make your own mind up - they're certainly both ancient enough). Smart dress required. Primarily a wine bar (175 varieties available). Bottled beer is also popular. No real ale.

Smoking policy: No restrictions.

NORTH

Alwyne Castle

83 St Paul's Road, N1 (0171 359 1108). Highbury and Islington tube/BR. Bars: 2 (main and conservatory). Food: Pub grub in conservatory, lunchtime. APPH: £4 per main course. Entertainment: None. Specialities: Conservatory. 9 tables outside.

Smoking policy: No restrictions.

Angel

37 Highgate High Street, N6 (0181 340 4305). Archway/Highgate tube. Bars: 1. Food: Pub grub, 1200-2000. APPH: £3.95 per main course. Entertainment: Live music (R & B, rock and roll), Sat. Specialities: Young clientele. Lively pub with loud music.

Smoking policy: No restrictions.

Antwerp Arms

168-170 Church Road, N17 (0181 808 4449). Tottenham Hale tube/White Hart Lane BR. Bars: 1. Food: Pub grub (24-seat dining area in conservatory). APPH: £9. Entertainment: None. Specialities: Garden. Village pub atmosphere in this tiny tavern. Real ale.

Smoking policy: No restrictions.

Black Cap

171 Camden High Street, NW1 (0171 485 1742). Camden Town tube. Bars: 2 (main and upstairs). Food: Pub grub, 1200-1730. APPH: £3-£6 per main course. Entertainment: Drag artistes. Specialities: Gay pub famous for its cabaret

Smoking policy: No restrictions.

Man's life is but a vapour!

Left: Dingwalls, Camden Town. Right: Eye to eye, outside Jamaica Wine House in the City.

Bull   13 North Hill, N6 (0181 340 4412). Highgate tube. Bars: 1. Food: Pub grub. APPH: £4.30-£5.50 per main course. Entertainment: None. Specialities: Side garden and front terrace. There has been a pub on the site for 400 years frequented at times by Charles Dickens and others.

Smoking policy: No restrictions.

Camden Head

Camden Walk, N1 (0171 359 0851). Angel tube. Bars: 2 (1 doubles as a function room). Food: Pub grub. APPH: £3.95 per main course. Entertainment: Comedy, Fri & Sat. Specialities: Terrace garden. Victorian gin palace with etched windows and engraved mirrors. Handy for the popular antiques market of Wed & Sat, nearby.

Smoking policy: No restrictions.

Compton Arms

4 Compton Avenue, N1 (0171 359 6833). Highbury and Islington tube/BR. Bars: 1. Food: None that we know of. Entertainment: None. Specialities: Dominoes.

Smoking policy: No restrictions.

Dublin Castle 94 Parkway, NW1 (0171 485 1773). Camden Town tube. Bars: 2 (main and in venue room). Food: None. Entertainment: Madness played here. Now there's Indie, R&B and Ska nights.
Smoking policy: No restrictions.

Flask Flask Walk, NW3 (0171 435 4580). Hampstead tube. Bars: 3. Food: Pub grub. Mon-Fri, 1200-1500; Sat & Sun, 1200-1600; Tues-Sat, 1800-2100. APPH: £3.50 per main course. Specialities: Strong local feel to this pub, still separated into public and saloon bars. Real ale.
Smoking policy: No restrictions

Flask 77 Highgate West Hill, N6 (0181 340 7260). Highgate tube. Bars: 2 (main and an overflow bar). Food: 2 areas. Pub grub. Mon-Fri, 1200-1400, 1800-2115; Sat, 1200-1430; Sun 1200-1430, 1500-2115. APPH: £3.75-£6.20 per main course. Bar snacks, Mon-Fri, 1400-1800. Entertainment: None. Specialities: It once sold flasks of water from Hampstead's mineral springs when it opened in 1663. Gets very crowded. Real ale.
Smoking policy: No restrictions.

Globe Tavern
43-47 Marylebone Road, NW1 (0171 935 6368). Baker Street tube. Bars: 2 (main and wine bar). Food: 3 areas, lunchtimes and evenings. Restaurant (30 seats) - English cuisine. APPH: £8.25 per main course. Ground floor bar - pub grub. APPH: £5.50 per main course. Wine bar - sandwiches. APPH: £4.25 per main course. Entertainment: None. Specialities: Majestic easy-to-spot Victorian pub opposite Baker Street tube, popular with tourists visiting Madame Tussaud's and Planetarium. Real ale.
Smoking policy: No restrictions.

Green Man 383 Euston Road, NW1 (0171 387 6977). Great Portland Street tube. Bars: 2 (main and cellar wine bar). Food: 2 areas. Ground floor bar - pub grub. Wine bar - traditional English home-cooked pies. APPH: £5.75 per main course. Entertainment: None. Specialities: Victorian pub close to Regent's Park. Real ale.
Smoking policy: No restrictions.

Holly Bush 22 Holly Mount, NW3 (0171 435 2892). Hampstead tube. Bars: 2. Food: Pub grub. APPH: £2-£4.50 per main course. Entertainment: Live music, jazz (Sun eve), 1960s-1970s covers (Wed). Poetry night (open to all budding bards), Tues (£2.50 entrance). Specialities: One of Hampstead's most picturesque pubs. Seats outside. Real ale.
Smoking policy: No restrictions.

Jack Straw's Castle

North End Way, NW3 (0171 435 8885). Hampstead tube. Bars: 2 (ground and first floor bars - latter only open weekends). Food: 2 areas. Restaurant (60 seats) - English and continental cuisine. Mon-Sat, 1200-1500, 1800-2200; Sun, 1200-2100. APPH: £13.95 3-course set menu. APPH: £9-£17 a la carte main course. Bar - home-cooked pub grub. Weekdays, 1200-2100. Sun, 1200-1600. APPH: £2.50-5.50 per main course. Entertainment: Shakespeare theatre, summer only (Briefly Shakespeare Co.). Specialities: Famous as the place where the leader of the Peasants' Revolt and associate of Wat Tyler took refuge, but - too late - he was caught and executed, just outside. Patio dining area, spacious ground floor bar and views of Hampstead Heath (the first floor bar/restaurant is the highest in London). Real ale.

Smoking policy: No restrictions at present.

King of Bohemia

10 Hampstead High Street, NW3 (0171 435 6513). Hampstead tube. Bars: 1. Food: Pub grub, Mon-Sun, 1200-1700. APPH: £2.95-£4.35 per main course. Breakfast, Mon-Sun, 0800-1100. APPH: £2 (crepe/croissant) - £3.25 (full English). Entertainment: None. Specialities: Modern, small pub. Seats in front. Good range of wines and real ales.

Smoking policy: No restrictions.

Narrow Boat 119 St Peter's Street, N1 (0171 226 3906). Angel tube. Bars: 1. Food: Home-cooked pub grub. Mon-Fri, 1200-1500; Wed-Fri, 1830-2030. APPH: £4.50 per main course. Summer barbecue, Sat & Sun (allowing for fine weather). Entertainment: Live music (including jazz), Fri. Specialities: This isn't a real narrow boat - it was built in the style of one - but looks the part, situated on the Regents Canal. Seats on the towpath and a terrace on the deck. Real ale.

Smoking policy: No restrictions.

Old Bull and Bush

North End Road, NW3 (0181 455 3685). Golders Green tube. Bars: 1. Food: Pub grub, 1200-2100. APPH: £4 per main course. Entertainment: None. Specialities: Home of the original "Come, come, come and make eyes at me down at the old Bull and Bush, da da da da da" refrain, now a modern, lively pub for over-21s only. Real ale.

Smoking policy: Designated non-smoking section in dining area, otherwise no restrictions.

Spaniard's Inn

Spaniard's Road, NW3 (0181 455 3276). Hampstead/Golders Green tube. Bars: 1, 1 function room/dining area. Food: 2 areas, Mon-Sun. Restaurant - English cuisine, 1800-2130. APPH: £14. Pub grub, 1200-2130, APPH: £3-£6 per main course. Entertainment: None. Specialities: Dickens, Shelley and Dick Turpin are just some of the many famous visitors to this 16th-century tavern over the years - the upstairs dining area overlooks the toll house where, rumour has it, the highwayman watched out for suitable prey. Dickens gave the pub a role in *The Pickwick Papers*. The garden is one of the best of any London inns, with flowers, plants and an aviary. Kenwood House and Hampstead close by. 4 real ales.

Smoking policy: Non-smoking area available, otherwise smoker-friendly.

SOUTH WEST

Admiral Codrington

17 Mossop Street, SW3 (0171 581 0005). South Kensington tube. Bars: 3 bars merged as one (main bar, snug, conservatory). Food: Home-cooked pub grub and ciabattas. APPH: £5.25 per main course. Entertainment: None. Specialities: Quiet, traditional pub without juke box or TV, ideal for chatting and smoking. Conservatory with pool/billiards table. Real ale.

Smoking policy: No restrictions.

Albert

52 Victoria Street, SW1 (0171 222 5577). St James's Park tube. Bars: 1. Food: 2 areas. Carvery restaurant (90 seats, first floor). APPH: £13.95. Bar pub grub. APPH: £4.25 per main course. Entertainment: None. Specialities: Listed Victorian building with beautifully etched windows. Listen to the ringing of the Division Bell from House of Commons and watch the MPs run. Real ale.

Smoking policy: No restrictions.

Antelope

22 Eaton Terrace, SW1 (0171 730 7781). Sloane Square tube. Bars: 2 (main and annexe). Food: 2 areas. Restaurant (separate dining area upstairs) - English food. APPH: £5-£6 per main course. At bar - bar snacks. Entertainment: None. Specialities: 200-year-old pub frequented by jolly pinstripes. Real ale.

Smoking policy: Non-smoking section in restaurant, otherwise no restrictions.

Blue Posts

6 Bennet Street, SW1 (0171 493 3350). Green Park tube. Bars: 1, 1 function room. Food: Separate dining area in function room upstairs, lunchtimes. APPH: £4 per main course. Entertainment: None. Specialities: Site dates back to 1667, although the current building was built after the Blitz of WW2. Once frequented by Lord Byron, who lived next door. Real ale.

Smoking policy: No restrictions.

Bunch of Grapes

207 Brompton Road, SW3 (0171 589 4944). Knightsbridge/South Kensington tube. Bars: 1. Food: Pub grub, 1100-2300. APPH: £4-£7 per main course. Entertainment: Live music (duo singing 'cover' songs), Thur. Specialities: Next

to Harrods. Ornate 18th century, classy pub.

Smoking policy: No restrictions.

Clarence   55 Whitehall, SW1 (0171 930 4808). Charing Cross/Embankment tube/BR. Bars: 1. Food: Pub grub, 1100-2100. APPH: £5-£6 per main course. Entertainment: None. Specialities: Tourist information centre is attached. Ancient pub with leaded windows and timbers from a Thames pier. 4 real ales.

Smoking policy: No restrictions.

Drayton Arms

153 Old Brompton Road, SW5 (0171 373 0385). Gloucester Road/South Kensington tube. Bars: 2. Food: Pub grub. APPH: £4.50 per main course. Entertainment: None. Specialities: Has a private theatre used by agents for drama student shows. Listed Victorian building. Seating outside. Real ale.

Smoking policy: No restrictions.

Duke's Head 8 Lower Richmond Road, SW15 (0181 788 2552). Putney Bridge tube. Bars: 2. Food: Pub grub, 1200-1500. APPH: £4.50 per main course. Sunday lunch (£6.50, 2-course set price). Entertainment: None. Specialities: Elegant Georgian building next to the river Thames, good place to be on the day of the Oxford v Cambridge Boat Race. Fine etched glass, comfortable banquettes, lofty ceilings and rowing memorabilia. No music as with all Young's pubs. Over 21s only. Real ale.

Smoking policy: No restrictions.

Hampstead Wine Bar.

Ferret & Firkin

114 Lots Road, SW10 (0171 352 6645). Fulham Broadway tube. Bars: 1. Food: Pub grub, 1200-2000. APPH: £3-£5 per main course. Entertainment: Live music (keyboard player, Fri; guitarist, Sat). Specialities: 5 real ales - own brewery on site. Busy pub popular with the 22-30 age group. Friday's keyboard player is especially popular.

Smoking policy: No restrictions.

> **Three things are men most likely to be cheated in -**
> **a horse, a wife and a cigar.**

Freedom & Firkin

196 Tooting High Street, SW7 (0181 672 5794). Tooting Broadway tube. Bars: 1. Food: Pub grub. APPH: £4-£5 per main course. Entertainment: Live music (cover duos), Sat & Sun. Specialities: Young, lively pub with background music. Real ale.

Smoking policy: No restrictions.

Grenadier   18 Wilton Row, Belgrave Square, SW1 (0171 235 3074). Hyde Park Corner tube. Bars: 1. Food: 2 areas. Separate dining area - a la carte English. APPH: £20.00. Bar pub grub. APPH: £4 per main course. Entertainment: Morris dancers, in summer. Specialities: Reputed to be haunted by the Duke of Wellington whose officers used it as their mess. Tudor bar is 300 years old. Real ale.

Smoking policy: No restrictions.

King's Head and Eight Bells

50 Cheyne Walk, SW3 (0171 352 1820). Sloane Square tube. Bars: 1. Food: Pub grub. Mon-Thurs, 1200-1500, 1900-2230; Fri-Sun, all day. APPH: £5 per main course. Entertainment: Live blues band, Fri. Specialities: Seats out front. Built in the 15th century this has been a local for sailors and boatmen on the Thames as well as a home for artists and writers such as Whistler, Turner and Augustus John, with Poets' Corner and Thomas Carlisle's house nearby. Diana Ross is a more recent visitor.

Smoking policy: No restrictions.

Man in the Moon

392 King's Road, SW3 (0171 352 5075). Sloane Square tube. Bars: 1. Food: Pub grub, 1100-2300. APPH: £4-£5 per main course. Entertainment: Occasional live music (jazz, blues). Specialities: The theatre out back is a major player on the London fringe scene, with performances Tues-Sun evenings. Real ale.

Smoking policy: No restrictions.

Orange Brewery

37 Pimlico Road, SW1 (0171 730 5984). Sloane Square tube. Bars: 2 (snug and main bar). Food: Home-made beer is used in all dishes. APPH: £3.25 per main course. Entertainment: None. Specialities: Brewing can be watched in action. Brewery tours available (£3-£4). Victorian pie and ale pub. 8 tables outside.

Smoking policy: No restrictions.

Pages

75 Page Street, SW1 (0171 834 6791). Westminster tube. Bars: 1. Food: Pub grub. APPH: £5 per main course. Entertainment: Karaoke evening, twice a month. Specialities: Real ale. Science fiction decor. Regular gathering of Sci-Fi fans (videos, quizzes, merchandising), Sat & Sun. Beam yourself in.

Smoking policy: No restrictions.

Pharaoh & Firkin

90-90a Fulham High Street, SW6 (0171 731 0732). Putney Bridge tube. Bars: 2 (main and a first floor bar which is only opened on Fri & Sat evenings). Food: Pub grub. APPH: £3.50 per main course. Entertainment: Live music (solo musician), Fri & Sat. Specialities: Real ale - own brewery on site. Busy, huge pub with mezzanine floor.

Smoking policy: Designated non-smoking area, otherwise no restrictions.

Plough

42 Christchurch Road, SW14 (0181 876 7833). Mortlake BR. Bars: 1. Food: Home-cooked pub grub. Mon-Sat, 1200-1500, 1900-2130; Sun, 1200-1600, 1900-2130. APPH: £4-£5 per main course. Entertainment: None. Specialities: Close to Richmond Park, friendly pub converted a century ago from three Queen Anne cottages. Tables outside in summer. 4 real ales.

Smoking policy: No restrictions.

Red Lion

23 Crown Passage, SW1 (0171 930 4141). Green Park tube. Bars: 1. Food: 2 areas. Restaurant (25-30 seats) - traditional English cuisine, 1200-1500, 1800-2130. APPH: £12-£13. Bar pub grub. APPH: £4 per main course. Entertainment: None. Specialities: Second oldest pub licence holder in the West End. A colourful historical pub near St James's Palace, serving real ales. Patronised by many royal figures over the years from Henry VIII and Charles II (both for romantic encounters.) to the late Duke of Windsor. Real ale.

Smoking policy: No restrictions.

Shakespeares Tavern

99 Buckingham Palace Road, SW1 (0171 828 4913). Victoria tube/BR. Bars: 2 (main and wine bar). Food: 3 areas. Fish & Chips restaurant. APPH: £5-£6 per main course. Pub grub. APPH: £4 per main course. Wine bar - sandwiches

and soup. APPH: £5 per sandwich and soup. Entertainment: None. Specialities: Popular with tourists. Real ale.
Smoking policy: No restrictions.

> Churchill, reflecting on the occasion he entertained the Saudi Arabian King, Ibn Saud, to lunch: "As I was host at luncheon I said to the interpreter that if it was the religion of His Majesty to deprive himself of smoking and alcohol I must point out that my rule of life prescribed as an absolutely sacred rite smoking cigars and also the drinking of alcohol before, after, and if need be during all meals and in the intervals between them."

Ship 10 Thames Bank, SW14 (0181 876 1439). Mortlake BR. Bars: 1. Food: Home-cooked pub grub and large salads, Mon-Sun, 1200-1430, 1800-2130. APPH: £4.90 per main course. Entertainment: Live jazz, Fri. Specialities: 16th-century riverside pub located at the end of the Oxford/Cambridge Boat Race route with optimum view. Large patio seating area. 4 real ales.
Smoking policy: No restrictions.

Slug and Lettuce 16 Putney High Street, SW15 (0181 785 3081). Putney Bridge tube. Bars: 2 (main and cellar), 1 function room. Food: Home-cooked pub grub, 1200-2200. APPH: £4 per main course. Entertainment: Live music (jazz, blues, soul), Thur. Live music some weekends. Specialities: Victorian ale house with bare floorboards. Popular and lively, especially at weekends. Garden. Real ale.
Smoking policy: No restrictions.

Star & Garter 4 Lower Richmond Road, SW15 (0181 788 0345). Putney Bridge tube. Bars: 1, 1 function room in cellar. Food: Pub grub, lunchtime. APPH: £4-£5 per main course. Entertainment: None. Specialities: Huge (5-storey) Victorian pub, situated at start of Oxford/Cambridge Boat Race. 40-foot bar counter is one of the longest in London.
Smoking policy: No restrictions.

Sun Inn 7 Church Road, SW13 (0181 876 5893). Barnes/Barnes Bridge BR. Bars: 3. Food: Pub grub, Mon-Sun, lunchtime. APPH: £5-£6 per main course. Entertainment: Live jazz, Tues. Specialities: Village pub atmosphere in this busy nook-and-cranny pub opposite Barnes Green pond. Tables seating 50 outside. Real ale.
Smoking policy: No restrictions.

Tattershall Castle

Kings Reach, Victoria Embankment, SW1 (0171 839 6548). Embankment tube. Bars: 3 (ward room, decks, Steamers Nightclub). Food: Pub grub in Paddles Bistro, 1200-2130 (from 1600 onwards a fuller menu is available). APPH: £5 per main course. Entertainment: Nightclub. (Year round) Fri & Sat, 2100-0300. (Seasonal: May-September) Thur, 2000-0100 & Sun, 1900-2400. Specialities: Converted paddle steamer on Thames. Near Cleopatra's Needle.

Smoking policy: No restrictions.

Windmill on the Common

Clapham Common South Side, SW4 (0181 673 4578). Clapham Common tube. Bars: 2. Food: 2 areas. Restaurant, weekday evening, weekend evening and lunchtime. APPH: £15. Bar pub grub, lunch and evening. APPH: £4-£5 per main course. Entertainment: Live music (opera, first Sun in month; jazz, second Thur in month). Specialities: Former coaching inn. Open hearth fire in winter. In the summer, drinkers spill out onto the Common. Real ale.

Smoking policy: No smoking in conservatory, otherwise no restrictions.

SOUTH EAST

Alleyns Head

Toby Carving Room. Park Hall Road, SE21 (0181 670 6540). Gipsy Hill/West Dulwich BR. Bars: 2. Food: Restaurant (90 seats). APPH: £10-£11. Entertainment: Occasional live music. Specialities: Patio area. Real ale.

Smoking policy: Non-smoking section in restaurant, otherwise no restrictions.

Anchor

Bankside, SE1 (0171 407 1577). London Bridge tube/BR. Bars: 6. Food: 3 areas. Restaurant (110 seats) - a la carte English cuisine. APPH: £13-ish (prices and menu changing at time of going to press). At bar - pub grub. APPH: £4.00 per main course. Barbecue occasionally (£3-£5). Entertainment: None. Specialities: Large terrace at front overlooking Thames. Barbecue patio. 18th-century pub with great view of St Paul's and Tower Bridge. Real ales.

Smoking policy: No restrictions.

Angel

101 Bermondsey Wall East, SE16 (0171 237 3608). Rotherhithe tube. Bars: 1. Food: 2 areas. Restaurant (upstairs) - a la carte traditional English cuisine. APPH: £35.00. Bar - home-cooked pub grub. APPH: £3.50-£5.50 per main course. Entertainment: Live music (acoustic rock group), Sun. Specialities: Historic pub on present site for five centuries with panoramic view of Thames. Clientele usually aged 30 plus. Seating outside.

Smoking policy: No restrictions.

> **"I do not believe that intelligence and creative thinking are injured by smoking." (Emile Zola)**

Beulah Spa Harvester

Beulah Hill, SE19 (0181 653 2051). Crystal Palace/South Norwood BR. Bars: 1. Food: Restaurant (100 seat, 'Harvester' chain). APPH: £8-£10. Entertainment: None. Specialities: Garden (no restaurant service).

Smoking policy: Restaurant: Mon-Fri - designated non-smoking section; Sat, Sun - non-smoking throughout. No restrictions at bar.

Cutty Sark Tavern

Ballast Quay, SE10 (0181 858 3146). Maze Hill BR. Bars: 1. Food: Pub grub. APPH: £5 per main course. Entertainment: Live trad. jazz, Thur. Specialities: Set in a charming quayside area this is a pub very much suited to the locale with a rich sense of history and a name to match. Georgian inn with 3 real ales.

Smoking policy: No restrictions.

Florence Nightingale

199 Westminster Bridge Road, SE1 (0171 928 3027). Westminster tube, Waterloo/Lambeth North tube/BR. Bars: 1, 1 function room. Food: Pub grub. APPH: £3.95 per main course. Entertainment: Karaoke evening, Thur. Specialities: Old-fashioned, friendly pub. 4 real ales.

Smoking policy: No smoking at lunchtime near food counter, otherwise no restrictions.

Mayflower 117 Rotherhithe Street, SE16 (0171 237 4088). Rotherhithe tube. Bars: 1. Food: 2 areas (dining area or at bar), pub grub, lunchtime and evening. APPH: £9-£11 per main course. Entertainment: Occasional live music (genre varies). Specialities: A small, dark pub next to the Mayflower's old mooring post, prior and post trips to the New World. It has excellent views of the Thames as well as great character and a sense of antiquity.

Smoking policy: No restrictions.

The Ring 72 Blackfriars Road, SE1 (0171 928 2589). Waterloo tube/BR. Bars: 1. Food: Pub grub, lunchtime. APPH: £3 per main course. Entertainment: None. Specialities: Home of boxers past and present, with an active ring in the gym upstairs. Real ale.

Smoking policy: No restrictions.

Trafalgar Tavern

Park Row, Greenwich, SE10 (pub - 0181 858 2437/restaurant - 0181 293 3337/banquet - 0181 858 2437). Maze Hill BR. Bars: 2, 1 function/banqueting room. Food: Banqueting room. Lunch - cold meat salad platter; evening meal - 3-course dinner. APPH: £36.50 (for the show and lunch/dinner). Entertainment: Elizabethan banquet with authentic food, music and song. Specialities: Evening Standard Pub of the Year 1996. Old-style riverside hostelry shuns TV and juke boxes in favour of friendliness and a warm welcome. Real ale.

Smoking policy: Banqueting area: no smoking during cabaret performance but allowed before, after and at all other times. Pub bar: no restrictions.

WEST

Archery Tavern

4 Bathurst Street, W2 (0171 402 4916). Lancaster Gate tube. Bars: 3. Food: Pub grub, 1100-2200. APPH: £3-£5.50 per main course. Entertainment: None. Specialities: Pretty, old-fashioned country-style pub. Garden. Real ale.

Smoking policy: No restrictions.

West London wine bar.

Bell & Crown

72 Strand-on-Green, W4 (0181 994 4164). Gunnersbury/Kew Gardens tube/BR. Bars: I. Food: Pub grub (25-seat dining area). APPH: £8. Entertainment: None. Specialities: Patio area. Overlooks Thames with a view of Kew Bridge. Busy, traditional pub with no background music. Real ale.

Smoking policy: No smoking in restaurant, otherwise no restrictions.

Black Lion 2 South Black Lion Lane, W6 (0181 748 2639). Stamford Brook tube. Bars: I. Food: Pub grub (sandwiches to steaks) (separate dining area). APPH: £2-£10 per main course. Entertainment: None. Specialities: Patio area overlooking Thames. 3 real ales.

Smoking policy: No restrictions.

Blue Anchor 13 Lower Mall, W6 (0181 748 5774). Hammersmith tube. Bars: 2 (main and upstairs/function room). Food: Pub grub. APPH: £4.50 per main course. Entertainment: None. Specialities: Riverside pub with seats and table facing the Thames. Especially popular with rowing club next door and anyone who enjoys an al fresco drink in summer. Wine bar planned. Real ale.

Smoking policy: No restrictions.

Bridge House

13 Westbourne Terrace Road, W2 (0171 286 7925). Warwick Avenue tube. Bars: 2 (main and I next to theatre). Food: Pub grub (served at downstairs bar and occasionally at the first floor bar, depending on number of customers). APPH: £4-£5 per main course. Entertainment: Theatre on first floor (audience seated, at tables). Specialities: Real ale.

Smoking policy: No restrictions in the bars or theatre.

Britannia I Allen Street, W8 (0171 937 1864). High Street Kensington tube. Bars: 2. Food: Pub grub (40-seat dining area in conservatory), Mon-Sat, 1200-1500, 1900-2230. APPH: £8. Entertainment: None. Specialities: Busy pub close to Kensington's shops. Mezzanine lounge floor and conservatory gives it character and adds to the friendly, chatty atmosphere. Real ale.

Smoking policy: No smoking in conservatory at lunchtime, otherwise no restrictions.

Builders Arms

I Kensington Court Place, W8 (0171 937 1614). High Street Kensington tube. Bars: I, I function room. Food: Pub grub. APPH: £4-£6 per main course. Entertainment: Occasional live music (R&B). 'Shot' night (American bar tradition with cheap shots/shorts e.g. tequila), Tues & Thur. Specialities: Real ale. Popular with nearby American college. Busy weekday evenings. Seating outside.

Smoking policy: No smoking near food counter, otherwise no restrictions.

Dove Inn 19 Upper Mall, W6 (0181 748 5405). Hammersmith tube. Bars: 1. Food: 2 cuisines. Pub grub, lunchtime. APPH: £4 per main course. Thai food, evening. APPH: £4.50 per main course. Entertainment: None. Specialities: Tiny 300-year-old pub down a side alley with one of the the smallest bars in Britain, and a main bar with oak ceilings and black panelling. 'Rule Britannia' was composed here. Graham Greene and Ernest Hemingway drank here. Real ales.
Smoking policy: No restrictions

Grange Tavern
Warwick Road, W14 (0181 567 7617). Ealing Broadway tube. Bars: 4 (1 lounge bar, 1 with darts board, 1 conservatory, 50-seat summerhouse), 1 function room. Food: 2 areas. Restaurant, 1100-2300 - a la carte. APPH: £10. Summer barbecue, Wed, Sat, Sun, evening (£5-£8.50). Entertainment: None. Specialities: Busy hostelry. Good food. Seating in summerhouse outside.
Smoking policy: No restrictions.

King's Head 214 High Street, W3 (0181 992 0282). Acton Town tube. Bars: 1, 1 function room. Food: Home-cooked pub grub. Mon-Sat, 1200-1430, 1700-2200; Sun, 1200-1500, 1700-2200. APPH: £3.50 per main course. Entertainment: Live music (big band jazz), Thur. Comedy club, Fri. Specialities: 3 real ales. Old coaching inn with small garden and extra seating in front.
Smoking policy: Designated non-smoking area at lunchtime, otherwise no restrictions.

Portobello Gold
95-97 Portobello Road, W11 (0171 460 4900). Notting Hill Gate tube. Bars: 1. Food: Garden restaurant with sliding roof. Modern British food, including fresh Irish oysters. Mon-Sun, 1930-2300, APPH: £9. Bar grub:1200-1600 hrs. Mon-Sat. APPH: £5. Entertainment: live piano music Sun evenings, otherwise canned World music. Photographic gallery. Claims to be first hotel (five rooms, all smoker-friendly, for £55 per night, including on-line time and continental breakfast) in London to provide Internet access in its bedrooms and first licensed premises in London to install a Web site found at http://w.w.w.buzzbar.co.uk. First floor dining room with open hearth fire for small functions and parties. Long wine list. 2 real ales.
Smoking policy: Smoker-friendly throughout, will make balcony non-smoking if required.

Scarsdale 23a Edwardes Square, W8 (0171 937 1811). High Street Kensington/Earls Court tube. Bars: 1. Food: Pub grub (waitress service at this Chef & Brewer pub). Mon-Sat, 1200-1430 (snacks 1830-2200); Sun 1230-1600. APPH: £5 per main course. Entertainment: None. Specialities: Ivy-clad and window-boxed pub with lofty ceilings and wooden fans. Fine Georgian pub with a good range of wines - 10 at the last count - plus a champagne selection. Seating at front. Real ale.
Smoking policy: No restrictions.

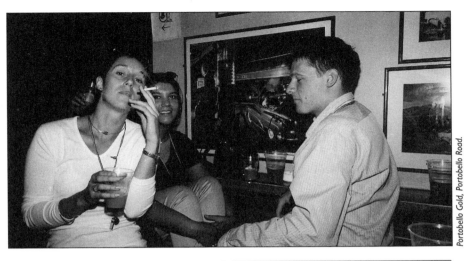

Portobello Gold, Portobello Road.

EAST

Blind Beggar 337 Whitechapel Road, E1 (0171 247 6195). Whitechapel tube. Bars: 2 (main and snug). Food: Pub grub. APPH: £5.95 per main course. Entertainment: None. Specialities: Frequented by the Krays, especially on one murderous occasion. Ask the bar staff to show you where it happened. Relax in the conservatory and beer garden. Real ales.

Smoking policy: No restrictions.

Cat and Canary
1-24 Fisherman's Walk, Canary Wharf, E14 (0171 512 9187). Canary Wharf DLR. Bars: 1, 1 function room. Food: Pub grub, Mon-Sat, 1200-1500, 1730-2100. APPH: £5 per main course. Entertainment: None. Specialities: New pub with old-style decor. Riverside seating overlooking dock.

Smoking policy: No restrictions.

Dickens Inn St Katharine's Way, E1 (0171 488 1226). Tower Hill/Tower Gateway DLR/tube. Bars: 1, 1 function room. Food: 3 areas. Restaurant - à la carte English cuisine. APPH: £22-£30. Restaurant - pizza/pasta dishes. APPH: £10-£12. Bar - pub food. APPH: £4 per main course. Entertainment: None. Specialities: Huge, old, former warehouse offers a plethora of cuisine, as well as five balconies for drinking and eating. It has no real connection with Charles Dickens except by name, but that hasn't quenched its popularity with tourists. Terrace area.

Smoking policy: Designated non-smoking section in both restaurants, otherwise no restrictions.

Outside West End Pub.

Hayfield 156-158 Mile End Road, E1 (0171 791 3427). Stepney Green tube. Bars: 1. Food: Pub grub, Mon-Sat, lunchtime and evening. APPH: £3-£4 per main course. Sunday roast and 2 other courses (£7.50). Entertainment: None. Specialities: Real ale.

Smoking policy: No smoking section in restaurant at lunchtime, otherwise no restrictions.

Henry Addington

20-28 Mackenzie Walk, Canary Wharf, E14 (0171 512 9022). Canary Wharf DLR. Bars: 1. Food: Pub grub, lunchtime. APPH: £4.95 per main course. Entertainment: None. Specialities: Seating available on dockside. Bright, airy pub. Its bar - at 97 feet - is one of the longest in London. 3 real ales.

Smoking policy: Designated non-smoking area at lunchtime, otherwise no restrictions.

Prospect of Whitby

57 Wapping Wall, E1 (0171 481 1095). Wapping/Shadwell DLR/tube. Bars: 1, 1 function room. Food: 2 areas. Restaurant (separate dining room upstairs) - a la carte English cuisine with good choice of fish dishes. APPH: £25. Bar pub grub. APPH: £4-£5 per main course. Entertainment: Live music (jazz band), once per month. Specialities: Famous East End riverside pub. Used to be very trendy with well-known punters from all over London. Patio overlooking river. 4 real ales.

Smoking policy: Designated non-smoking area in restaurant, otherwise no restrictions.

Pub on the Park

19 Martello Street, E8 (0171 275 9586). Bethnal Green tube. Bars: 1. Food: Pub grub. APPH: £3 per main course. Barbecue every evening in summer (good weather permitting) (£3). Entertainment: Live music (jazz, Celtic, folk), Tues, Fri or Sat, & Sun lunchtime. Specialities: Light, airy pub near London Fields. Boules played outside. 70-seat patio area.

Smoking policy: No restrictions.

OUTSIDE LONDON POSTCODES

Albion   34-36 Bridge Road, East Molesey, KT8 (0181 979 1035). Hampton Court BR. Bars: I. Food: Restaurant (40 seats) serving an original menu including the usual venison and steaks, but also swordfish, ostrich, kangaroo and crocodile. APPH: £12-£15. Entertainment: None. Specialities: Riverside pub built in 18th century for farmworkers at nearby Hampton Court. Patio area outside. Real ale.

Smoking policy: Non-smoking section in restaurant (50%), otherwise no restrictions.

Flicker & Firkin

Dukes Yard, Dukes Street, Richmond, TW9 (0181 332 7807). Richmond tube/BR. Bars: I. Food: Pub grub. APPH: £4-£5 per main course. Entertainment: Live music (soloist/two-piece soft rock cover band), Wed & Thur. Specialities: Brews its own real ale (the only pub in Richmond that does). Popular with an eclectic clientele.

Smoking policy: Designated non-smoking area (2 tables) during day, otherwise no restrictions.

George   5 The Town, Enfield, EN2 (0181 363 0074). Enfield Town BR. Bars: 3 (2 ground floor, I next to restaurant on first floor). Food: Restaurant (50 seats, first floor, Toby restaurant). APPH: £9-£15. Entertainment: None. Specialities: Lively pub, popular with a young crowd, especially at weekends. Seating outside. Real ale.

Smoking policy: No smoking in restaurant, otherwise no restrictions.

Horse and Chains

79 High Street, Bushey, WD2 (0181 950 1767). Bushey BR. Bars: I. Food: Pub grub. APPH: £3.50-£6 per main course. Entertainment: None. Specialities: Patio area. Listed 17th-century pub. Friendly local. Real ale.

Smoking policy: Designated non-smoking area at lunchtime, otherwise no restrictions.

London Apprentice

62 Church Street, Isleworth, TW7 (0181 560 1915). Hounslow East/ Richmond/Isleworth tube/BR. Bars: I. Food: Restaurant (in conservatory) - a la carte English cuisine. APPH: £22. Bar pub grub. APPH: £5-£6 per main course. Entertainment: Quiz night, Tues. Specialities: Traditional pub in Tudor building near Syon House. Once frequented by Dick Turpin, Charles I, Oliver Cromwell and Lady Jane Grey, but not all at once. Patio area leads on to river. Real ale.

Smoking policy: No smoking in food area in conservatory during day, otherwise no restrictions.

Orange Tree 45 Kew Road, Richmond TW9 (0181 940 0944). Richmond tube/BR. Bars: 3 (merged into one). Food: 2 areas. At bar - pub grub. Mon-Sun, 1200-1430; Mon-Sat, 1800-2200. APPH: £4.40 per main course. Restaurant (55 seats) - a la carte English cuisine. Mon-Fri, 1200-1430; Mon-Sun, 1800-2200. APPH: £7.90 two courses. Entertainment: Fringe theatre above pub and a theatre across side alley offer a range of dramatic interludes. Specialities: Large Victorian pub. An amiable place for a drink, especially of a weekend, with a garden out back and tables on the forecourt. Real ale.

Smoking policy: No restrictions.

Roebuck Richmond Hill (0181 948 2329). Richmond tube/BR. Bars: 1. Food: Home-cooked pub grub, Mon-Sun, 1200-1500, 1900-2100. APPH: £4-£5 per main course. Entertainment: None. Specialities: With a view of a bend in the meandering Thames that has been painted by both Turner and Reynolds, this pub perched on the top of Richmond Hill has an aspect to die for. It is popular inside as well as out and serves a range of people with its age 21+ licence. 3 real ales.

Smoking policy: Non-smoking section in dining area, otherwise no restrictions.

White Cross Hotel

Water Lane, Richmond, TW9 (0181 940 6844). Richmond tube/BR. Bars: 3 (outside terrace bar, main bar, upstairs bar/function room). Food: Home-cooked pub grub, Mon-Sun, 1200-1800. APPH: £5.95 per main course. Entertainment: Occasional live music. Specialities: Riverside pub with excellent views, a busy terrace bar in summer and a balcony in the top bar overlooking the Thames. 4 real ales.

Smoking policy: No restrictions.

White Swan 25-26 Old Palace Lane, Richmond TW9 (0181 940 0959). Richmond tube/BR. Bars: 1, 1 function room. Food: 2 areas. Restaurant - English cuisine (speciality is fish dishes e.g. rainbow trout), Mon-Sun, 1900-2130. APPH: £6.50 per main course. Bar pub grub, Mon-Sun, 1200-1430. APPH: £4 per main course. Entertainment: None. Specialities: Painted white like the nearby cottages, this is one of London's most picturesque riverside pubs, tucked down a country lane. Conservatory and patio garden. Real ale.

Smoking policy: No restrictions.

Cocktail bars

Alfred 245 Shaftesbury Avenue, WC2 (0171 240 2566). Tottenham Court Road tube. Open: 1200-1530 hrs and 1800-2330 hrs, Mon-Fri. 1800-2330 hrs Sat.

Seating: 58 inside, 40 garden. Food: Knuckle of bacon. Rabbit in beer and sage sauce. APPH: £22.

Smoking policy: No restrictions. Free matches.

The American Bar

Savoy Hotel, Strand, WC2 (0171 836 4343). Charing Cross tube/BR. Open: 1100-1500 hrs and 1730-2300 hrs, Mon-Sat. 1200-1500 hrs and 1900-2230 hrs, Sun. Seating: 100. Food: Light lunches and snacks. APPH: £12.

Smoking policy: No restrictions. Free matches.

Café Royal 68 Regent Street, W1 (0171 437 9090). Piccadilly Circus tube. Open: 1000-2300 hrs, Mon-Sun. Seating: 650. Food: Various. APPH: £33. Specialities: Once frequented by Oscar Wilde.

Smoking policy: No restrictions in reception area, bar or restaurant. Free matches.

The Library Lanesborough Hotel, Hyde Park Corner, SW1 (0171 259 5599). Hyde Park Corner tube. Open: 1100-2300 hrs, Mon-Sun. Seating: 70. Food: Between 1200 and 1500 hrs one free glass of house wine with sandwiches. APPH bar meal: £10.

Smoking policy: No restrictions. Free matches.

Trader Vic's Basement, London Hilton, Park Lane, W1 (0171 208 4113). Hyde Park Corner tube. Open: 1700-0100 hrs, Mon-Sat. 1700-2230 hrs, Sun. Seating: 120 restaurant, 60 bar. Food: Barbecue, seafood and cocktails. APPH: £30.

Smoking policy: No restrictions in reception, bar or restaurant. Free matches.

Wine Bars

> **"A cigar has a fire at one end and a fool at the other."**
> **(Horace Greeley, founder of the New York Tribune)**

Balls Brothers

6/8 Cheapside, EC2 (0171 248 2708). St Paul's tube. Open: 1130-2100 hrs, Mon-Sun. Seating: 50 inside, 50 outside. Food: Sandwiches. APPH: Snack prices.

Smoking policy: No restrictions. Free matches.

Balls Brothers

Ryder Street, St James's, SW1 (0171 321 0882). Green Park tube. Open: 1130-2100 hrs. Mon-Fri. Food: Good selection of fish and cold meats.

Smoking policy: No restrictions.

Butler's Wharf Wine Bar

31 Shad Thames, SE1 (0171 403 2089). London Bridge tube/BR. Open: 1100-

2300 hrs, Mon-Sat. 1200-2230 hrs, Sun. Seating: 80. Food: Tapas. APPH: Two dish meal £6-£7.

Smoking policy: No restrictions.

Bucci's   62a Goodge Street, W1 (0171 580 5362). Goodge Street tube. Open: 1100-midnight. Mon-Fri. Food: Well-cooked Italian and French dishes. Daily specials on the blackboard.

Smoking policy: No restrictions. Say hello to your friendly hosts, Simon and Micheala.

The Connaught

Carlos Place, W1 (0171 499 7070). Green Park tube. Open: 1230-1430 hrs and 1800-2245 hrs, Mon-Sun. Seating: 100. APPH: £65-£70.

Smoking policy: No restrictions but the management expects customers to be considerate of others. Free matches.

Corney and Barrow

10 Cabot Street, E14 (0171 512 0397). Canary Wharf DLR. Open: 1100-2300 hrs, Mon-Fri. Seating: 350 inside, 200 outside. Food: Sandwiches and snacks. APPH: Snack prices.

Smoking policy: No restrictions. Free matches.

Ebury Wine Bar

139 Ebury Street, SW1 (0171 730 5447). Sloane Square tube, Victoria tube/BR. Open: 1100-2300 hrs, Mon-Sat. 1200-2200 hrs, Sun. Seating: 70. APPH: £20-£25.

Smoking policy: No restrictions.

Paradise Bar 2 George Court, Adelphi, WC2 (0171 839 4012). Charing Cross tube/BR. Open: 1200-2300 hrs, Mon-Sat. 1200-2230 hrs, Sun (food served between 1200 and 1500 hrs). Seating: 50. Food: cafe-style lunches and salads. APPH: £5-£10.

Smoking policy: No restrictions.

Pimlico Wine Vaults

19-22 Upper Tachbrook Street, SW1 (0171 834 7429). Pimlico tube, Victoria tube/BR. Open: 1030-2300 hrs, Mon-Sun. Seating: 90. Food: Salmon, rump steak. APPH: £20.

Smoking policy: No restrictions.

Tiles   36 Buckingham Palace Road, SW1 (0171 834 7761). Victoria tube/BR. Open: 1100-2300 hrs, Mon-Fri. Seating: 65. Specialities: English and Mediterranean cuisine. APPH: £14.

Smoking policy: No restrictions.

Vat's   51 Lamb's Conduit Street, WC1 (0171 242 8963). Holborn/Russell Square tube. Open: 1200-2300 hrs, Mon-Sun. Seating: 70-80. Food: British. APPH: £25-£30.

Smoking policy: Pipe and cigar smokers must remain at the bar. Free matches.

Yorks   344/346 Old York Road, SW18 (0181 877 1633). Wandsworth Town BR. Open: 1830 hrs-Close, Mon-Sun. Seating: 50-60. Food: British. APPH: £15.

Smoking policy: No restrictions.

Japanese cigar oficionado lights up at Bucci's, Goodge Street.

THEATRES

You are not allowed to light up in any of London's theatre auditoriums, although most still allow smoking in the foyer and bar. When in doubt, ask an usher or another member of staff.

Some theatres we have talked to are considering turning up to half of their bars into non-smoking zones. Ironically, many of them will probably continue to stage productions which feature actors smoking. Can you imagine a play by Oscar Wilde, Sir Noel Coward or PG Wodehouse which doesn't include at least one smoker?

The 88th edition of Samuel French's Guide to Selecting Plays, 1994-97, lists the following: *Lighting Up Time*, *Secret Rapture* (which is what London's smokers will be condemned to, if we're not too careful), *Gone Up in Smoke* and *Matchmaker*.

Lord Laurence Olivier is, as far as we know, the only actor who gave his name to a cigarette brand. AJ Raffles, the Amateur Cracksman (also the subject of a stage play) used to smoke Sullivan's, but like Olivier cigarettes, they're no longer available.

Some thirsty theatregoers who can't face fighting their way to the bar head to the nearest pub, for a quick sharpener. If any more of London's theatres insist on turning their bars into non-smoking areas, those few drinkers may soon be joined by a much larger number of London's theatre-loving smokers.

WEST END

Adelphi   Strand, WC2 (0171 344 0055). Charing Cross tube/BR
Smoking Policy: Smoking allowed in the foyer and all four bars, two of which may become non-smoking by the end of 1996.

Albery   St Martin's Lane, WC2 (0171 369 1730). Leicester Square tube
Smoking Policy: Smoking allowed in all three bars but the stalls bar may become non-smoking by the end of 1996.

Aldwych   Aldwych, WC2 (0171 416 6048). Covent Garden tube.
Smoking Policy: No smoking in auditorium but allowed everywhere else, front-of-house.

Apollo. Shaftesbury Avenue, W1 (0171 494 5070). Piccadilly Circus tube.
Smoking Policy: Smoking allowed in both bars.

Apollo Victoria
17 Wilton Road, SW1 (0171 416 6070). Victoria tube/BR.
Smoking Policy: Smoking allowed in foyer bar. Non-smoking area being tested in the circle bar (July 1996).

Arts 6/7 Great Newport Street, WC2 (0171 836 3334). Leicester Square tube.
Smoking Policy: Smoking allowed in the bar.

Bloomsbury 15 Gordon Street, WC1 (0171 388 8822). Holborn tube.
Smoking Policy: Smoking allowed in the bar.

Cambridge Earlham Street, WC2 (0171 494 5054). Leicester Square tube.
Smoking Policy: Smoking allowed in all three bars.

Comedy Panton Street, SW1 (0171 369 1731). Piccadilly Circus tube.
Smoking Policy: Smoking allowed in the bar.

Criterion Piccadilly Circus, W1 (0171 369 1747). Piccadilly Circus tube.
Smoking Policy: Smoking allowed in the dress circle bar but not the stalls bar.

Dominion Tottenham Court Road, W1 (0171 416 6060). Tottenham Court Road tube.
Smoking Policy: Smoking allowed in only two of its four bars.

Duchess Catherine Street, WC2 (0171 494 5075). Covent Garden tube.
Smoking Policy: Smoking allowed in both bars.

Duke of York's
St Martin's Lane, WC2 (0171 836 5122). Leicester Square tube.
Smoking Policy: Smoking allowed in both bars.

Fortune Russell Street, WC2 (0171 836 2238). Covent Garden tube.
Smoking Policy: No smoking in the bar. Smoking allowed in the foyer.

Garrick Charing Cross Road, WC2 (0171 494 5085). Leicester Square tube.
Smoking Policy: No smoking in the stalls bar but it is allowed in the other two bars.

Gielgud Shaftesbury Avenue, W1 (0171 494 5065). Piccadilly Circus tube.
Smoking Policy: No smoking in the foyer bar but it is allowed in the other two bars.

Her Majesty's
>Haymarket, SW1 (0171 494 5400). Piccadilly Circus tube.

Smoking Policy: Smoking allowed in all three bars.

London Palladium
>Argyll Street, W1 (0171 494 5020). Oxford Circus tube.

Smoking Policy: Smoking allowed in all three bars.

Lyric Shaftesbury Avenue, W1 (0171 494 5045). Piccadilly Circus tube.

Smoking Policy: Smoking allowed in all three bars.

Lyric Hammersmith & Lyric Studio
>King Street, W6 (0181 741 2311/8701). Hammersmith tube.

Smoking Policy: No smoking in the foyer. Smoking area in the restaurant.

Mermaid Puddle Dock, EC4 (0171 236 1919). Blackfriars tube/BR.

Smoking Policy: Smoking allowed in both bars and the foyer.

National Theatre (Cottesloe, Lyttelton and Olivier)
>South Bank, SE1 (0171 928 2252). Waterloo tube/BR.

Smoking Policy: Smoking allowed in all four bars. Smoking areas in both restaurants.

New London Drury Lane, WC2 (0171 405 0072). Covent Garden tube.

Smoking Policy: Smoking allowed in the bar.

Old Vic Waterloo Road, SE1 (0171 928 7616). Waterloo tube/BR.

Smoking Policy: Smoking allowed in all the bars.

Palace Shaftesbury Avenue, W1 (0171 434 0909). Leicester Square tube.

Smoking Policy: Smoking is not allowed in the stalls bar but it is allowed in the other three bars.

Phoenix Charing Cross Road, WC2 (0171 369 1733). Leicester Square tube.

Smoking Policy: Smoking allowed in all five bars.

Piccadilly Denmark Street, W1 (0171 369 1734). Piccadilly Circus tube.

Smoking Policy: Smoking allowed in all four bars.

Players The Arches, Villiers Street, WC2 (0171 839 1134/976 1307). Charing Cross tube/BR or Embankment tube.

Smoking Policy: Smoking allowed in the foyer bar only.

Criterion Theatre, Piccadilly Circus.

Playhouse   Northumberland Avenue, WC2 (0171 839 4401). Embankment tube or Charing Cross tube/BR.
Smoking Policy: Smoking allowed in all three bars. Smoking area in the restaurant.

Prince Edward
                  Old Compton Street, W1 (0171 734 8951). Piccadilly Circus tube.
Smoking Policy: Smoking allowed in all three bars and the foyer.

Prince of Wales
                  Coventry Street, W1 (0171 839 5972). Piccadilly Circus tube.
Smoking Policy: Smoking allowed in both bars.

Queen's   Shaftesbury Avenue, W1 (0171 494 5040). Piccadilly Circus/Leicester Square tube.
Smoking Policy: Smoking allowed in all three bars.

Royal Court & Royal Court Theatre Upstairs
                  Sloane Square, SW1 (0171 730 1745/2554). Sloane Square tube.
Smoking Policy: No smoking in the stalls bar. Smoking is allowed in the circle bar.

RSC Barbican & RSC The Pit
                  Barbican, EC2 (0171 638 8891). Barbican tube or Moorgate tube/BR. Follow the yellow line.
Smoking Policy: Smoking allowed in the foyer bar only.

Theatre Royal, Drury Lane.

St Martin's West Street, WC2 (0171 836 1443). Leicester Square tube.
Smoking Policy: Smoking allowed in the foyer and all three bars.

Savoy Savoy Court, WC2 (0171 836 8888). Charing Cross tube/BR.
Smoking Policy: No smoking, anywhere.

Shaftesbury Shaftesbury Avenue, WC2 (0171 379 5399). Tottenham Court Road/Covent Garden tube.
Smoking Policy: Smoking allowed in the foyer and bar.

Shakespeare's Globe
New Globe Walk, Bankside, SE1 (0171 928 6406). Mansion House tube, London Bridge tube/BR.
Smoking Policy: No smoking, anywhere, in London's newest theatre.

Strand Aldwych, WC2 (0171 930 8800). Covent Garden tube.
Smoking Policy: Smoking allowed in all four bars and the foyer.

Theatre Royal Drury Lane
Catherine Street, WC2 (0171 494 5062). Covent Garden tube.
Smoking Policy: Smoking currently allowed in all six bars and foyer but this will soon change to allow for some non-smoking bars.

Theatre Royal Haymarket
Haymarket, SW1 (0171 930 8800). Piccadilly Circus tube.
Smoking Policy: Smoking allowed in all three bars and the foyer.

Vaudeville 404 Strand, WC2 (0171 836 9987). Charing Cross tube/BR or Embankment tube.
Smoking Policy: Smoking allowed in all three bars and the foyer.

Victoria Palace
Victoria Street, W1 (0171 834 1317). Victoria tube/BR.
Smoking Policy: Smoking allowed in all five bars.

Whitehall Whitehall, SW1 (0171 369 1735). Charing Cross tube/BR.
Smoking Policy: Smoking allowed in both bars and the foyer.

Wyndhams Charing Cross Road, WC2 (0171 369 1736). Leicester Square tube.
Smoking Policy: Smoking allowed in all three bars.

In Russia, Michael Feodorovich (1596-1645), the first Romanov Czar, declared the use of tobacco a deadly sin and forbade possession for any purpose. A Tobacco Court was established to try breaches of the law, its usual punishments were slitting of the lips, or a terrible and sometimes fatal flogging. In Turkey, Persia and India, the death penalty was prescribed as a cure for the habit.

Passion thrillingly fulfills, Shaftsbury Avenue.

OFF-WEST END

Warning: Some of the theatres in the Off-West End and Fringe sections require membership so check with them first, before setting out, as if you do not comply with their membership requirements they may be forced to refuse entry.

BAC 176 Lavender Hill, SW11 (0171 223 2223). Clapham Junction BR.
Smoking Policy: No smoking, anywhere.

The Bush Shepherds Bush Green, W12 (0181 743 3388). Goldhawk Road/Shepherd's Bush tube.
Smoking Policy: Smoking allowed in the foyer. (NB: the theatre is over a smoker-friendly pub).

Donmar Warehouse
Earlham Street, WC2 (0171 369 1732). Covent Garden tube.
Smoking Policy: Smoking allowed in the circle bar but not the stalls bar.

Drill Hall 16 Chenies Street, WC1 (0171 637 8270). Goodge Street tube.
Smoking Policy: No smoking, anywhere, on Thursday evenings. On other days, smoking allowed in the bar and foyer.

The Gate 11 Pembridge Road, W11 (0171 229 5387). Notting Hill Gate tube.
Smoking Policy: No smoking, anywhere.

Hampstead Avenue Road, NW3 (0171 722 9301). Swiss Cottage tube.
Smoking Policy: No smoking in the conservatory attached to the theatre. Smoking allowed in the bar and foyer.

King's Head 115 Upper Street, N1 (0171 226 1916). Angel tube, Highbury & Islington tube/BR.
Smoking Policy: Smoking allowed in the auditorium during dinner but not when the performance starts. Smoking allowed in the bar.

Old Bull Arts Centre
68 High Street, Barnet, Hertfordshire (0181 449 0048). High Barnet tube.
Smoking Policy: Smoking allowed in the bar.

Orange Tree 1 Clarence Street, Richmond, Surrey (0181 940 3633). Richmond tube/BR.
Smoking Policy: Smoking allowed in the bar but not the upstairs reception room.

Riverside Studios
Crisp Road, off Queen Caroline Street, W6 (0181 741 2255). Hammersmith tube.
Smoking Policy: No smoking in the cinema, or theatre auditorium. Smoking allowed in the foyer, gallery and café.

Tricycle 269 Kilburn High Road, NW6 (0171 328 1000). Kilburn tube.
Smoking Policy: No smoking in the gallery café. Smoking allowed in the bar and foyer.

Warehouse 62 Dingwall Road, Croydon, Surrey (0181 680 4060). East Croydon BR.
Smoking Policy: No smoking, anywhere.

Young Vic 66 The Cut, SE1 (0171 928 6363). Waterloo tube/BR.
Smoking Policy: Smoking allowed in the café bar.

> **Ernest Hemingway once sent a cigar band to Ava Gardner (who lived in London for many years) as a souvenir of their first encounter. He was devoted to Havana cigars.**

FRINGE

Albany   Douglas Way, SE8 (0181 692 4446). New Cross BR.
Smoking Policy: No smoking in the auditorium for theatrical performances but it is allowed for some events. Smoking allowed in the bar but not the foyer.

Almeida   Almeida Street, N1 (0171 359 4404). Angel tube, Highbury & Islington tube/BR.
Smoking Policy: Smoking allowed in the foyer and a section of the bar.

The Bridewell
Bride Lane, EC4 (0171 936 3456). Blackfriars tube/BR, Holborn Viaduct BR.
Smoking Policy: No smoking, anywhere.

Canal Café Theatre
Bridge House, Delamere Terrace, W2 (0171 289 6054). Warwick Avenue tube.
Smoking Policy: "Smoking is allowed everywhere but the stage," said the nice man who answered the phone. "It's practically obligatory".

Chelsea Centre
World's End Place, King's Road, SW10 (0171 352 1967). Sloane Square tube, then 11, 22 or 211 bus.
Smoking Policy: Smoking allowed in the bar only (but "it is permitted on stage during performance, in the presence of a fireman").

Hackney Empire
291 Mare Street, E8 (0181 985 2424). Hackney BR, or 22a, 22b, 30, 38, 56, 106, 236, 253, 277 bus.
Smoking Policy: Smoking allowed in all four bars.

Jackson's Lane
269a Archway Road, N6 (0181 341 4421). Highgate tube.
Smoking Policy: No smoking in the café. Smoking allowed in the foyer, except on Saturdays after 1800.

> **LADY BRACKNELL: Do you smoke?**
> **ERNEST: Well, yes, I must admit I smoke.**
> **LADY BRACKNELL: I am glad to hear it. A man should always have an occupation of some kind.**
> **(Oscar Wilde, 'The Importance of Being Earnest')**

> **Better to have smoked and coughed, than never to have smoked at all. (Russian proverb)**

Leighton House Museum
12 Holland Park Road, W14 (0171 603 9115). Holland Park tube.
Smoking Policy: No smoking, anywhere.

Man in the Moon
392 Kings Road, SW3 (0171 351 2876/5701). Sloane Square tube.
Smoking Policy: No smoking in the foyer but you can smoke in the pub (which is handy as this is a pub theatre).

New End
27 New End, NW3 (0171 794 0022). Hampstead tube.
Smoking Policy: No smoking in the bar or foyer but it is allowed in the box office area. Just take your time buying the tickets!

Southwark Playhouse
62 Southwark Bridge Road, SE1 (0171 620 3494). Borough tube.
Smoking Policy: Smoking allowed in the bar only.

Steiner
35 Park Road, NW1 (0171 723 4400). Baker Street tube.
Smoking Policy: Smoking allowed in the foyer.

Theatre Royal
Gerry Raffles Street, E15 (0181 534 0310). Stratford tube/BR.
Smoking Policy: Smoking allowed in the bar and foyer.

Theatre Technis
26 Crowndale Road, NW1 (0171 387 6617). Camden Town tube.
Smoking Policy: No smoking, anywhere, except in the garden next to the bar.

Tower
Canonbury Tower, Canonbury Place, N1 (0171 226 3633). Highbury & Islington tube/BR.
Smoking Policy: Smoking allowed in the bar.

Watermans Arts Centre
49 High Street, Brentford, Middlesex (0180 568 1176). Kew Bridge BR.
Smoking Policy: No smoking in the cinema or café. Smoking allowed in the bar.

> In 1949, American importers presented **Edward G Robinson** with the title **"Mister Cigar"** in recognition of the publicity he had given the cigar in films like **'Little Caesar'**

Only one cinema in London allows its customers to smoke while viewing films:

Notting Hill Coronet
Notting Hill Gate, W11 (0171 727 6705). Notting Hill Gate tube.
Smoking Policy: Half of its 396 seats are allocated to smokers.

The general rule for cinemas in London is that smoking is not allowed anywhere in the auditorium. However, smoking is often allowed in their cafés, bars and foyers. Meanwhile, they are still showing films (old and new) with people smoking. Is this sadistic, or what!

> **FOOTBALL REFEREE:**
> What are you doing with that cigar in your mouth?
> **GROUCHO MARX:**
> Why, do you know another way to smoke it? (Scene from the Marx Brothers film, 'A Night in Casablanca')

WEST END

ABC   Panton Street, SW1 (0171 930 0631, bookings: 0181 970 6021). Piccadilly Circus tube.
Smoking Policy: No smoking, anywhere.

ABC   Shaftesbury Avenue, W1 (0171 836 6279, bookings: 0181 970 6013). Tottenham Court Road/Leicester Square tube.
Smoking Policy: No restrictions in the foyer or bar.

Barbican Centre
Silk Street, EC2 (0171 638 8891). Moorgate tube/BR, Barbican tube - and follow the yellow line.
Smoking Policy: No restrictions in the bar.

Chelsea Cinema
Kings Road, SW3 (0171 351 3742). Sloane Square tube.
Smoking Policy: No restrictions in the foyer.

Curzon Mayfair
Curzon Street, W1 (0171 369 1720). Hyde Park Corner/Green Park tube.
Smoking Policy: No restrictions in the foyer.

Curzon Phoenix
Phoenix Theatre, Charing Cross Road, WC1 (0171 369 1721). Tottenham Court Road tube.
Smoking Policy: Smoking allowed in the foyer only.

Curzon West End
Shaftesbury Avenue, W1 (0171 369 1722). Leicester Square/Piccadilly Circus tube.
Smoking Policy: No smoking, anywhere.

Empire   Leicester Square, WC2 (0171 437 1234, bookings: 0990 888990). Leicester Square tube.
Smoking Policy: No restrictions in the bar.

Gate   Notting Hill Gate, W11 (0171 727 4043). Notting Hill Gate tube.
Smoking Policy: No smoking, anywhere.

ICA Cinema   Nash House, The Mall, SW1 (0171 930 3647). Charing Cross tube/BR or Piccadilly Circus tube and walk down Haymarket.
Smoking Policy: No restrictions in the foyer or bar.

Lumiere   St Martin's Lane, WC2 (0171 836 0691). Leicester Square tube.
Smoking Policy: No restrictions in the foyer or bar.

MGM Baker Street
Marylebone Road, NW1 (0171 935 9772). Baker Street tube.
Smoking Policy: No restrictions in the foyer.

MGM Chelsea
279 King's Road, SW3 (0171 352 5096, bookings: 0181 970 6010). Sloane Square tube, then 11, 19, 22, 211, 249, 319 bus.
Smoking Policy: No smoking, anywhere.

MGM   Piccadilly, W1 (0171 437 3561). Piccadilly tube.
Smoking Policy: No smoking, anywhere.

MGM   Shaftesbury Avenue, W1 (0171 836 6279/379 7025). Tottenham Court Road/Leicester Square tube.
Smoking Policy: No restrictions in the foyer.

MGM   Swiss Centre, Wardour Street, WC2 (0171 439 4470, bookings: 0181 970 6017). Leicester Square/Piccadilly Circus tube.
Smoking Policy: No smoking, anywhere.

MGM   Tottenham Court Road, W1 (0171 636 6148). Tottenham Court Road tube.
Smoking Policy: No restrictions in the foyer.

MGM   Trocadero Centre, 13 Coventry Street, W1 (0171 434 0031). Piccadilly Circus/Leicester Square tube.
Smoking Policy: Smoking allowed on floors 2 and 3 where there is a coffee shop and bar.

Minema   45 Knightsbridge, SW1 (0171 369 1723). Knightsbridge/Hyde Park tube.
Smoking Policy: No restrictions in the foyer or bar.

Odeon   Haymarket, SW1 (01426 915353). Piccadilly Circus tube.
Smoking Policy: No smoking, anywhere.

Odeon   263 Kensington High Street, W8 (01426 914666). High Street Kensington tube.
Smoking Policy: No smoking, anywhere.

Odeon   Leicester Square, WC2 (01426 915683). Leicester Square tube.
Smoking Policy: No smoking, anywhere.

Odeon Marble Arch
                 10 Edgware Road, W2 (01426 914501, bookings: 0171 723 2011). Marble Arch tube.
Smoking Policy: No smoking, anywhere.

Odeon Mezzanine
                 22/24 Leicester Square, WC2 (01426 915 683, bookings: 0171 930 3232). Leicester Square tube.
Smoking Policy: No smoking, anywhere.

Odeon Swiss Cottage
                 Finchley Road, NW6 (01426 914098, bookings: 0171 722 5905). Swiss Cottage tube.
Smoking Policy: Ask at the box office.

Plaza   Lower Regent Street, W1 (0171 437 1234). Piccadilly Circus tube.
Smoking Policy: No restrictions in the foyer or bar.

American comedians and comic actors who have enjoyed a smoke (at least while performing, many also smoked in private life) include the cross-eyed silent star, Ben Turpin, George Burns (who smoked several cigars a day and lived to a 100 while the doctor who tried to get him to quit, died years before), WC Fields, Groucho Marx and his brothers, Harpo and Chico, Danny Kaye, Phil (Bilko) Silvers, Lucille Ball, Mae West, Buster Keaton, Jimmy Durante and Bill Cosby.

Prince Charles
2-7 Leicester Place, WC2 (0171 437 8181). Leicester Square/Piccadilly Circus tube.
Smoking Policy: Ask at the box office.

Renoir Brunswick Square, WC1 (0171 837 8402). Russell Square tube.
Smoking Policy: No restrictions in the foyer or bar.

Screen on Baker Street
96 Baker Street, NW1 (0171 935 2772). Baker Street tube.
Smoking Policy: No restrictions in the foyer or bar.

UCI Whiteley's
2nd Floor Whiteley's Shopping Centre, Queensway, W2 (0171 792 3303, bookings: 0990 888990). Bayswater/Queensway tube.
Smoking Policy: No restrictions in the foyer.

Virgin Fulham Road, SW10 (0171 370 2636, bookings: 0181 970 6011). South Kensington tube.
Smoking Policy: No restrictions in the bar.

Virgin Haymarket, W1 (0171 839 1527). Piccadilly Circus tube.
Smoking Policy: No restrictions in the foyer.

Warner West End
Leicester Square, WC2 (0171 437 4347, bookings: 0171 437 4343). Leicester Square tube.
Smoking Policy: No restrictions in the foyer or bar.

REPERTORY

Clapham Picture House
Venn Street, SW4 (0171 498 3323). Clapham Common tube.
Smoking Policy: No restrictions in the foyer or bar.

Everyman Hollybush Vale, NW3 (0171 435 1525). Hampstead tube.
Smoking Policy: No restrictions in the foyer. Smoking section in the café. Members only.

National Film Theatre
South Bank, SE1 (0171 928 3232). Waterloo tube/BR.
Smoking Policy: Smoking allowed in the café and lobby only. Not the bookshop or auditoriums. Members only. Best repertory cinema in London.

Rio Cinema Kingsland High Street, E8 (0171 254 6677). Dalston/Kingsland BR.
Smoking Policy: Smoking is not allowed in the café. No restrictions in the foyer.

Ritzy Cinema
Brixton Oval, Coldharbour Lane, SW2 (0171 737 2121). Brixton tube.
Smoking Policy: No restrictions in either bar.

Screen on the Green
Islington Green, N1 (0171 226 3520). Angel tube.
Smoking Policy: No smoking, anywhere.

Screen on the Hill
230 Haverstock Hill, NW3 (0171 435 3366). Belsize Park tube.
Smoking Policy: No restrictions in the foyer or bar.

Richmond Filmhouse
3 Water Lane, Richmond, Surrey (0181 332 0030). Richmond tube/BR.
Smoking Policy: No restrictions in the foyer.

> **Australia is considering introducing an 'S' certificate for films featuring smokers. Does this mean they'll be shelving all those excellent movies starring, among many other screen icons, Humphrey Bogart, W C Fields, Sean Connery (as James Bond), Clint Eastwood (the man with no name in Sergio Leone's spaghetti westerns), Marlene Dietrich, Eddie Murphy or John Wayne? Perhaps they should also introduce 'V', for Violence, 'A', for Alcohol, and 'IAT', for Intolerant Aussie Twits.**

Institut Francais
> 17 Queensbury Place, SW7 (0171 838 2144). South Kensington/Gloucester Road tube.
>
Smoking Policy: No smoking, anywhere.

London Film Makers Co-op
> 3rd Floor, The Impact Centre, 12-18 Hoxton Street, N1 (0171 739 7117). Old Street tube.
>
Smoking Policy: No restrictions.

Museum of London Cinema
> London Wall, EC2 (0171 600 3699). Barbican tube.
>
Smoking Policy: No smoking anywhere in the museum. Smoking area in café, opposite.

Riverside Studios Cinema
> Crisp Road, W6 (0181 741 2255). Hammersmith tube.
>
Smoking Policy: No restrictions in the foyer bar or café.

British comedians and comic actors who enjoyed a smoke (at least while performing) include Eric Morecambe and Ernie Wise, Tony Hancock and Sid James, Bob Hope, Charlie Chaplin, Will Hay, many British music hall stars including Jimmy James and The Crazy Gang (Bud Flanagan smoked cigars), John Cleese, Frankie Howard, Alastair Sim, Arthur Askey, Max Bygraves, Harry H Corbett and Wilfrid Brambell as Steptoe and Son, Rik Mayall, 'Professor' Jimmy Edwards, Harry Worth, both of The Likely Lads (played by James Bolam and Rodney Bewes), Roy Hudd, several characters in Dad's Army and Are You Being Served, Alf Garnett (the foul-mouthed bigot played by Warren Mitchell in Till Death Us Do Part, created by another noted cigarette smoker, Johnny Speight) and Absolutely Fabulous's politically incorrect Patsy (Joanna Lumley).

10

MUSIC

> The composer Franz Liszt always carried a large supply of Havanas
> in a large cedarwood chest. He used to say, "A good imported cigar
> shuts you off from the vulgarities of this world." Maurice Ravel was
> also a cigar aficionado, as was the famous pianist, Arthur Rubinstein,
> who once owned a plantation in Cuba.

Many of the world's greatest classical musicians have smoked, including Mozart, but not while performing. The same is not true for countless rock, jazz and pop musicians, including Jimi Hendrix, Count Basie, Eric Clapton and the Beatles.

Nobody is allowed to smoke in the auditoriums of London's classical concert halls, but most of the capital's nightclubs, jazz, latin, rock, reggae, soul, roots, dance, country and folk clubs still allow you to light up.

It's probably not a good idea to smoke and play a saxophone or flute at the same time but it's a neat trick if you can manage it.

If you're a paying guest and not sure that smoking's allowed, look around to see if anyone else is doing it, or ask the staff. Most of the bars are still smoker-friendly.

CLASSICAL/OPERA

Barbican Silk Street, EC2 (0171 638 4141). Barbican tube or Moorgate tube/BR - and follow the yellow line.
Smoking Policy: No smoking in the auditorium. It is allowed on Level 1, by the café, and some tables are designated for smokers.

London Coliseum
St Martin's Lane, WC2 (0171 632 8300). Leicester Square/Charing Cross tube/BR.
Smoking Policy: No smoking in the auditorium or Dutch bar. Smoking is allowed in the remaining five bars, and the lobby.

Purcell Room
South Bank, SE1 (0171 928 8800/0171 960 4242). Waterloo tube/BR or Embankment tube and walk across the foot bridge over the Thames.
Smoking Policy: No smoking in the auditorium. Smoking is allowed in the foyer.

Queen Elizabeth Hall
South Bank Centre, SE1 (0171 928 8800/0171 960 4242). Waterloo tube/BR or Embankment tube and walk across the foot bridge over the Thames.
Smoking Policy: No smoking in the auditorium. Smoking is allowed in the foyer.

Royal Albert Hall

Kensington Gore, SW7 (0171 589 8212). Knightsbridge/High Street Kensington tube.

Smoking Policy: No smoking in the auditorium. Smoking is allowed in the corridors and the bars.

Royal Festival Hall

South Bank, SE1 (0171 960 4242). Waterloo tube/BR or Embankment tube and walk across the footbridge over the Thames.

Smoking Policy: No smoking in the auditorium. Certain areas in the foyers are non-smoking but smoking is allowed at "quite a lot" of tables in the bar areas.

Royal Opera House

Covent Garden, WC2 (Box Office: 0171 304 4000). Covent Garden tube.

Smoking Policy: No smoking in the auditorium or Pit lobby bar. Smoking is allowed in the foyer bar. Smoking and non-smoking areas in the amphitheatre and crush bars.

Sadler's Wells

Rosebery Avenue, EC1 (0171 713 6000). Angel tube.

Smoking Policy: No smoking in the auditorium. Smoking allowed in the bars and foyer. (NB Theatre closed until 1998, when we hope this policy will remain unchanged.)

Wigmore Hall

36 Wigmore Street, W1 (0171 935 2141). Oxford Circus/Bond Street tube.

Smoking Policy: No smoking in the auditorium. You may smoke in the smoking section of the bar.

Jimi Hendrix in Gerrard Street, Soho, 1967.

JAZZ

These are just a few of London's better-known traditional haunts of the jazz-lover. In some of them it's difficult to see the musicians through the haze. The tube stops around midnight so check with London Transport (0171 222 1234) on the late-night buses that will take you home. Or get a smoker-friendly black cab.

Ronnie Scott's

47 Frith Street, W1 (0171 439 0747). Leicester Square/Tottenham Court Road tube.

Smoking Policy: You can smoke anywhere in this club, which first opened nearby in 1959 and has since showcased the world-class talents of countless jazz musicians, including Louis Armstrong (who smoked and drank B'n'Bs, ie brandy and Benedictine, mixed) and the late Ella Fitzgerald. We had a great evening in July 1996 listening to the Art Porter Sextet and the music of Ray Gaskins. Art attended the inauguration of fellow-saxophonist, Bill Clinton (the American President who isn't allowed to smoke his cigars inside the White House!).

You can always tell when the jazz musicians have finished their final set - they take the cigarettes and matches with them instead of leaving them behind (for an encore).

Jazz Cafe 5 Parkway, NW1 (0171 344 044). Camden Town tube.
Smoking Policy: Smoke anywhere, upstairs or downstairs.

Blue Note (named after the famous jazz record label)
Hoxton Square, N1 (0171 729 8440). Old Street tube.
Smoking Policy: Smoke anywhere.

100 Club 100 Oxford Street, W1 (0171 636 0933). Tottenham Court Road/Oxford Circus tube.
Smoking Policy: Smoke anywhere.

Pizza on the Park

11 Knightsbridge, SW1 (0171 235 5273). Hyde Park tube.

Smoking Policy: Smoking allowed in downstairs music room. Two smoking areas by the windows in the restaurant. Very classy.

> **"No woman should marry a teetotaller, or a man who does not smoke." (Robert Louis Stevenson)**

Art Porter at Ronnie Scott's, July 1996.

Johnny Cash at Hammersmith Odeon, 1966.

ROCK/POP

There are lots of places in London to listen to rock, reggae, soul, latin, roots, folk and country music - far too many to list here. Most of them usually allow smoking, at least in their bars and foyers.

The Forum Club
9 Highgate Road, NW5 (0181 963 0940). Kentish Town tube/BR.
Smoking Policy: No smoking in theatre. Smoking allowed in the bar and foyer.

Labatt's Apollo Hammersmith
Queen Caroline Street, W6 (Box Office: 0171 416 6080). Hammersmith tube.
Smoking Policy: No smoking in the auditorium. Smoking allowed in all three bars

> **Smoke Rings, Two Cigarettes in the Dark, While a Cigarette Was Burning, The End of Me Old Cigar** and **Maurice Chevalier's Cigarette** - which apparently was the name of the girl he was singing to - are just a few of 50 titles in the **BBC Record Library** with the word **Smoking** in them. There's another 25 with **Smokin'**. That well-known song, **Smoke Gets in Your Eyes**, refers to people in love, blinded from the fumes when their heart is on fire. **Puff the Magic Dragon** is also not what it seems...

If you want more details on the latest clubs and music, check the listings section in Time Out, What's On In London or ES (free with Friday's *Evening Standard*) magazines.

The Beatles, Chapel Street, Belgravia, May 1967.

11

SMOKERS

Clubs

St James's has long been the haunt of elegant smokers, many of them members of the aristocratic gentlemen's clubs at the top half of the street, just off Piccadilly, including: Boodles, founded in 1762 and famous for its gambling, at no. 28; White's, founded in White's Chocolate Shop in the 1690s, and still open at no. 37-38; Brook's, at no. 60, founded in 1764 and including among its celebrated Whig members, William Pitt; and, not least, The Carlton, at no. 69, founded in 1832 in opposition to Brook's. All of them still have smoking rooms for members.

An unofficial smoker's club that anyone can join is Simpson's-in-the-Strand (0171 836 9112), which opened in 1828 as the 'Home of Chess' and became the 'Great Cigar Divan', with chess players seated, puffing away on divans or sofas. Its roast beef is celebrated, worldwide.

Another informal cigar divan can be found at 19 St James's Street (0171 930 3787). The tobacco merchant's shop, believed to be the longest established in the UK, has been trading as Robert Lewis since 1787, until it was acquired by JJ Fox in 1992. It supplies cigars to some of the afore-mentioned clubs. Chairs provided.

In its basement there's a small museum where, if you ask them nicely, you can check the old ledgers to see what Oscar Wilde smoked (and still owes), sniff one of the oldest cigars in the world, and find out what Winston Churchill spent on his favourite smokes.

The cigar room on the first floor of Alfred Dunhill's (0171 499 9566) shop at 30 Duke Street, is just round the corner from St James's. Customers relax

> In 1986, The Rt Hon Lord Mason of Barnsley convened The Lords and Commons Pipe Smokers Club, renamed a decade later as The Lord and Commons Pipe and Cigar Smokers Club. "Membership has doubled to about 65 as a result of bringing in cigar smokers," explained the club's secretary, Arthur Butler, who helps organise 3-4 smoking related outings a year.

on the comfy chairs, with a cigar. If you're passing Davidoff's (35 St James's Street, SW1. 0171 930 3079), light up in memory of its deceased founder, the one and only Zino Davidoff.

Cross Piccadilly and drop in at Benson and Hedges, 13 Old Bond Street, W1. 0171 493 1825) - there's a spacious smoking area with chairs, in the back of the shop, which was first opened in 1865.

A rainy day outside JJ Fox of St James's.

At G Smith & Sons (0171 836 7422) at 74 Charing Cross Road, you will find the largest selection of snuff in England, and hankies to blow it into. If it's Wednesday, ask if you can watch their weekly snuff sieving in the basement. According to the shop manager, Barry Monaghan: "Snuff is the safest way of taking tobacco. It clears the head, helps catarrh sufferers and is very popular with people who can't be seen to be smoking, such as doctors, lawyers, priests and, in the old days, miners."

Sneezing loudly, nip round to Inderwicks (0171 734 6574) at 45 Carnaby Street, W1, the oldest pipe makers in England (founded around 1707).

If you're fond of a bowlful of hot tobacco, The Pipe Club of London (40 Crescent Drive, Petts Wood, Orpington, Kent, BR5 1BD) was founded in 1969 and today has about 500 members in 19 countries.

It usually meets on the third Thursday of the month at the Royal British Legion, 4 Grotto Passage, off Paddington Street.

Whatever you smoke, you can light up from the permanent (during shop hours, anyway) flame on the counter at Shervingtons, 337-338 High Holborn, WC1 (0171 405 2929). The shop was established in 1864 in the famous Staple Inn building (built 1545).

Finally, return to Mayfair for a quiet smoke in Desmond Sautter's shop at 106 Mount Street, W1 (0171 499 4866). Sir Winston Churchill lived upstairs from 1900-1905.

SMOKERS CLUBS

The Havana Club, Fulham Broadway.

Tobacco is probably the most sought-after commodity in London's prisons and rations are often mortgaged for a smoke. A Tobacco Baron is a prisoner who wields power by trading in tobacco, or snout. According to the Home Office, prisoners can smoke in every cell in all six of London's prisons, ie Brixton, Pentonville, Holloway (women only), Wandsworth, Wormwood Scrubs and the capital's latest penal institution, Belmarsh, which opened next to Woolwich's secure court in 1993. Visitors aren't so lucky as many of prisons' waiting rooms are non-smoking. There's no limit on the amount of loose or cigarette tobacco prisoners can buy from their average weekly wage of £7. London's prisons hold a total of about 4,700, on a bad day. So if you're desperate for a smoke, get arrested.

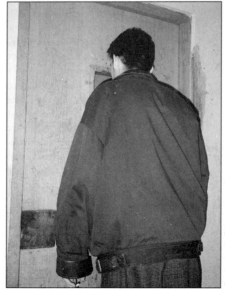

Smoker inside Ealing police cell.

146

Entertainment

12

In the days of music hall many stand-up comedians smoked cigarettes on stage as this was the perfect means of timing their act, and not overstaying their welcome. Even better, they could offset the cost of the tobacco against their income tax!

Brick Lane Music Hall

152 Brick Lane, E1 (0171 739 9997). Aldgate East tube. Open: Bar from 1830 hrs. Dinner from 1900 hrs. Show 2100-2300 hrs, Mon-Sun. Seating: 200-250. Entertainment: Modern music hall with a new artist every week. APPH: Dinner and show £20.

Smoking Policy: Half of the music hall is reserved for smokers. No pipes or cigars in restaurant or bar.

Canal Café Theatre

The Bridge House, corner of Westminster Terrace Road and Delamere Terrace, W2 (0171 289 6054/6056). Warwick Avenue tube. Open: 1200-1500 hrs and 1800-2200 hrs, Mon-Sun. Seating: 60. Entertainment: Comedy plays, satire, reviews, cabaret and drama. Food: English pub grub. APPH: £8.

Smoking Policy: No restrictions.

Centre Stage, The Theatre Restaurant

Radisson Mountbatten Hotel, Seven Dials, off Monmouth Street, WC2 (0171 379 6009). Covent Garden/Leicester Square tube. Open: 1000-0100 hrs, Thur-Sat. Entertainment starts 2320 hrs. Seating: 70-75. Entertainment: Cabaret. APPH: Show, dinner and wine £35.

Smoking Policy: No restrictions in the bar or restaurant.

"If you give up smoking, drinking and loving, you don't live any longer, it just seems longer." (Old Music Hall joke)

> **The great Italian lover, Casanova (1725-1798)**
> **was one of the first Europeans to smoke**
> **cigarettes. Later, the French Emperor,**
> **Napoleon III (1808-1873) did much to popularise**
> **the cigarette in France, his own consumption**
> **of them running to what was then thought the**
> **remarkable number of 50 a day. He so entirely**
> **lacked his uncle's disregard for the lives of others**
> **that he could only bear to watch his battles by**
> **chain smoking throughout.**

The Green Room

Café Royal, 68 Regent Street, W1 (0171 437 9090). Piccadilly Circus tube. Open: 1900-0300 hrs, Tues-Sat. Seating: 150. Entertainment: Cabaret. APPH: Dinner £28, show £20, Tues-Thur; dinner £30, show £25, Fri-Sat.

Smoking Policy: No restrictions.

R S Hispaniola

Victoria Embankment, WC2 (0171 839 3011). Embankment tube, Charing Cross tube/BR. Open: 1200-1400 hrs and 1830-2200 hrs, Mon-Sun (no lunch Sat). Seating: 80. Entertainment: Latin-American harpist, Mon-Wed. Jazz pianist, Thur-Sun. Extensive wine list. APPH: Lunch £14.50, dinner £30.

Smoking Policy: No restrictions. Free matches.

The New Restaurant at the V & A

Victoria and Albert Museum, Cromwell Road, SW7 (0171 581 2159). South Kensington tube. Open: 1000-1700 hrs, Mon-Sun. Seating: 200. Entertainment: Live music every lunchtime. Sunday Jazz Brunch. APPH: £10.

Smoking Policy: Half of restaurant is allocated to smokers, but you still can't smoke anywhere else in the museum.

Salsa

96 Charing Cross Road, WC2 (0171 379 3277). Leicester Square/Tottenham Court Road tube. Open: 1730-0200 hrs, Mon-Sat. Seating: 220. Entertainment: Dancing to Latin-American music every evening. APPH: £17

Smoking Policy: Pipe and cigar smokers asked to use bar.

The Sports Café

80 Haymarket, SW1 (0171 839 8300). Piccadilly Circus tube. Open: 1200-0200 hrs, Mon-Sun. Seating: 280. Entertainment: TV and video sports, arcade games, dancing, pool and basketball. Food: Steaks and burgers. APPH: £15

Smoking Policy: No restrictions in the restaurant or bars. Free matches.

Thunder Drive

24 Shaftesbury Avenue, W1 (0171 734 6161). Leicester Square tube. Open: 1800-late, Mon-Sun. Seating: 180. Entertainment: Late night dancing to Latin and modern dance music. Food: Beef chilli with rice. Pizza. APPH: £20.

Smoking Policy: Smoking and non-smoking sections in the restaurant. No restrictions in the bars.

Up the Creek

302 Creek Rd, SE10, (0181 858 4581). Greenwich BR. Open: 2000-0200 hrs, Fri-Sat Seating: 300. Entertainment: Wide range of stand-up comedy and live music. Disco after the show Fri-Sat. Food: Thai. APPH: £6-£10.

Smoking Policy: No restrictions in the bar or restaurant. Free matches.

Windmill on the Common

Clapham Common Southside, SW4 (0181 673 4578). Clapham Common/ Clapham South tube. Open: 1900-2200 hrs, Mon-Sat. 1200-1500 hrs, Sun. Seating: 29. Entertainment: Live opera the first Mon and live Jazz the first Thur of the month. Food: Rabbit with shallots and red wine, quail breast with paté and chives. APPH: £15.

Smoking Policy: No restrictions.

COMEDY

The Comedy Café

60 Rivington Street, EC2 (0171 739 5706). Old Street tube. Open: 1900-0100 hrs, Wed-Thur. 1900-0200 hrs, Fri-Sat. Seating: 150. Entertainment: Stand-up comedy, Wed-Thur. Disco, Fri-Sat. Food: Tex-Mex. APPH: £12.

Smoking Policy: No restrictions.

Jongleurs Camden Lock

Middle Yard, Camden Lock, Chalk Farm Road, NW1 (0171 924 2766). Camden Town/Chalk Farm tube. Open: 1800-1900 hrs for tickets, 1900-2030 hrs for pre show restaurant, Fri-Sat only. Seating: 420 for the show. Entertainment: Stand-up comedy, with a disco after Fri show. Food: Snacks at snack prices.

Smoking Policy: No restrictions. Lighters can be purchased.

A lady who liked her Havanas
Played hot rags on upright pianas
She polished her toes
On the end of her nose
And was distinctly lacking in manners   (James Leavey)

13

GAY & lesbian London

Perhaps it's because they've had to fight intolerance themselves, most of London's Gay pubs, bars, restaurants and clubs are still smoker-friendly, including:

Drill Hall Women Only Bar

16 Chenies Street, WC1 (0171 631 1353). Goodge Street tube. Open: 1800-2300 hrs, Mon. Entertainment: On Monday evenings the entire building is for women only. Busy and lively atmosphere with relaxing background music and low prices. Food is available from the Greenhouse restaurant downstairs.

Smoking Policy: No restrictions.

Heaven

The Arches, Villiers Street, WC2 (0171 930 2020). Embankment tube, Charing Cross tube/BR. Open: 2230-0330 hrs, Mon-Sat. 1200-1800 hrs and 2230-0330 hrs, Sun. Music: Dance/House music. Thursday night is mixed (Gay/straight). Lots of heteros also turn up on Friday night. Three areas to smoke in: Main dance floor, Dakota and Star bar.

Smoking Policy: No restrictions on smoking. No membership required. As the pleasant man on the phone said, "Just turn up as loud and funky as you can be."

Madame Jo Jo's

8 Brewer Street, W1 (0171 734 2473). Piccadilly Circus tube. Open: 2230-0300, Sun-Thur. 2230-0430, Fri-Sat. Seating: 200. Entertainment: Transvestite cabaret. Entry: £10.

Smoking Policy: No restrictions.

If you'd like more information on the enormous range of Gay meeting places in London, contact: London Lesbian and Gay Switch board (0171 837 7324), for 24 hour advice. (minicom service for the deaf).

Galleries & Museums

> At the end of his life Raoul Dufy didn't want any more money so he exchanged many of his paintings for Havana cigars.

You are not allowed to smoke in any of London's museums or art galleries although we have seen people light up during private and press views. If you know of any tobacco-related exhibits not listed here, do let us know.

The British Museum

Great Russell Street, WC1 (0171 636 1555). Tottenham Court Road tube. Edward Wharton-Tigar bequeathed a collection of one million cigarette and trade cards. According to the Guinness Book of Records, this is the largest known collection in the world. They can be viewed by appointment.

Museum of Mankind

6 Burlington Gardens, W1 (0171 437 2224). Green Park tube. There are a few pipes in the Philippines exhibit. The rest of their pipe collection is not on display. Ask to view it.

National Gallery

Trafalgar Square, WC2 (0171 839 3321). Charing Cross tube/BR. Currently displays the following smoker-friendly paintings:

Room 23:   - Two men with pipes by William Duster (no. NG1387)
             - Pipesmoker by Jacob van Velsen (no. NG2575)
Room 26:   - Still life of a pipe and a skull by Jan Jansz Treck (no. NG6533).
Gallery A (Orange Street entrance):
             - Alchemist with pipe by A. Van Ostade (no. NG846)
             - Peasant, smoking by A. Diepram (no. NG3534)
             - Cavalier, with pipe by Pieter Quast (no. NG2856)
             - To paintings of Pipes by A. Van Ostade (nos. NG2543 and 2543)
             - Portrait of J. de la Chambre by Franz Hals (no. NG6411)

Horniman Museum

London Road, SE20 (0181 699 1872). Forest Hill BR. Several smoking pipes used to be on permanent display in the world culture section on the second floor, above the aquarium, but have been temporarily put away while the museum is being refurbished. You can't smoke anywhere in the museum, although that you shouldn't stop you making the journey to South London to enjoy 19th c tea merchant Frederick Horniman's charming, eclectic collection.

Tourist Attractions

About 25 per cent of the world's adults smoke, but the figures vary enormously, per country. FOREST estimates that at least 10 per cent of all adult foreign visitors smoke - and this is a very conservative estimate. You could probably double this figure, at least, for tourists from Greece, Japan, USA, Canada, Switzerland, Spain, Germany, Austria, Australia and New Zealand.

The following London attractions each get over half a million visits a year. The latest figures (for 1995) are shown in brackets.

British Museum (5.7 million)
Great Russell Street, WC1 (0171 636 1555). Tottenham Court Road tube.
Smoking Policy: Total ban. Smokers gather on the steps outside.

National Gallery (4.4 million).
Trafalgar Square, WC2 (0171 839 3321). Charing Cross tube/BR.
Smoking Policy: Total ban. Smokers gather on steps outside, or sit on the short perimeter wall in front of the building.

Madame Tussauds (2.7 million)
Marylebone Road, NW1 (0171 935 6861). Baker Street tube.
Smoking Policy: Total ban. As there is virtually a permanent queue outside most of the year you have plenty of time to enjoy a smoke before you go in.

Tower of London (2.5 million)
Tower Hill, EC3 (0171 709 0765). Tower Hill tube, Fenchurch Street BR, Docklands Light Railway.
Smoking Policy: No smoking in any of the buildings but you can smoke while moving around between them. We once saw a beefeater enjoying a crafty fag, not that long ago.

Tate Gallery (1.8 million)
Millbank, SW1 (0171 887 8000). Pimlico tube.
Smoking Policy: Total ban - smoke on the steps outside.

Science Museum
Exhibition Road, SW7 (0171 938 8008). South Kensington tube.
Smoking Policy: Total ban. They even had an anti-smoking exhibit recently. Smoke outside, in the doorway, or nearby.

Trafalgar Square.

Left: British Museum. Right: Big Ben.

St Paul's Cathedral (2.2 million)

St Paul's Churchyard, EC4 (0171 248 2705). St Paul's tube.

Smoking Policy: Total ban. We think it would be sacriligous to smoke inside a place of worship, although many of the clergy are habitual smokers. Incense doesn't count, apparently.

Victoria & Albert Museum (1.2 million)

Cromwell Road, SW7 (0171 938 8500). South Kensington tube.

Smoking Policy: Total ban. Smoke outside, where you can.

Natural History Museum (1.1 million)

Exhibition Road, SW7 (0171 938 9123). South Kensington tube.

Smoking Policy: Total ban. Join the smokers outside, perhaps on the seats in the garden.

Royal Botanic Gardens (Kew Gardens - 1.0 million)

Kew Road, Kew, Surrey (0181 332 5622/0181 940 1171). Kew Gardens tube.

Smoking Policy: No smoking in Orangery café. Smoking allowed in outdoor Bakery (it has a covered section). No smoking inside the greenhouses. You're not allowed to take cuttings of the tobacco plant, that's if you can find it. Do take your smokers' litter with you, as it will otherwise spoil the gardens.

London Zoo (1.0 million)

Regent's Park, NW1 (0171 722 3333). Camden Town tube.

Smoking Policy: No smoking inside any of the buildings or eating areas. You really shouldn't smoke close to the animals - there are plenty of open spaces.

National Portrait Gallery (0.8 million)

2 St Martin's Place, WC2 (0171 306 0055). Leicester Square tube or Charing Cross tube/BR.

Smoking Policy: Total ban. Smoke outside.

Westminster Abbey (2.2 million)

Dean's Yard, SW1 (0171 222 5152/0171 222 7110). Westminster tube.

Smoking Policy: Total ban. See St Paul's Cathedral above.

Rock Circus (0.7 million)

London Pavilion, Piccadilly Circus, W1 (0171 734 7203). Piccadilly Circus tube.

Smoking Policy: Total ban. Which is ironic as many of the world's rock icons smoked all kinds of substances, not all of them legal. The following have been seen with a cigarette in their mouth, at one time or another: various members of the Beatles and Rolling Stones, Jimi Hendrix, Johnny Cash, Cher - the list is endless. You may smoke outside the building, of course.

They're changing the guard at Buckingham Palace.

The last drag outside Madame Tussauds.

Hampton Court Palace (0.6 million)

East Molesey, Surrey (0181 781 9500). Hampton Court BR.

Smoking Policy: Total ban inside the buildings. You may smoke outside but only if you're careful where you leave your litter. If you must smoke in the Maze, try not to set fire to it.

National Maritime Museum (0.6 million)

Romney Road, SE10 (0181 858 4422). Greenwich or Maze Hill BR.

Smoking Policy: Total ban inside the buildings. You may smoke freely while wandering around outside.

Carnaby Street.

16

OTHER

Attractions in London

Now that you've smoked next to the Eros statue in Piccadilly Circus, under Nelson's column (145 foot high) in Trafalgar Square, in front of the Houses of Parliament, in a theatre bar, and while leaning on the railings of Buckingham Palace, where next?

> A fag-end was the coarser part of cloth that hangs loose, and came to be applied to the last and poorest part of anything. It was first used to describe inferior cigarettes about 1883.

Over the past 40 years or so, London's Chinese community has moved from Victorian slums in the East End dockland area of Limehouse to the livelier streets around Gerrard Street, W1, now known as Chinatown. It's full of oriental restaurants (in which almost every table has an ashtray) and shops selling everything from Chinese medicines to Mah-Jong.

Three Chinese arches straddle Gerrard Street (there are also oriental-style telephone boxes), where the annual street festival celebrates Chinese New Year with loud music and paper offerings hung from windows and lamposts for the Chinese Dragon to eat.

SOHO

London's sex industry in this former red light district has mostly gone underground in the last few years, and the streets are now walked by a growing number of visitors in search of the pleasures of the table, and ashtrays, rather than the pleasures of the flesh.

Cross Shaftesbury Avenue to walk up Berwick Street Market and through the alley on which Raymond's Revue Bar has presented its festival of erotica since 1958 (you could smoke there, the last time we looked). Get to the northern end of the market then turn left, for Carnaby Street.

Swinging London swung by almost 30 years ago and the clothing in the shops is no longer quite as trendy. Most of them now don't allow smoking, either, apart from Inderwick's (at no.45 Carnaby Street), England's oldest pipe maker, founded in 1797.

Backtrack east to Soho Square, W1, to rest for a while on one of the benches. The square was laid out in 1681, but the tidy mock-Tudor garden shed in the centre was added two centuries later. Some of the best-known music publishers in the world have offices in the square and it's not unusual to see their protégés, ie. pop or rock stars, being photographed on the grass, some of them with cigarettes in their mouths.

A few minutes down the road, Old Compton Street is the heart of Soho and has many restaurants, bars and pubs, many of them now frequented by young Gay men and women.

In Frith Street, Louis Armstrong, Ella Fitzgerald and nearly all the other great names of jazz have played at Ronnie Scott's club, although at times it may have been difficult to see them through the haze of smoke. The club first opened nearby, in 1959, and is still smoker-friendly.

The writer, Jeffrey Bernard, one of England's most famous smokers (and former bon viveur) used to frequent The Coach and Horses pub in Romilly Street, W1.

When you're sipping capuccino in Bar Italia at 22 Frith Street, spare a thought for the room upstairs where John Logie Baird first demonstrated television in 1926. In the Fifties, Britain's tv's allowed the advertising of cigarettes. Mozart lived next door to 22 Frith Street with his family in 1764 and 1765, when he was a child.

COVENT GARDEN

The Piazza, London's first square, was laid out by Inigo Jones in the 1630s. Until 1974, it was the home of the capital's wholesale fruit and vegetable market, and you could listen to the singers at the Royal Opera House rehearsing while you bought a pound of oranges.

Since then, the Piazza, Central Market and surrounding streets have been transformed into central London's liveliest area, full of cafés, restaurants, umpteen shops, markets and street entertainers.

It's one of the best places to smoke outside as there is so much to see and enjoy.

In the former Victorian Flower Market, the London Transport Museum (0171 379 6344) has a fine collection of old buses, trams and underground trains, which once upon a time allowed their passengers to smoke. Now you cannot smoke on any part of the London Underground, London's buses, or in the museum.

Opposite is the Theatre Museum (7 Russell Street, WC2. 0171 836 7891), with its theatrical memorabilia, including original play bills, programmes, props, costumes and bits of vanished theatres.

You can't smoke here either, but if you look carefully, some of those old

Chinatown, Soho.

performers often used cigarettes, cigars or pipes as props.

The first theatre on the site of the Royal Opera House (0171 240 1066) was built in 1732 and staged plays as well as concerts. The present (and third) building was designed in 1858 by E M Barry, son of Charles Barry, the architect of the Houses of Parliament.

Charles Barry, conscious of his limitations as an architect in the Gothic style, enlisted the help of the French architect, Augustus Pugin. Barry provided the practical plans for 'the Mother of Parliaments', and Pugin, the ornamentation.

Back in Covent Garden, his son's famous building is now the home of the Royal Opera and Royal Ballet. Some performances have been relayed on giant screens to non-paying audiences in the Piazza, the only place they get to smoke while enjoying live opera.

The London Coliseum (St Martin's Lane, WC2. 0171 836 3161) is the capital's largest theatre, and home of the English National Opera. Its singers, musicians, office and backstage workers are still allowed to smoke, in the staff restaurant and bar, downstairs.

THE STRAND

Smokers have been strolling down this famous street, just over three quarters of a mile long, for hundreds of years. During the day, office and other workers smoke in its doorways. At night, they're replaced by the homeless. If they ask for a smoke why not give them one; they've not much else to look forward to, poor devils.

You can't smoke in the auditoriums of any of the theatres along its route (see Theatre section), or anywhere in the Savoy Theatre. Victoria Embankment Gardens (open 7am to dusk) is a better place, especially near the bandstand a few minutes from Embankment tube station.

BLOOMSBURY

Take the Northern Line to Leicester Square, then the Piccadilly Line to Russell Square and you will find yourself in Bloomsbury, synonymous with literature and art from the turn of the 20th century until the 1930s.

The Bloomsbury Group, nicknamed the Bloomsberries, was an exclusive circle of talented young writers and artists who began meeting in the house of Virginia Woolf (1821-1941) and her sister, Vanessa Bell, at 46 Gordon Street, not far from the British Museum, around 1905. They rejected Victorian social and sexual propriety and followed their beliefs in the vital importance of art and human relationships. Many of them smoked.

Among its best-known members were E M Forster (1879-1970), who wrote A Room with a View (1908), A Passage to India (1924) and Howard's End (1910), Roger Fry (1866-1934), the most influential art critic of his time, and

Left: T-shirt stall, Embankment. Right: Lighters for sale, Tottenham Court Road.

John Maynard Keynes (1883-1946), the economist who argued that governments could spend their way out of recession by commissioning work on public projects and encouraging consumers to spend by increasing the available money supply. His 'Keynesian economics' weren't fully rejected until the late 1970s.

FITZROVIA

Fitzrovia's boundaries are Marylebone Road (to the north), Tottenham Court Road (to the east), Oxford Street (south) and Great Portland Street (west). Dylan Thomas, George Orwell and the artist, Augustus John, all drank at the Fitzroy Tavern (16 Charlotte Street, W1. 0171 580 3714).

As London's upper classes moved away from Bloomsbury in the early 19th century, a flood of artists and immigrants moved in, some setting up small workshops to service the furniture stores on Tottenham Court Road and the clothing shops of Oxford Street.

For many years, John Constable (1776-1837), one of England's greatest painters, lived and worked at 76 Charlotte Street.

Today's Fitzrovia boasts a variety of fine restaurants and pubs, especially in Charlotte Street. It's also the home of the clothing industry (known as the Rag Trade), student hostels, media and communications companies and the headquarters of The Family Planning Association (27 Mortimer Street, W1. 0171 636 7866). What a good place to work, relax, drink, eat and smoke.

THE CITY

The City of London's square mile is the world's most vital financial centre, home to the Stock Exchange, the Bank of England, Lloyd's and branches of most, if not all, of the world's banks and commerce.

You can still light up in the doorway of Mansion House, Walbrook, EC4, the official residence of the Lord Mayor of London, although he has banned smoking, we're told, from his functions.

Natwest Tower, City of London.

Anyone born within earshot of the Bow Bells of the Wren church, St Mary-le-Bow, is said to be a true Londoner, or Cockney, whether they smoke or not.

A short walk westwards along Cheapside will take you to Sir Christopher Wren's masterpiece, St Paul's Cathedral. Smoke on the steps if you must, but not inside. A longer stroll in the opposite direction heading south will take you to the Tower of London and Tower Bridge. You can't smoke inside the historic buildings, but you can outside while you are admiring their exteriors.

The Tower of London has twenty towers, and two bastions (count them yourself, if you don't believe it). Tower Green was the site of numerous executions, including those of three Queens of England. The last person beheaded there and the last to lose his head by the axe in England was Lord Lovat, executed in 1747. The axe used is still on display. No doubt some vehement anti-smokers would like to see its return, for smokers.

Next door is St Katharine's Dock (E1. 0171 481 8350), a good place for a wander after visiting the Tower. A short taxi ride will take you to Tobacco Dock in Wapping. D A Alexander's large, secure warehouse (1811-1814) was built beside London Docks to store tobacco before serving as a wool store for 100 years, and a fur skins store after World War II.

Not long ago it housed several bars, shops and restaurants until it was bankrupted. Any time now it is expected to re-open as a Factory Goods outlet. The restaurant, now closed, has a 'no smoking' sign.

Leadenhall Market.

SOUTHWARK AND BANKSIDE

The Anchor (34 Park Street, SE1. 0171 407 1577) has been a favourite riverside pub for centuries, and dates from after the Southwark fire of 1676 which devastated this area south of the river, almost as much as the Great Fire of London had done a decade earlier to the north side of the Thames.

Close by is Shakespeare's Globe Museum (Bear Gardens, SE1. 0171 620 0202), built on the site of a 17th century bear-baiting venue. William Shakespeare wrote his plays for the actors of the original Globe Theatre, which has been reconstructed.

The George Inn (77 Borough High Street, SE1. 0171 407 2056) also dates from the 17th century, and is the only remaining example of a traditional galleried coaching inn left in London.

If you walk up to London Bridge and turn right into Tooley Street, SE1, stop off at Hay's Galleria as this former wharf, used for unloading tea and other provisions - and one of the first places in London to use cold storage - has been transformed into a very pleasant upmarket venue of eating and drinking places, market stalls and shops.

SOUTH BANK

In 1951, the bomb-damaged area between Waterloo Station and the Thames was chosen as the site of the Festival of Britain, celebrating the centenary of the Great Exhibition. The only remaining building from 1951 is the Royal Festival Hall, but London's main arts centre has grown around it, including the

HMS Belfast.

Left: Brixton welcomes Nelson Mandela. Right: Outside Royal Exchange.

UK's showcases for theatres, film, music and art.

The Royal National Theatre (South Bank Centre, SE1. 0171 928 2252) was subject to 200 years of debate in Parliament and elsewhere before it finally got designed by Sir Denys Lasdun, built, and opened in 1976. The company was formed in 1963 under Sir (later Lord) Laurence Olivier, perhaps the greatest actor ever produced in Britain. Olivier, a brand of cigarettes (no longer available) was named after him.

A short walk under Waterloo Bridge takes you to the Museum of the Moving Image (South Bank Centre, SE1. 0171 401 2636), otherwise known as MOMI.

It's an extension of the National Film Theatre (0171 928 3232), without doubt the best repertory cinema in London and on whose screens you can still see the world's most celebrated smokers, even if you can't join them with a smoke in the auditoriums.

A walk along the bland concrete pathways takes you back to the Royal Festival Hall (South Bank Centre, SE1. 0171 928 3191), which has weathered well over the last 45 years or so. You should pay a visit to its cafés, bars and bookshops, even if you aren't attending one of the concerts by the world's greatest musicians. If you're short of cash, there's free music, some weekday lunchtimes.

The Museum of Garden History (Lambeth Palace, SE1. 0171 261 1891) is

> **The name for a person who collects cigar bands is Infulaphilist, from the Latin Infula for a band.**

housed in and around the 14th century tower of St Mary's Church. Smoke outside, in the garden.

Further south is the Imperial War Museum (Lambeth Road, SE1. 0171 416 5000), with its tanks, artillery, bombs, aircraft and displays of food rationing and air raid precautions. Maybe it's time they included an exhibit on the role of smoking during the war. Nowadays it seems to be more acceptable to be seen with a smoking gun, than a smoking cigarette.

CHELSEA

The trendy shoppers of 1960s King's Road have long gone, but this former riverside village, fashionable since Tudor times when Henry VIII's chancellor, Sir Thomas More, lived here, still has much to offer the passing smoker.

Some of its more recent inhabitants are immediately recognisable from their scarlet coats and tricorne hats. This is the uniform of the Chelsea Pensioners, who live in the Royal Hospital (Royal Hospital Road, SW3. 0171 730 0161). Quite a few of them still smoke and are not above accepting the polite offer of a cigarette.

Many famous writers and artists have lived in the 18th century houses in Cheyne Walk, SW3, including, in Carlyle Mansions, Henry James, T S Eliot, and Ian Fleming (who created James Bond, another famous literary smoker). The painter, J M W Turner, lived quietly at No 119; George Eliot, the novelist, died at No 4.

Chelsea Physic Garden (Swan Walk, SW3. 0171 352 5646) was first established by the Society of Apothecaries in 1673 to study plants for medicinal use, including tobacco. If you light up here perhaps they'll study yours.

SOUTH KENSINGTON AND KNIGHTSBRIDGE

One of the most desirable areas in London, at least if you're an ambassador or consulate (the place is full of them), perhaps because of the royal residence, Kensington Palace, home of Princess Margaret who used to be a heavy smoker, Hyde Park, Harrods (which has an excellent smokers' department), and some of the most famous museums in the world.

Smoking is banned inside all of London's museums, but this is no reason why you shouldn't visit the Victoria and Albert Museum (founded in 1852 and known as the V&A), National History Museum (especially its new dinosaur exhibition), or the Science Museum. J M Barrie, the creator of Peter Pan, whose pipe-playing (not smoking) statue can be seen in Kensington Gardens, was himself a pipesmoker.

KENSINGTON AND HOLLAND PARK

The Commonwealth Institute (Kensington High Street, W8. 0171 603 4535) is a shrine to the history, industries and culture of the 50 member nations of the Commonwealth. Years ago, it used to openly display tobacco plants. Perhaps it's time they dusted them off and put them out again. In adjacent Holland Park (Abbotsbury Road, W14. 0171 603 9487), planes en route to Heathrow and peacocks occasionally disturb the genteel tranquillity, but not for long.

At the northern end of the Park, Notting Hill is the home of Europe's biggest street carnival (August Bank Holiday weekend), which started in 1966. It's enjoyed by countless smokers, though what they inhale is not always legal.

Since 1937, Notting Hill has also been the home of Portobello Road market, which still gets crowded on Saturdays. The south end consists mostly of stalls and shops selling antiques, souvenirs and other collectables, while the north end is mostly fruit, vegetables and, under the bridge, ethnic goods.

REGENT'S PARK AND MARYLEBONE

Madame Tussauds and the Planetarium (Marylebone Road, NW1. 0171 935 6861) have permanent, long queues throughout the year so there's plenty of time to enjoy a smoke, while you're waiting to get in. A year or so ago the anti-smoking lobby rang Madame Tussauds and asked them to remove the

Portobello Road.

167

cigarette from Humphrey Bogart's waxwork. This request, we're glad to say, was politely ignored. Regent's Park (NW1. 0171 486 7905) is one of the finest open spaces in London, and was first enclosed in 1812. There's a boating lake, with a wonderful variety of water birds that flock to it from all over the world, including Mandarin ducks and Black swans, over which drifts music from the bandstand on summer days.

Queen Mary's Gardens are a mass of colours and smells and visitors can enjoy Shakespeare's plays and modern musicals in the Open Air Theatre nearby. The scents from the rose garden are at times overwhelming, and shouldn't be spoiled with too much exhaled tobacco smoke.

London Zoo (0171 722 3333) opened in 1828 and has been a major tourist attraction ever since, as well as a world famous research centre. It does allow smoking, but not inside or too near the animals' cages.

HAMPSTEAD

If you head north, cross the canal, up past Primrose Hill, you'll eventually find yourself perched on top of Hampstead. This is one of London's most desirable neighbourhoods and has long been the home of the famous.

Keats House (Keats Grove, NE3. 0171 435 2062) is actually two semi-detached dwellings, built in 1816, knocked into one. John Keats wrote Ode to a Nightingale there, under a plum tree in the garden. He died of consumption when he was just 25 years old.

There are three square miles of Hampstead Heath (0181 348 9945) to walk across, including woods, meadows, hills, swimming ponds (Men only, Women only, and Mixed bathing).

If you're in need of refreshment, stop off at Spaniards Inn (Spaniards Road, NW3. 0181 455 3276) and, on dry days, drink your pint in the garden. On winter evenings you can light your cigarettes from the open fireplace in the small upstairs Turpin bar, named after Dick Turpin, the notorious 18th century highwayman who is said to have frequented the pub when he wasn't holding up stagecoaches.

GREENWICH

A short train ride from Charing Cross or London Bridge stations will take you to the chosen site of Britain's millenium celebrations. Elizabeth I and her sister, Mary, were born in their father's, Henry VIII, palace here, but it has long gone.

The National Maritime Museum (Romney Road, SE1. 0181 858 4422) is a tribute to the role of the sea in Britain's history, and includes exhibits on Sir Walter Raleigh, and many other celebrated English mariners.

Nearby is Greenwich Park (0181 858 2608), in which you can stand with your feet on either side of the Meridien line that divides the earth's eastern

Ancient Smoker.

Camden Town.

> **Sackville Street, W1, is the longest street in central London without a turning out of it.**

and western hemisphere. It has been suggested that one day all of London's smokers will stand on one side, and non-smokers, the other.

The majestic Cutty Sark (King William Walk, SE10. 0181 858 2698) is a surviving clipper that crossed the Atlantic and Pacific a century ago. It was launched as a tea carrier in 1869.

You can't smoke in the 1,200 feet Greenwich Foot Tunnel between Greenwich Pier and the Isle of Dogs (E14, 5am-9pm, daily), unlike some of the South London labourers who used to walk through it to work in Millwall Docks for many years after it opened in 1902.

Above the ground, East London's skyline has been dominated by the 50-storey, 800 feet Canada Tower since it opened at Canary Wharf in 1991. It's the tallest office building in Europe, at the moment.

CAMDEN TOWN

Millions of young tourists flock to Camden Town every year, partly because it's the home of MTV, and partly because it offers a good selection of budget-conscious entertainment in its clubs, pubs, bars and markets, especially at weekends.

If you arrive at Camden Town tube station, take the right-hand exit and turn right again. Walk up Camden High Street to Chalk Farm Road and on the way you'll pass Camden Market, which recently celebrated its 20th anniversary. Over the bridge and to the left is the Camden Canal Market, with mountains of bric-a-brac, new and old.

Continue under the railway bridge and you'll see lots of small trendy shops and bars on your right, and the Victorian Railway Arches and Stables, on your left, overflowing with food and yet more bric-a-brac stalls.

The City branch of the Northern Line from Chalk Farm tube station will (if London Transport aren't still busy upgrading it) take you to Angel, in the heart of gentrified Islington. Evelyn Waugh, George Orwell and Joe Orton lived here, for a while.

It's the home of several fringe theatres, a decent cinema (Screen on the Green), numerous (and crowded) restaurants and bars, and two markets: Chapel Road - for its fruit, veg and inexpensive clothing, Camden Passage - for overpriced 'antiques'.

17

THE London smoker's Social Calendar

> "In any case we agree that pleasure-seeking is among the greatest virtues. Wherever it is neglected or maligned, something is rotten." (Bertolt Brecht, 1898-1956)

January
New Year's Day Parade (for those who are still celebrating from the night before) along Regent Street and Piccadilly.
International Boat Show, Earls Court (you can smoke while wandering around, but usually not when you're viewing the latest water craft).
London International Mime Festival (outdoors, so perfect for the smoker - who is sometimes the subject of the silent artistes).
January shopping sales (there's plenty of time to smoke in the queue outside while waiting for the doors to open).

February
Blessing the Throats Service at St Etheldreda's Church in Ely Place, just off Holborn. (Extinguish your cigarette before you enter).
Chinese New Year Parade, Gerrard Street, W1 (most Chinese restaurants are smoker-friendly).
Pancake Races at Covent Garden and Lincoln's Inn - but not with a fag in your mouth as it ruins the batter.
Royal Gun Salutes on Accession Day (February 6), fired by King's Troop Royal Horse Artillery in Hyde Park. They're also fired on April 21 (the Queen's real birthday), June 2 (Coronation Day), June 10 (Prince Philip's birthday) and Aug 4 (Queen Mother's birthday). If one of these dates falls on a Sunday, the salute is held the following day.
Similar salutes are held in Green Park for Trooping the Colour (the Queen's official birthday), the State Opening of Parliament and to honour some visiting heads of state. On all these special days, the Honourable Artillery Company fires a 62-gun salute (41 for the royal Tower, 21 for the City of London) at 1pm from the Tower of London. As there's lots of smoke anyway they won't mind you lighting up.

March
St Patrick's Day (17th), when you should drink a pint of Guinness with your smoke, in one of London's growing number of Irish pubs.

	Daily Mail Ideal Home Exhibition, Earls Court (where you'll find on display the latest smoke extractors).

Easter weekend   Easter Sunday Parade at Battersea Park.

Harness Horse Parade of working horses in Regent's Park (Easter Monday).

Hot Cross Bun Ceremony (Good Friday) at Widow's Son Inn, 75 Devons Road, E3.

The first of the year's Bank Holiday fairs on Hampstead Heath and other open spaces around London.

April   Canal cavalcade of narrow boats at Little Venice (you can smoke anywhere along London's 40 miles of towpath, and on most of the boats).

St George's Day, patron saint of England (23rd) - when English smokers should light up and celebrate with something red.

May   Covent Garden May Fayre in St Paul's Churchyard (dance round the Maypole with a fag in your mouth).

Piccadilly Festival.

Beating the Retreat (the soldiers, not the smokers) at Horse Guards Parade.

Chelsea Flower Show (no tobacco on display, alas).

June   Open Air Theatre, Regent's Park.

Morris Dancing, Wednesday evenings, by Westminster Abbey.

Open-air concerts at Kenwood House and Marble Hill House.

July   City of London Festival (some of it outdoors).

Swan Upping (Sunbury-on-Thames to Whitchurch).

Royal Garden Parties.

Fitzrovia Fair (outdoors, in Fitzroy Square, under the shadow of the BT Tower).

August   Cart making in Guildhall Yard. More traditional fairs on Hampstead Heath and elsewhere in London. An annual blessing of horses and their riders takes place every year on Horseman's Sunday, near Hyde Park.

> "I have never seen a single neurosis or psychosis which could definitely be attributed in any way to tobacco. On the other hand one is more justified in looking with suspicion at the abstainer...most of the fanatic opponents of tobacco I have known were all bad neurotics."
> (A A Brill, 'Tobacco and the Individual', International Journal of Psychoanalysis, 1922)

> The first Cuban seegars (as they were then known)
> arrived in London at the shop of Robert Lewis in St
> James's Street in 1830. By the end of the 19th century,
> smoking jackets and hats had been introduced for
> gentlemen smokers, and the after-dinner cigar (with
> a glass of port or brandy) was an established tradition.

September   Henry Wood Promenade Concerts at the Royal Albert Hall (you can smoke in the bars, but not the auditorium).
Autumn Equinox (22nd or 23rd) celebrated by the Druids on Primrose Hill, the top of which has one of the finest views of London.
Private Fire Brigades Competition in Guildhall Yard (see how quickly they can extinguish your cigarette).
Antique fairs at Burlington House, Piccadilly, and in Chelsea (check the prices of old lighters and ashtrays).

October   Harvest Festival services in many churches (can smokers give thanks for crops of tobacco?).
Annual conferences of political parties elsewhere in England (Conservative and Labour alternate between Blackpool and Brighton) - a lot of hot air.

November   London Film Festival (see how many new films still feature smokers).
Guy Fawkes Day (5th) - when you can get a light from bonfires throughout the country.
London-Brighton Veteran Car Run (1st Sunday, from Hyde Park Corner) - most of the vintage cars (watch the film, 'Genevieve', for a sample of the fun) are open-topped so perfect for the smoker, provided he or she can a) light their cigarette, and b) stop it being blown out of their mouth when they're zooming down the road.
World Travel Market exhibition at Earls Court (how many airlines have banned smoking? Are there any other smoker-friendly countries?).
Lord Mayor's Show (2nd Saturday).
Christmas illuminations switched on in Oxford Street, Regent Street, Jermyn Street and Bond Street.

December   Carol-singing around the Christmas Tree in Trafalgar Square and throughout London.
Christmas Day, as good a day to light up as any other.
New Year's Eve, in one of London's pubs or restaurants. Be careful if you light up in Trafalgar Square at midnight as it gets very crowded.

18

GAMBLING

London's 21 casinos, bookmakers and numerous bingo clubs welcome smokers, for obvious reasons, although some have non-smoking areas, usually an area of a bar or restaurant.

Section 42 of the British Gaming Act 1968 currently forbids us telling you the actual names and addresses of the London clubs where gaming takes place. This law has become increasingly stupid and archaic, especially when you consider the enormous promotion and money spent on the National Lottery every week.

London's casinos aren't hard to find, just stroll around Mayfair (Park Lane, Curzon Street, Hertford Street, Berkeley Street), Piccadilly Circus (Shaftesbury Avenue, Archer Street) and other central areas (Baker Street, Knightsbridge, Queensway, Kensington High Street, Palace Gate, Hamilton Place, Bryanston Street, Edgware Road, and Russell Square).

London's casinos are all members only establishments so you'll need to produce a current driving licence or passport, wait 48 hours, and be prepared to pay a one-off joining fee after you have found a friendly member to nominate you.

Once you're inside, if you can convince them you are a high roller they may provide you with free cigarettes and cigars; winners still celebrate with the latter, losers with the former.

It is believed that you can increase your credibility (and credit rating) by sauntering in, smartly dressed, puffing on a large Havana. Those lucky few whose chips are in will probably take the taxi or limo back to their home, or hotel. If you're determined to lose, try to do it early in the day as the last tubes stop running around midnight.

James Leavey's politically correct definitions of a smoker:
Discretionary fumerist, fresh-air re-offender,
nicotine companion, alternatively oxegenated,
environmentally unhygienic, natural substance
abuse survivor, person of differing inhalation,
temporary orally dysfunctional, individual with
differential breathing requirements.

19

SPORT

> **If you don't smoke or drink, you die in good health.**
> **(Old Russian saying)**

You can smoke outside virtually everywhere in London's sports grounds, arenas and stadiums, but not on the actual playing areas or in some of the stands and buildings. Lots of players enjoy a smoke after the game, even if their PR managers don't like them to mention it.

> **"I would argue that every man, whatever his race, whatever his rank, whatever his profession, whatever his work, is helped by smoking." (Sir Compton Mackenzie, the prolific author, of 'Whiskey Galore,' among many other books, who believed that without his continual pipe-smoking, he would not have written half of what he did)**

CRICKET

Lord's Cricket Ground
St John's Wood, NW8 (0171 289 8979). St John's Wood tube.
Smoking Policy: No restrictions.

The Oval Kennington, SE11 (0171 582 6660). Kennington tube.
Smoking Policy: 80% of the stand available to smokers. Smoking and non-smoking sections in the bar and food areas.

GOLF

The English Golf Union
1-3 Upper Kings Street, Leicester (01526 354500).
UK Policy: The Union has stated that golfers can smoke at all times while playing. In the event of dry weather conditions smoking may be temporarily restricted due to fire risk. Some areas in club houses may be restricted to non-smokers.

LAWN TENNIS

Wimbledon The All England Lawn Tennis and Croquet Club, Church Road, SW19 (0181 944 1066). Wimbledon Park or Southfields tube.
Smoking Policy: Smoking is not permitted in courts 1, 2, 13, 14, 17 and the centre court, otherwise feel free to light up.

FOOTBALL - SOME OF LONDON'S LEADING CLUBS

Arsenal Football Club
Avenell Road, Highbury, N5 (0171 704 4000). Highbury & Islington tube/BR.
Smoking Policy: Smoking allowed in all areas except the family enclosure. If in doubt ask.

Charlton Football Club
The Valley, Floyd Road, SE7 (0171 293 4567). Charlton BR.
Smoking Policy: You can smoke in most of the stand. There are a few small non-smoking areas. If in doubt, ask.

Chelsea Football Club
Fulham Road, SW6 (0171 385 5545). Fulham Broadway tube.
Smoking Policy: No restrictions.

Crystal Palace Football Club
Selhurst Park, White House Lane, SE25 (0181 768 6000). Selhurst or Thornton Heath BR.
Smoking Policy: Most of the club is smoker-friendly. There are a few small non-smoking areas. If in doubt, ask.

Fulham Football Club
Craven Cott, Stevenage Road, SW6 (0171 736 6561). Putney Bridge tube.
Smoking Policy: No restrictions.

Leyton Orient Football Club
Leyton Stadium, Brisbane Road, Leyton, E10 (0181 539 2223). Leyton tube.
Smoking Policy: Smoking is not allowed in the main centre stand (1,000 seats). If in doubt, ask.

Millwall Football Club
The Den, Zampa Road, SE16 (0171 232 1222). New Cross Gate tube/South Bermondsey BR.
Smoking Policy: No restrictions.

Queen's Park Rangers
Loftus Road/South Africa Road, Shepherds Bush, W12 (0181 743 0262). White City tube.
Smoking Policy: No restrictions.

Tottenham Hotspurs
748 High Road, Tottenham, N17 (0181 365 5000). White Hart Lane BR or

Seven Sisters tube.

Smoking Policy: Smoking is not allowed in the member's stand (7,000), otherwise the club is smoker-friendly. If in doubt, ask.

West Ham United Football Club

Boleyn Ground, Green Street, Upton Park, E13 (0181 548 2748). Upton Park BR.

Smoking Policy: Half of the family enclosure is reserved for non-smokers. If in doubt, ask.

Wimbledon Football Club

Selhurst Park Stadium, White House Lane, SE25 (0181 771 2233). Selhurst or Thornton Heath BR.

Smoking Policy: You can smoke everywhere except for the few small non-smoking areas. If in doubt, ask.

TEN PIN BOWLING

The Lewisham Bowl

11-29 Belmont Hill, SE13 (0181 318 9691). Lewisham BR.

Smoking Policy: No restrictions.

MULTI SPORT EVENT VENUES

Alexandra Palace

Wood Green, N22 (0181 778 0131). Wood Green tube.

Smoking Policy: Private hire venue policy depends on who is organising the event.

Royal Albert Hall

Kensington Gore, SW7 (0171 589 8212). South Kensington tube.

Smoking Policy: No smoking in the auditorium.

Wembley Stadium and Arena

Empire Way/Stadium Way, Middlesex (0181 902 1234). Wembley Stadium BR, Wembley Park tube.

Smoking Policy: No restrictions in the Stadium. The Arena is a non-smoking venue.

HORSE RACING

Ascot Racecourse,

Ascot, Berkshire SI5 7JN (0134 422211). Ascot BR.

Smoking Policy: No restrictions.

Epsom Grandstand Association

Race-Course Paddock, Esher, Surrey (0132 726311). Epsom BR.

Smoking Policy: No restrictions.

Goodwood   Chichester, Sussex (01243 774107). Chichester BR.
Smoking Policy: No smoking in the house.

Newmarket   High Street, Newmarket, Suffolk (01638-663482).
Smoking Policy: No restrictions.

MOTOR RACING

Brands Hatch Fawkham, Kent (01474 872331). Swanley BR.
Smoking Policy: No restrictions.

GREYHOUND RACING

Catford Stadium
              Catford Bridge, SE6 (0181 690 8000). Catford Bridge BR.
Smoking Policy: No restrictions.

Hackney Stadium
              Waterden Road, E15 (0181 986 3511). Hackney Wick BR, Stratford tube/BR.
Smoking Policy: No restrictions.

Walthamstow Stadium
              Chingford Road, E4 (0181 531 4255). Walthamstow Central BR.
Smoking Policy: No restrictions.

Wembley Stadium
              Empire Way, Wembley (0181 902 1234). Wembley Park BR, Wembley Stadium
              tube.
Smoking Policy: No restrictions.

> **Queen Victoria's guests at Balmoral, including
> the Prince of Wales, had to lie on the floor of
> their bedrooms and puff their cigarette or
> cigar smoke up the chimney, to avoid giving
> offence to the Her Majesty. Balmoral is not
> very large and Victoria's sense of smell was
> acute. Years later, Queen Victoria reported
> in her diary that she, her daughter, Beatrice,
> and a lady-in- waiting started smoking
> cigarettes in the garden at Balmoral,
> to keep the midges away.**

20

HEALTH

& Fitness Centres

A matter of choice.

Pineapple 7 Langley Street, WC2 (0171 836 4004). Covent Garden tube. Mixed (male/female).
Smoking Policy: Smoking sections in the cafeteria.

St James's Health Club
7 Byron House, 7-9 St James's Street, SW1 (0171 930 5568). Green Park tube. Mostly a male only club, but women are permitted to use the gym.
Smoking Policy: Smoking is permitted in most parts of the club.

Sanctuary 11 Floral Street, WC2 (0171 240 0695). Covent Garden tube. Women only.
Smoking Policy: You can smoke in the gallery overlooking the swimming pool.

YMCA   112 Great Russell Street, WC1 (0171 637 1333). Tottenham Court Road tube. Mixed (male/female).
Smoking Policy: Smoking is permitted in sections of the café and the spectator gallery.

PRIVATE SPORTS CLUBS

Well, well, what a surprise, some of the members smoke. Shame on them for not owning up before they joined.

A study in the Journal of the American Medical Association in mid-1996 which checked the fitness of 32,421 people (25,341 men and 7,080 women) over eight years found moderately fit men and women - even if they smoked - were less likely to die than unfit non-smoking couch potatoes.

The Dallas researchers said people could get moderately fit by briskly walking for 30 minutes every day, and even fitter by additional swimming two or three times a week.

Barbican Health & Fitness Centre
97 Aldersgate Street, EC1 (0171 374 0091). Barbican tube.
Smoking Policy: No smoking, anywhere, but we've seen members light up in the changing rooms.

Broadgate Club
1 Exchange Place, EC2 (0171 375 2464). Liverpool Street tube.
Smoking Policy: No smoking anywhere, except when they open the place for celebrations, parties or private functions.

Hurlingham Club
Fulham, SW6 (0171 736 8411). Putney Bridge tube. Mixed (male/female).
Smoking Policy: No smoking in the conservatory. Smoking allowed in the long gallery, drawing room and bars.

Roehampton Club
Roehampton Lane, SW15 (0181 876 5505). East Putney tube. Mixed (male/female).
Smoking Policy: Smoking is permitted in the bar but not the restaurant.

> **"I am not following your interdict on smoking: do you think it is then so lucky to have a long miserable life?"**
> **(Sigmund Freud to his doctor)**

21

OPEN

Spaces

Around 67 square miles of Greater London is covered in grass. The capital's parks, commons, heaths, squares, gardens and allotments are the envy of the world, and the perfect place for a relaxed smoke on a fine day.

Royal Parks, total acreage, 6000 acres
St James's Park - 93 acres
Green Park - 53 acres
Hyde Park - 360 acres
Kensington Gardens - 275 acres
Regent's Park and Primrose Hill - 472 acres
Greenwich Park - 200 acres
Richmond Park - 2,500 acres
Hampton Court Home Park - 1,000 acres
Bushy Park - 1,100 acres

Left: Portobello Road. Right: Where's the lighter?

Hyde Park concert.

Other major open spaces in the greater London area include:
Epping Forest - 6,000 acres
Hampstead Heath - 800 acres

> For a time after WW2, smoking was sometimes prescribed by doctors as soothing to the nerves. Perhaps it was with this in mind that Britain's Chancellor of the Exchequer introduced tobacco coupons for old age pensioners in his 1947 Budget. They were discontinued in 1958.

Within the City of London, there are 35 acres of open space, mainly gardens, squares, walks and churchyards. The largest are the Barbican (8 acres), Finsbury Circus Gardens (3 acres) and St Paul's Churchyard (2 acres).

All of London's street markets are also smoker-friendly, including:

Berwick Street
(Piccadilly Circus tube), Mondays to Saturdays
Camden Market
(next to Camden Town tube), Saturdays and Sundays
Camden Canal Market
(Camden Town or Chalk Farm tube), mostly Saturdays and Sundays - gets VERY crowded
Portobello Road
(Notting Hill Gate tube) - general market most weekdays, antiques market, Saturdays
Petticoat Lane
(Aldgate, Aldgate East or Liverpool Street tube) - Sunday morning
Brick Lane
(Aldgate East tube), 5am to 2pm, Sundays
Columbia Road
(Shoreditch or Old Street tube), Sunday mornings
Brixton Market
(Brixton tube), Mondays, Tuesdays, Thursdays and Saturdays from 8am to 5.30pm
Leadenhall Market
(Bank tube), Monday to Friday, 7am to 3pm
Smithfield Market
(Farringdon tube), the last-surviving wholesale produce market in central London. Monday to Friday, 5am to 10.30am

22

SHOPPING

> Hamleys, 188 Regent's Street, W1 (0171 734 31610), the world's most famous toyshop, has stopped selling exploding cigars, but will sell you an exploding golfball for £2.99. The difficult bit is trying to get someone to smoke it...

Smoking is discouraged in almost every shop in London, except for tobacconists. Legally, shops can't force you not to smoke but London's smokers have long been tolerant of this informal ban, and tend to extinguish whatever they are enjoying before they enter the premises.

You will still find staff in smaller high street shops enjoying a quiet puff behind the counter. Not long ago we saw the owner of a pet shop in Victoria, with a lit cigarette. Perhaps he planned to smoke the fish before he sold it.

More of a problem are London's major shopping precincts as many of them now ban smoking completely, forcing customers to leave the building for a fag. The same ban doesn't apply to the capital's street markets, which may be one of the reasons they are still popular.

If you know of any shops that still allow smoking, do let us know.

> Founded in 1676, James Lock & Co Ltd, 6 St James's Street, SW1 (0171 930 5849) are the oldest hatters in London. One day a gentleman named William Coke asked them to design a hat for hunting and stood on the finished article to test its strength. It was called the Billycock after its originator, and eventually developed into the world famous Bowler hat. Lock still sells velvet smoking hats in various colours, with a tassle at the side, for £55 each.

Versace, Knightsbridge.

For years, people have been celebrating April Fool's Day by playing practical jokes on each other. The Davenport Magic Shop, Charing Cross Underground Concourse, off Adelaide Street, WC2 (0171 836 0408) sells vanishing cigarettes, and fags that won't light - perfect presents for non-smokers. It all started in 1898 when Lewis Davenport began selling stink bombs to London's schoolboys. And yes, you can smoke in the shop.

Cigar Indian, Harrods.

TOP 23

Valuers & Auctioneers

Some auctioneers include vintage cigars with 'lots' of fine wines. Cigarette cards, unusual humidors, lighters and pipes are often valuable - so check with one of the following companies before you think of selling. Old cigarette packs, tobacco jars and tins are also worth holding on to.

Bonhams   Montpelier Street, SW7 (0171 393 3900). Knightsbridge tube.
Smoking Policy: Total ban on smoking in the building. In occasional sales of 'objects of vertu' they may include pipes etc. Their Devon branch very occasionally auctions cigarette cards.

Christie's   8 King Street, St James's, SW1 (0171 404 0670). Green Park tube.
Smoking Policy: Total ban in public areas.

Christie's   South Kensington. 85 Old Brompton Road, SW7 (0171 581 7611). South Kensington tube.
Smoking Policy: No smoking in the public areas. Bi-monthly sales of 'objects of vertu' sometimes include cigar and cigarette cases or boxes. The rarest item sold - a silver humidor.

Phillips   101 New Bond Street, W1 (0171 629 6602). Bond Street tube.
Smoking Policy: Total ban on smoking in the building. Sales of cigarette cards and postcards three times a year.

Sothebys   34-35 New Bond Street, W1 (0171 493 8080). Bond Street tube.
Smoking Policy: Total ban on smoking in the building. Their Billingshurst branch holds sales of portrait miniatures and 'objects of vertu' five times a year, and these may include pipes etc.

> **Calumet, otherwise known as the Peace-pipe, was presented by North American Indians to a stranger as a mark of hospitality and goodwill. If you refused the offer this was seen as an hostile act of defiance. Wonder if they still use it...?**

John MacGregor came up with the idea of employing boys of the Ragged Schools as London's shoeblacks in 1851, to take advantage of the crowds attending the Great Exhibition. He started with two boys and soon dozens of societies were formed, some named after the colours of their uniforms - Marylebone Whites, Central Reds, Westminster Blues. They mostly disappeared after 1917. Today the few remaining shoeblacks are organised by a firm of shoepolish manufacturers but they still wear the red coats.

Anti-smoking non-smokers sometimes complain that their clothing reeks after they have been in close proximity to a smoker, but usually conveniently forget to mention the far worse pollution from London traffic, and the horrible pong of junk food. London has lots of dry cleaners, so there's no reason to go around for months on end smelling of petrol fumes, cheap hamburgers or even stale smoke.

On a positive note, the Harrods lighter repair department (next to lost property in the basement of the Knightsbridge store, via the Basil Street entrance), has been servicing the world's most exclusive lighters for the past 25 years or so.

"We've had to deal with gold, silver, platinum and jewel-encrusted lighters," explained Jim Cassidy, who does all the repairs personally, and whose repair service is one of the few left in the UK, "from royalty, stars of film, tv and stage, well-known politicians and business people."

Richard Ball, founder and deputy chairman of the Lighter Club of Great Britain (membership details from 351a Whitehorse Road, Croydon, Surrey, CR0 2HS. 0181 665 9578), which was formed in 1990 and now has over 200 members, worldwide, agreed that the Harrods department was unique in London.

Ball added: "Lighters are becoming increasingly collectable and some are fetching up to £2,500, so it's a good idea to look after them."

One of his members in Cornwall has about 25,000 lighters. The Lighter Museum in Neunen, near Eindhboven, Holland, has around 50,000.

Our favourite is Fred, who recently moved to the Great Marlborough Street end of Carnaby Street and charges £2 a shine, while he chainsmokes over your footwear. He's been cleaning shoes for 49 years.

25

EXHIBITIONS,

Seminars & Conferences

> They say figures can't lie - but political figures have been known to tell or fib or two, especially when it comes to ranting against smoking.

Every year over four million people from all over the world attend London's exhibitions, seminars and conferences, for business or pleasure. The last recorded combined annual attendance figure for Earls Court and Olympia alone was 3.3 million.

Visitors can still smoke anywhere in Earls Court, Olympia and Alexandra Palace exhibition halls, and the Business Design Centre in Islington.

Cigar Dinner in the City.

26

OUTSIDE

London

The good news is that most of Britain is still smoker-friendly, but the bad news is that there's too much of it to write about here. You'll have to wait for The FOREST Guide to Smoking in Britain.

Meanwhile, if you go nowhere else, try a long weekend on the Isle of Wight, one of the most smoker-friendly places in England.

The island's famous visitors over the years include John Keats, who is said to have recited the opening lines of his newly written Endymion poem in the grounds of Carisbrooke Castle; Charles Dodgson (also known as Lewis Carroll), who spent three idyllic summers in Sandown.

J M W Turner painted his first oil here, a study of fishing boats off The Needles; and D H Lawrence's novel, *The Trespasser*, drew on the magical summer he spent at Freshwater in 1909. Turgenev began the first draft of *Fathers and Son* while bathing at Ventnor; and Karl Marx, who made three visits to Ryde and Ventor for the sake of his health, described it in a letter to Engels as 'a little paradise.'

Former residents include Queen Victoria, at Osborne House (where A A Milne and Robert Graves recuperated after being invalided out of the trenches in World War I); Alfred Lord Tennyson at Farringford; J B Priestley (the pipe-smoking author) near Godshill, and David Niven smoked cigarettes at Seaview.

Take the Southampton train from Waterloo and a boat to Cowes (you can smoke on the Red Funnel car ferry, not the catamaran), the world's mecca of yachting. All the pubs and restaurants are smoker-friendly, and you can light up in every yacht club, including the Royal Yacht Squadron, where, during Cowes Week, you will meet some of the finest sailors in the world.

You'll also get a warm welcome from the following smoker-friendly businesses outside London:

The Barley Mow
Gower Street, Telford, Shropshire (01952 613565).

The Business Club
60 Marine Parade, Brighton, East Sussex (01273 620130).

Cheers   6a Queen Street, Rushden, Northamptonshire (01933 410803).

The Church Inn
422 Huddersfield Road, Millbrook, Stalybridge, Cheshire (0161 338 2813).

The Coach House
The Street, Cowfold, Horsham, West Sussex (01403 865016).

Pipe smoker in Cowes, Isle of Wight.

Cocker's Garden Centre
Whitemyres, Lang Stracht, Aberdeen (01224 313261).
Dolphin Hotel
218 Central Drive, Blackpool, Lancashire (01253 290915).
Empire Café 19 Cheap Street, Newbury, Berkshire (01635 41424).

Everybody's Inn
Addington Street, Margate, Kent (01843 223907).
The Fittie Bar
18 Wellington Street, Aberdeen (01224 582911).
Hayman's Bakery & Coffee House
8 Institute Road, Swanage, Dorset (01929 422594).
The Heath Tavern
Uxbridge Road, Hillingdon, Middlesex (0181 569 2369).

> **In WW2 virtually all of the armed forces smoked, except in submarines. One submarine captain took to embroidery and did several chair covers for his mother, to keep his mind off smoking. When asked how his crew coped, he said he never asked.**

Kingswood Hotel
  55 Rodwell Road, Weymouth, Dorset (01305 784926).
The Lion's Den
  Little Clacton Road, Great Holland, Frinton-on-Sea, Essex (01255 675137).
The Pavilion Vaults
  Westborough, Scarborough, North Yorkshire (01723 503170).
The Pig & Whistle
  Grafty Green, Kent (01622 850501).
The Queen's Head
  Iron Cross, near Evesham, Worcestershire (01386 871012).
The Red Lion Inn
  Church Street, Coltishall, Norfolk (01603 737402).
Rawlings Club, Hotel and Restaurant
  30 Sun Hill, Cowes, Isle of Wight PO31 7HY (01983 297507).
Royal Lion Hotel
  Lyme Regis, Dorset (01297 445622).
The Shepherd's Rest
  Ridgeway, Wiltshire (01793 790266).
The Skipworth Arms
  Station Road, Moortown, Lincolnshire (01472 851770).
The Somerset Arms
  231 North Road West, Plymouth, Devon (01752 663846).
The Sportsman
  9/11 Cantelupe Road, East Grinstead, West Sussex (01342 311944).
The Stag   65 Wainscott Road, Wainscott, Rochester, Kent (01634 718359).
The Waterloo
  41 Mill Street, Brierly Hill, West Midlands (01384 828066).
The Water Gipsies
  Ashburnham Road, Ham, Richmond, Surrey (0181 940 3169).
The Waterwitch
  Cockcroft Road, Didcot, Oxfordshire (01235 812786).
The Wheel Inn
   Burton Road, Midway, Swadlincote, Derbyshire (01283 221759).
The White Horse
  Church Hill, Eythorne, Dover, Kent (01304 830252).
Ye Jolly Farmers of Olden Times
  Dalton, Thirsk, Yorkshire (01845 577359).

> BT's Central London residential phone book, September 1996, lists the following: 30 telephone users sharing the surname Ash, 6 sharing Forest and 1 with the surname Smoker.

THE LONDON

of Sherlock Holmes

James Leavey dogs the footsteps of one of the most famous smokers in the world

Every year, thousands of tourists arrive in London in search of a myth that has been closely interwoven with Victorian history. Their quarry is Sherlock Holmes, the world's greatest consulting detective; perennial star of countless books, comics, radio and stage plays, tv series, films, videos and a growing mountain of merchandise.

Back in 1887 when his first case, *A Study in Scarlet*, was published, Sir Arthur Conan Doyle's gimlet-eyed know-all received a modest reception from the public.

Now all you've got to do is don a deerstalker, stuff a Calabash pipe in your mouth and ask someone the way to Baker Street. You'll immediately be recognised as a keen Sherlockian, if not the man himself. Coachloads of Japanese or Americans tourists will dog your steps and, if you can find a suitably drooling mask for your mutt, Baskerville (as in Hound of), you'll make a small fortune in signed photographs.

So, suitably garbed, with a magnifying glass in one hand and some dog biscuits in the pocket of my Inverness cape, I set off across London in search of the Great Detective's haunts.

"The game's afoot!" I cried, indicating my destination on the map to Bert, the driver of the black four-wheeler cab (there wasn't a Hansom in sight) hailed outside Charing Cross station. The latter was where a criminal named Matthews knocked out Holmes's left canine in the waiting room, in *The Empty House*.

"There's the White House, the Kremlin and 10 Downing Street, but they're probably not as well known as 221b Baker Street, immortalised as the address of Sherlock Holmes from around 1881 to 1903, until his retirement to Sussex Downs to study beekeeping," said Bert over his shoulder as he drove off. I sat back astonished by this unexpected barrage of knowledge.

"It's elementary, mate," explained Bert, "when you get as many tourists as I do, all asking to be taken to the same address."

As we transversed the city, I noticed that the Victorian pea-souper fog had been replaced by fumes from countless horseless carriages. Alas, most of the 50,000 horses that had worked in London a century ago had long gone. As had the manure-coated cobbles. Only the street vendors, itinerants, vagrants and traffic jams remained, and the average Hansom cab speed of about 9

Sherlock Holmes Museum, Baker Street.

miles per hour.

When we eventually arrived at 221b Baker Street, I found it had been Abbey National's London headquarters since 1944, and Abbey House since 1932. A bronze plaque celebrating the company's special relationship with Sherlock Holmes was unveiled by the late, and much celebrated television Sherlockian actor, Jeremy Brett, in 1985.

Apart from that the only visible homage to Holmes was a mock antique leather-topped desk in the company's press office, manned by Gug Kyraicou, official secretary to Holmes since April 1994.

"Since 1949, Abbey National has received and dealt with between 30 and 40 letters a week, sometimes whole bagfuls, addressed to Sherlock Holmes," said Gug. "They're mostly from kids who sometimes ask for help in solving minor mysteries such as finding lost pets."

> The chief doorkeeper's snuff-box at the House of Commons is filled at Government expense and available for members' nostrils only. Before World War II, up to about 100 members used to take a pinch before they blew their tops. Now they blow them anyway, often without the benefit of a good excuse. The box was one of the many victims of the Blitz but Sir Winston Churchill donated a Georgian replacement to keep alive yet another tradition of the House. It resides at the doorkeeper's chair next to the main entrance to the chambers and is still used most days by a handful of MPs.

Gug dutifully replies to every letter, enclosing a free goody bag containing a booklet, a highly collectable set of commemorative stamps, and a badge, informing enquirers that: "Mr Holmes has now retired to Sussex where he spends his time reviewing the records of his cases and keeping bees..."

A short stroll led me to other dedications to the Great Detective, which abounded everywhere I looked. Even Baker Street underground station's ticket hall (refurbished for the opening of the Jubilee line in 1979), middle concourse and Bakerloo line platforms were clad in duo-tone tiling featuring a total of about 50 silhouettes of Holmes.

Baker Street itself now boasts a Sherlock Holmes pharmacy and newsagent. At No.108, you can unwind in a large Victorian porcelain bath in the Sherlock Holmes Hotel's (0171 486 6161) Reichenbach Suite. Or enjoy Mrs Hudson's Tea of finger sandwiches, hot toasted crumpets, muffins, scones, cake, clotted cream and preserves, served from midday till 6pm, in the Dr Watson's bar and lounge, or dinner in the 221b Eating House restaurant.

On the north side of Marylebone Road, the entrance charge to the Sherlock Holmes Museum at the other "221b" Baker Street (0171 935 8866) seemed a trifle expensive. Also the exhibition wasn't located on what most Sherlockians believe to be the actual site of 221B. Nonetheless, it was a charming reconstruction of a Victorian three storey lodging house (17 steps from the front door to Holmes's first floor study) and you were allowed to handle the curious range of exhibits, while the flames from mock coal fires helped shake off the chill.

Dr Watson's bedroom was on the second floor, next to Mrs Hudson's quarters. On display downstairs were fan letters to Holmes, including one from an 8-year-old in Japan, which ended: "PS Please give my love to your friend." The mind boggled at the unseemly possibilities.

I was met just outside the museum's front door by Sherlock's shorter lookalike, actor Stewart Quentin 'Holmes', who had been immersed in the role, full-time, for five years. His colleague, John Barrett 'Watson', now only works weekends, preferring to spend the rest of the week in medical publishing.

Strangely, neither could be found in BT's London Residential Phone Book, which currently lists the following entries: J Moriarty - 9, S Holmes - 19, Dr J Watson - 1, and J (as in Inspector?) Lestrade - 1.

"I live round the corner from Baker Street so it's quite handy," said Stewart under his deerstalker, who hands out business cards and is the popular subject of foreign snapshooters. "Watson and I often go out in costume and recently turned up in a Hansom cab at Buckingham Palace for the Changing of the Guard, where we caused quite a sensation."

A keen cryptologist, like his namesake, 'Holmes' directed me across the road to the Sherlock Holmes Memorabilia Society at 230 Baker Street, NW1 (0171 486 1426), where from Monday to Saturday they sell over 1,000 items of merchandise (including a deerstalker hat, £24.95, a selection of magnifying glasses from £9.95 - £29.95, miniature violins, Meerchaum pipes, Persian slippers - £9.99, bound copies of the original Strand Magazine, Sherlock Holmes Teddy Bears and fridge magnets).

Opened in July 1992 on the site known to Holmes's followers as *The Empty House*, part of the first floor has since been converted into a Victorian first class railway carriage - a scene from the story, *Silver Blaze*. Customers can have their photos taken sitting next to a life-sized model of the Great Detective, whose unlit pipe, unfortunately, dangles from its hand rather than its mouth.

The genuine Holmes displayed a vast knowledge of the uses and properties of tobacco in solving cases. He was an avid lover of the pipe, cigar and cigarette, which prompted his equally famous friend and biographer, Dr John Watson, himself an occasional pipesmoker, to note bitterly that Holmes was

"…a self-poisoner by cocaine and tobacco."

Holmes would often sit for hours enshrouded in smoke, pondering cases, and kept his shag (strong coarse tobacco, best avoided these days) in the toe end of a Persian slipper, and in assorted tobacco-pouches littered across the mantelpiece of his bedroom.

Cigars were stashed in a coal-scuttle, as were pipes and tobacco. Perhaps his most disheartening custom was to smoke a pre-breakfast pipe filled with the dottles and plugs left from the smokes of the previous day, which had all been carefully dried and collected on a corner of the mantelpiece.

Keenly interested only in anything relevant to his work, Holmes wrote a famous monograph based on his long study of tobacco ash. "I found the ash of a cigar, which my special knowledge of tobacco ashes enables me to pronounce as an Indian cigar," he informed Watson in the course of the investigation, *The Boscombe Valley Murder*.

"I have, as you know, devoted some attention to this, and written a little monograph on the ashes of 140 different varieties of pipe, cigar, and cigarette

> **"Pipes are occasionally of extraordinary interest. Nothing has more individuality save, perhaps, watches and bootlaces." (Sherlock Holmes in 'The Yellow Face', by Arthur Conan Doyle)**

tobacco. Having found the ash, I then looked round and discovered the stump among the moss where he had tossed it. It was an Indian cigar, of the variety which are rolled in Rotterdam."

In *The Sign of the Four*, Holmes again demonstrated his expertise with the statement: "…there is as much difference between the black ash of a Trichinopoly and the white fluff of bird's eye as there is between a cabbage and a potato."

It appears, unfortunately, that Holmes's extensive knowledge of tobacco was largely ignored by the police at Scotland Yard, who have since made up for this startling oversight.

Perhaps the most interesting place I encountered was The Sherlock Holmes Collection at the Marylebone Library, Marylebone Road, NW1 (0171 798 1206), although this closed collection of magazines (including a complete run of the Strand Magazine up to 1930), society journals, comics, film and stage scripts, cuttings, photographs, complete bibliography and about 1,000 books on Arthur Conan Doyle and his creation can only be viewed by special appointment. You can also buy a series of eight prints celebrating the centenary of Holmes, greetings cards or a tea-towel.

"The collection was started in 1951 when, for the Festival of Britain, St Marylebone Borough Council held a Sherlock Holmes exhibition of printed materials, artefacts - such as the Stuffed Giant Rat of Sumatra and the now famous reconstruction of Sherlock Holmes's sitting room," explained curator, Catherine Cook.

"The books and magazines formed the nucleus of the present collection, while the sitting room was permanently transferred and displayed on the first floor of what is now the Sherlock Holmes Pub in Northumberland Street, when it opened in 1957."

Footweary, my brain reeling, I flagged down another black cab, hastening to James Taylor & Son at 4 Paddington Street, W1 (0171 935 4149). Established in 1857, the shoemaker now offers a range of Sherlock Holmes handmade footwear from about £680 plus VAT (boots from £780, plus VAT), each taking about three months in the making. You can choose between The Sherlock Shoe (an elastic sided Cambridge), The Lestrade (suede chukka boots) or the Mrs Hudson (high laced Balmoral).

My cab passed St Bartholomew's Hospital where Young Stamford introduced Watson to Holmes, and the British Museum - an invaluable source of information used by Holmes in solving several cases.

> **Nicotine gets its name from Jean Nicot, French Ambassador to Portugal in the 16th century. He presented seeds of the tobacco plant to Catherine de Medici, queen of Henry II of France, in 1561. She is reputed to be the first woman to popularise snuff-taking.**

I perceived that Holmes's old haunts - Simpson's restaurant in the Strand, the Café Royal - in front of which he was attacked by the henchmen of Baron Gruner in *The Illustrious Client*, and the Langham Hotel - were still thriving as we weaved our way through the traffic to the Diogenes Club (also known as The Athenium, in Waterloo Place off Pall Mall, SW1), of which Sherlock's brother, Mycroft, was a founding member.

It was there where I bumped into Peter Harkness, publisher of the *Sherlock Holmes Gazette*. "I received a letter from a retired police detective in America asking me for an endorsement from Sherlock Holmes for his new agency," he said. "I wrote back politely to break the news that he might be on the wrong trail."

If I hadn't already possessed one, a real Inverness cape, made from Harris Tweed, could have been purchased from Cording's, the gentlemen's outfitters at 19 Piccadilly, W1 (0171 734 0830) either off-the-peg for about £250-£300, or made-to-measure for around £400.

Sherlock Holmes Memorabilia Company, Baker Street.

Sherlock Holmes' study, Baker Street.

Later, I made my way to the Sherlock Holmes section in the Murder One bookshop, Charing Cross Road, WC2 (0171 734 3484), which stocks over 1000 different titles - anything in print on the subject in the English language. The most expensive item was the first bound volume of the complete works, signed by Conan Doyle, at £900.

Of the dozen or so different published versions of Sherlock Holmes's complete 56 stories and four novels in one volume, the best are those published by John Murray (out of print but available from good second-hand bookshops), Penguin and Wordsworth (complete facsimile, from the original set of *Strand Magazine*, including illustrations).

Undoubtedly, the most interesting title was the authoritive and entertaining *The Sherlock Holmes Encyclopedia* by Matthew E Bunson (Pavilion).

Round the corner was Chinatown, which had moved from its original location in Limehouse to the area between Leicester Square and Shaftesbury Avenue. There was no sign of the vile opium den, the Bar of Gold, from *The Man with the Twisted Lip*, but Holmes's vice, cocaine, was still readily available in the usual 7 per cent solution from well-dressed scoundrels skulking in the West End's night clubs and bars.

My next steps took me along Whitehall, where Holmes made frequent

Rodriguo de Jerez, one of Christopher Columbus's fellow explorers, took his first puff of the New World's version of the cigar in Cuba on 28 October 1492, and became the first European smoker in history. When he returned home he made the mistake of lighting up in public and was thrown into prison for three years by the Spanish Inquisition - becoming the world's first victim of the anti-smoking lobby.

visits, particularly to the diplomatic service and the headquarters of the Metropolitan Police at Scotland Yard. I was en route to The Sherlock Holmes Pub at 10 Northumberland Avenue, WC2 (0171 930 2644) where I met the co-manager, Robert Davie, in the first floor restaurant, the menu of which is in six languages, while peering through the glass wall into Holmes's recon-structed study.

"All the London walks come here," said Davie, who is convinced the tav-ern is haunted by the ghost of a cellarman. "On some days the police have to move on five or six coachloads."

A telephone call to a communicative friend revealed that Holmes's fame had reached the ether. A freely available news conference on the Great Detective can now be accessed on the Internet. In a query regarding Holmes's relationship with Watson, one net surfer replied: "There is as much canonical evidence that Holmes was gay as there is that he was Mr Spock's ancestor."

It all seemed too much and I dashed out to hail another four-wheeler. "Quick, take me to 221b Baker Street," I cried. "Which one?" asked the dri-ver, a cigarette dangling from the corner of his mouth.

Aha! That will be a three-pipe problem.

For more information:
The Sherlock Holmes Society of London,
> c/o Commander Geoffrey Stavert, 3 Outram Road, Southsea, Hants, PO5 1QP. Formed in 1951, it now has about 1400 members worldwide, holds six meetings a year in London, and an annual weekend out-of-town excursion.

The Arthur Conan Doyle Society,
> Grasmere, 35 Penfold Way, Dodleston, Chester, CH4 9ML.

Sherlock Holmes Gazette,
> 46 Purfield Road, Wargrave, Berkshire. RG10 8AR. 01734 402801. Back num-bers available.

Doorways to light up in

There you are in one of London's doorways, puffing away in the rain while the non-smokers remain inside, dry, hard at work or trying to enjoy themselves. Your only consolation is the pleasure gained from whatever you're smoking and the comradeship of fellow nicotine-lovers.

If you are one of the capital's habitual smokers, you're likely to spend even more of your time over the coming years banished from a growing number of London's buildings. So you may as well make the most of it and take a closer look at your surroundings.

While you're looking, it's best to avoid posting fag-ends through the letterbox (which was first introduced in London in about 1840), or dumping matches and other smokers' litter on the step or immediate vicinity, as this can make it awkward for any other smokers who follow in your wake.

Also, you shouldn't argue if someone comes out and asks you to move on, especially if you're in the doorway of a private house.

There are plenty more buildings to choose from, some with the typical six-panelled door of the early Georgian period, or 18th century Palladian-style doors with glass fanlights (from about 1720 these allowed light to penetrate London hallways for the first time). Other doors are adorned with Regency lion's head knockers; later came so many different designs, they'd fill a book on their own.

Then there's the simpler 19th century door (whose panels were reduced to 2-3) which eventually got decorated with Victorian and Edwardian glass.

According to the Royal Institute of British Architects, London has probably the greatest diversity of doors and doorcases in the UK, although few examples of the Medieval, Tudor and Early Stuart periods have managed to survive the Great Fire of 1666 or subsequent, thoughtless urban vandals.

Westminster Abbey's medieval door is still an impressive place to light up out of the wind, as long as you don't attempt to smoke inside the building. Even better, and quieter, is the doorway of the Abbey Gardens tucked round the back of this famous place of worship.

Doors have long been a vital clue to the wealth and pretensions of a build-

> **"To cease smoking is the easiest thing I ever did; I ought to know because I've done it a thousand times." (Mark Twain)**

ing's resident; witness the mock Doric columns guarding the entrances of London's surburban semi-detached houses. Or the flamboyantly over-the-top front entrances to multi-million pound houses in Bishops Avenue, between East Finchley and Hampstead. Not for nothing has it been known for years as the 'burglar's road'.

There's nothing pretentious about the most famous door in the world, Number 10, Downing Street, but very few people are likely to get closer to it than the guarded iron gates at the end of the road, in Whitehall.

I received my first invitation to a press conference at Downing Street a

The hand.

203

Money, Money, Money...

couple of years ago and cautiously walked up to the celebrated entrance, looking at the policeman on duty, wondering if I was supposed to knock. Seconds later, the door opened and I was pulled inside and to the side of the large hallway by a press officer who muttered in my ear: "Hurry! This way! The Greek Ambassador's right behind you."

Through this door have walked several Prime Ministers who enjoyed smoking, including Ramsey Macdonald, Stanley Baldwin, Winston Churchill and Harold Wilson. Downing Street's present (at the time of writing) incumbent, John Major, doesn't smoke.

Smoking is banned in all Government buildings in London, at least for the ordinary working members of the Civil Service. This hasn't stopped Ministers and VIPs lighting up during meetings at 10 Downing Street, no doubt because it would look bad to see them standing outside next to the policeman with a cigarette in their mouths.

The casual visitor to London is also not likely to get beyond the railings to admire any doorways in that other world-famous building, Buckingham Palace. If you are lucky enough to be invited to one of the Queen's annual Royal Garden Parties, you'll be pleased to know that you will be allowed to smoke. Just make sure you use the ashtrays provided.

You can't smoke in the Royal Mews but there are another 600 mews in London to light up in, most of them housing former stable blocks that date back to the time when the horse, not the car, was the city's main form of transport. In these small cobbled, hidden sidestreets you will find some of the capital's least-known doorways, but most of them are privately-owned so be on your best behaviour.

For instance, Montagu Mews North, W1, is a charming galleried yard in Marylebone, named after Mrs Elizabeth Montague, who came to London in 1781. She was often referred to as the 'original bluestocking' (a derogatory term for a pretentiously intellectual woman), as she used to lavishly entertain writers and artists. One of her guests used to attend the gatherings in informal attire, wearing blue worsted stockings instead of the usual black silk ones, which led to the social evenings being gently mocked as 'blue stocking'.

Every May Day, Mrs Montague gave a great feast for chimney-sweeps "so they might enjoy one good day a year." Nobody knows if she also provided them with free tobacco.

A short walk will take you to 94 Baker Street, W1, the former site of the Beatles' famous Apple shop which opened in a blaze of publicity on December 7 1967 and closed, after giving away its remaining stock, on 31 July 1968.

No. 3 Savile Row, W1, was the headquarters of the Liverpool supergroup's Apple Corps. On its roof, the Beatles gave their famous, unannounced live show at lunchtime on Thursday 30 January 1969. Traffic came to a standstill in all the nearby streets while office workers and passers by stood around, enjoying the music.

After 42 minutes, constables from Savile Row police station ordered the lads to cease playing, but it wasn't too late for the rest of us as the event was recorded for posterity in the film, *Let It Be*.

Another good doorway to stand in, preferably while you're smoking something impregnated with garlic, is 138 Piccadilly, W1, as this house to the left of the Hard Rock Café was Dracula's main lair while he prowled the capital in search of victims. Today 'ole red eyes' would probably join the permanent queue next door for a bite of rare hamburger, and get his ears punctured by the loud music.

> "You are quite a philosopher, Sam," said Mr Pickwick.
> "It runs in the family, I b'lieve, sir," replied Mr Weller.
> "My fahter's wery much in that line, now. If my mother-in-law blows him up, he whistles. She flies in a passion, and breaks his pipe; he steps out and gets another. Then she screams wery loud, and falls into 'sterics; and he smokes very comfortably till she comes to agin. That's philosophy, sir, ain't it?" (Charles Dickens, 'The Pickwick Papers')

> **Smoker-friendly London streetnames: Ash (Close, Court, Croft and Grove), Churchill (Avenue, Court, Gardens, Mews, Place, Road, Terrace, Walk and Way), Columbus Courtyard, Hawkins (Close, Court and Road), Raleigh (Avenue, Close, Court, Drive, Gardens, House, Mews, Road, Street and Way), Tobacco (Dock and Quay).**

Bram Stoker's bloodthirsty literary creation has been well-played in Hammer film's gory epics by Christopher Lee, who enjoys pipes and cigars. His chief adversary, Professor Van Helsing, was usually portrayed by the late Peter Cushing, a former Pipe Smoker of the Year.

The love affair between Miss Helene Hanff of New York and Messrs Marks and Co, sellers of rare and secondhand books, at 84 Charing Cross Road was the subject of a best-selling book, and film. The bookshop has long gone, but why not light up in its former doorway, for the memory. We believe she enjoyed a cigarette.

According to Ike Ong, the managing director of Skoob Books (11a - 17 Sicilian Avenue, WC1. 0171 404 3063) who used to work at Joseph Poole's when it briefly took over 84 Charing Cross Road, most of London's second-hand bookshops still allow smoking, even if their first-hand rivals (Dillons, Foyles, Blackwells, Waterstones, WH Smith etc), don't.

Ike should know. He also publishes the excellent *Skoob Directory of Secondhand Bookshops* in the British Isles, now in its sixth edition, smokes like a chimney and will allow you to light up and browse.

The smallest police station in Britain can be found in the bottom south-east corner of Trafalgar Square. There's just enough room inside for two coppers, if they're good friends. Lighting up in its tiny doorway won't get you arrested, although you may become another target of the perishing pigeons. Try not to drop your butts in the fountains, as this makes them too soggy for other more desperate smokers to light.

If you enjoy smoking near water, try the entrance to the Westbourne Grove public lavatories at the junction of Colville Road, W11. The triangular site accommodates toilets at its wider end and a friendly florist at its pointed bit.

Ramesses II, Sainsbury's Homebase do it yourself store in Warwick Road, W8, was vilified by journalists in June 1987, who asked, "is this architecture, and if it isn't, then what is it?" Why not light up in its Egyptian-style colonnade and decide for yourself.

Another temple (well it looks like one, anyway) of London architecture is Marco Polo House in Queenstown Road, W8, where you can try to figure out how to get inside. The main entrance is not immediately obvious.

If you can't get into Imagination's headquarters at 25 Store Street, WC1, it's a pity as there's more behind the Edwardian facade than meets the eye. If you are around at Christmas, light up in a doorway opposite, and admire the company's fabulous annual Yuletide display.

City House in Britton Street, Smithfield, EC1, looks for all the world like a windmill merged with a French chateau, or a yacht's sails stuck on the end of the Titanic.

On the other side of the City, lots of smokers nip out of the Lloyd's of London Insurance building (Lime Street, EC3), one of the world's most famous financial institutions, designed by the Richard Rodgers Partnership. But then the structure is inside-out, anyway. It must be an interesting job being a broker, bumping up the insurance premiums for smokers.

If you're on the South Bank under Waterloo Bridge, shelter in a concrete doorway out of the wind to observe the roof of the Hayward Gallery, on which there's a kinetic neon sculpture which changes colour, depending on which way the wind blows. It could be better situated elsewhere, in front of the House of Commons.

In Kew Gardens you will find a 163 foot high, ten-storied wooden Pagoda, one of the great landmarks of South London. It is not open to the public because the staircase, which takes up most of the interior space, is only wide enough to allow one person to ascend or descend at a time.

The BT Tower (originally known as the Post Office Tower when it first

You can't smoke here - what a load of rubbish!

> **"When smoking began to go out of fashion, learning began to go out of fashion also." (Richard Porson, celebrated scholar).**

opened in 1965) is, at 620 feet high, one of London's tallest buildings and dominates the West End's skyline. It has 34 floors, the top one of which revolves for VIP visitors. I used to be its PR manager, years ago, and smoked several cigars at official functions watching London circle by.

A couple of decades ago the revolving floor used to house a restaurant, but it was closed after a bomb attack by the IRA. The other reason BT gives for not reopening the tower for the public is that it only has two lifts so London's Fire Brigade won't allow it (because if one is faulty, there's no safe way of getting people down in an emergency).

When you stand puffing away on the pavement in front of the main entrance, wave to the security men watching you on the closed-circuit camera. They may even let you finish your smoke, before asking you to move on.

The editorial floors of Express Newspapers' new-ish headquarters on the south side of Blackfriars Bridge are smoker-friendly, although cigars and pipes are firmly discouraged. But then this is probably true of the offices of most of Britain's national media. Stressed-out journalists, especially when they're close to a deadline, have long found their concentration helped by a smoke and prefer not to waste time dashing outside.

There is at least one unofficial smoking room in Broadcasting House, Portland Place, W1, despite the BBC ban of smoking throughout the well-known building. The official smoking room, if it still exists, is somewhere in the basement, but nobody bothers to go down there.

Instead, you'll find producers and other radio personnel smoking outside on the roof, or in a certain office above the 3rd floor. Ironically, one of the male smokers who enjoys a sly cigarette in that same unofficial smoking room is also the person who signed the ban.

The entrance to the Law Courts in the Strand is a good place to observe aggrieved former couples trying to settle alimony disputes, while they smoke to calm their nerves. Famous plaintiffs in divorce cases are always snapped up by press photographers, many of whom smoke while waiting for their chance of an exclusive.

A stroll up Fleet Street and Ludgate Hill will take you to the Old Bailey where you can stand outside and guess who's about to come up in front of the judge in the Central Criminal Court.

Just watch that you don't end up there yourself, for enjoying a smoke in public.

The Suite Room, City of London.

Smokers in London

> Some English chroniclers of 1618 claim Sir Walter Raleigh was still smoking on the executioner's block.

Start in Leicester Square, with the statue of Charles Spencer Chaplin (1889-1977), the London-born comedian famous for his baggy trousers, bowler hat, cane and little moustache. In his early silent films, he could often be seen smoking a cigarette.

Walk south through Trafalgar Square to Whitehall, where you will find on the left a small statue of Sir Walter Raleigh (1552-1618), the Elizabethan adventurer who first popularised tobacco in London.

On the same lawn, you'll find another statue, of the great British General Montgomery (1887-1976), who once told Churchill, "I don't drink. I do not smoke. I sleep a great deal. That is why I am in one hundred per cent form." Churchill replied, "I drink a great deal. I sleep little, and I smoke cigar after cigar. That is why I am in two hundred per cent form."

Near the Post Office at the end of Whitehall is a dusty-looking building with a shop on the ground floor, No. 38 Parliament Street. In the 1920s, visitors were greeted by personally-signed photographs of King George V and the Duke of York, then offered a cigarette from a silver case with an inscription which indicated it was a present from the king.

More famous than Fidel Castro for his love of cigars, Sir Winston Spencer Churchill (1874-1965) has a statue erected to his memory on the corner of Parliament Square, half-facing the House of Commons. It was unveiled by Lady Randolph Churchill in 1973.

Another statue of Sir Winston, this time with a cigar in his hand, sitting and chatting with former American President Franklin D Roosevelt, can be found on a bench near Aspreys, 165 New Bond Street. This is believed to be the only statue in London where you can see someone actually enjoying a smoke.

Another man who gave his name to Havana cigars was Simon Bolivar (1783-1830), who devoted his life to the cause of freeing the South American countries from Spanish domination. His statue can be found on the southeast corner of Belgrave Square. On the plinth are the words: "I am convinced that England alone is capable of protecting the world's precious rights as she is great, glorious and wise." Let us hope this is still true when it comes to the rights of British smokers.

Some believe there are probably more statues of Queen Victoria (1819-1901) in London than any other personage in the history of the human race. One of them can be found under the porchway of the National Portrait Gallery annexe at 15 Carlton House Terrace. Although she discouraged smokers most of her life (her son, Edward VII, said the famous words, after her death: "Gentlemen, you may smoke."), she is believed to have taken up the habit in later life, to ward off midges in Balmoral.

Further north, the International Student's Hostel at 1 Park Crescent at the corner of Marylebone Road and facing Regent's Park has a memorial bust of President John Fitzgerald Kennedy, who was born in 1917 and assassinated in 1963.

Most people have heard how Kennedy, the day before he signed the USA's official blockade of Cuba, asked one of his aides to buy as many Havana cigars as possible.

No.18 Park Lane was once the London home of the biggest business man in 19th century Britain, Whitaker Wright. It has since been replaced by an extension of the Londonderry Hotel. Wright was sentenced to seven years' penal servitude for transferring capital from one company to another to give the appearance of assets, but never reached prison. A few minutes after the trial he lit up a cigar, gave his gold watch and a few other possessions to his friends, and bit on a cyanide capsule.

On the north side of Fleet Street is the church of St Dunstan-in-the-West, over whose door is a figure of Elizabeth I. She may have taxed tobacco, but at least she didn't ban it.

Sir Winston Churchill and Roosevelt.

> During the Blitz of London a German bomb destroyed the Dunhill shop. At two o'clock in the morning, having surveyed the damage, the manager of the shop rushed to the phone to inform Sir Winston Churchill, "Your cigars are safe, sir."

Mary Frith, also known as Moll Cutpurse, lived and died in what is now 134 Fleet Street "within 2 doors of the Globe Tavern over against the Conduit." One of the 17th century's most colourful underworld characters, she dressed as a man, carrying a sword and smoking a long clay-pipe. At various times she was a pickpocket, forger, receiver, highwaywoman and transvestite. Further along on the north-west side of Ludgate Circus is a tablet with a relief portrait of Edgar Wallace (1875-1932), the prolific crime novelist and journalist, and a noted smoker.

North from London Bridge is King William Street, to the east of which is the Monument to the Great Fire of London, 1666. This fluted Doric column is 202 feet high and exactly 202 feet from the point in Pudding Lane where the fire started. About 46 years ago, it was the temporary shelter of a tame mouse, fed by visitors, which died when a thoughtless smoker dropped his cigar butt, still lit, on its head.

A bronze bust of Samuel Pepys (1633-1703), the great London diarist is in Seething Lane Gardens, on the site of his old home. During the Black Plague, Pepys used tobacco to ward off the terrible smell of death.

Over the centuries since that dreadful period, London has been the home of many famous smokers, including the actor Charles Laughton (1899-1962), who lived at 15 Percy Street, W1, from 1928-1931.

James Joyce (1882-1941) lived in 28 Campden Grove, Kensington, W8, in 1931. Another nicotine-lover, Alfred, Lord Tennyson (1809-1892), the great poet, lived in 9 Upper Belgrave Street, SW1, in 1880 and 1881.

JB Priestley (1894-1984), the pipe-smoking novelist, playwright and essayist lived at 3 The Grove, Highgate, N6, when he was not on the Isle of Wight. The fine writer, and poet, Robert Graves (1895-1985), a cigarette smoker, was born at 1 Lauriston Road, Wimbledon, SW19.

One of the most elegant smokers of his time, usually via a cigarette-holder, Sir Noel Coward (1899-1973), songwriter, actor and playwright, was born at 131 Waldegrave Road, Teddington, Middlesex. Another musical smoker, Wolfgang Amadeus Mozart (1756-1791), lived for a while at 121 Ebury Street, SW1. Pipe-smoker George Frederic Handel (1685-1759) lived at 22 Brook Street, W1.

England's greatest novelist, Charles Dickens (1812-1870), smoked and lived at 48 Doughty Street, WC1. In 1849, Karl Marx (1818-1883) moved to London where he remained for the rest of his life, smoking. He lived at 28 Dean Street, W1.

Sir Walter Raleigh statue, Whitehall.

30

PLACES

To Avoid

Smokers are not welcome on the tube, buses, in auditoriums of theatres, cinemas and concert halls, or in any of the following places:

Burlington's Park Café Chiswick House, Burlington Lane, W4
Coffee Gallery 23 Museum Street, WC1
HaVoc (private hire river boat) Wen Lock Basin, Whale Road, N1
Museum Street Café 47 Museum Street, WC1
The Orangery Kensington Palace, Kensington Gardens, W8
Oshabasho Café Highgate Wood, Muswell Hill Road, N10
Primrose Patisserie 136 Regent's Park Road, NW1
Queen's Park Pavillion Café Kingswood Avenue, NW6
Villandry Dining Room, 89 Marylebone High Street, W1
Wagamama, 4 Streatham Street, Off Coptic Street, WC1

Warming up in a City doorway.

31

LAST WORD

by Jeffrey Bernard

Photograph: Bob Barknay.

London has always been one of the bastions of smokers, but now the world and the authorities have decided to persecute us it is in serious danger of no longer being, for the smoker at least, a free city.

I've always thought one's choice is bloody sacrosanct.

The people who looked after me when I collapsed in north Africa a couple of weeks ago told me later that they knew I was out of danger as soon as I asked for a cigarette. This was the first sign that they could take me off the drip. My nurse said that she knew if I went more than half an hour without a cigarette then I was getting seriously ill. It's a barometer of my good health, plenty of fags.

I started smoking the day after I left school in 1948, when I was 16. I used to smoke cigars occasionally but I don't like them anymore. Although I'm a heavy smoker, one of my brothers smokes a pipe and oddly enough I find that can be offensive. It's too much.

Incidentally, I've noticed that girls that are very difficult to get into bed usually don't smoke. Women who are healthily promiscuous, not to the extent of being whores or something, nearly always are smokers. It's odd that. I suppose it's something to do with temperament. Non-smokers tend to be more judgemental.

There's a whole generation of puritans growing up which I can't bear the thought of. Thank God I won't be here to put up with them all in twenty years' time.

The next thing is these anti-smoking people will move on, inevitably, to drinking and people will start talking absolute crap about passive drunks. I know drunks are a bore but at least smokers aren't.

Soho, August 1996.

Smokers & The Law

Britain, unlike many other countries, has so far refrained from passing laws prohibiting or restricting smoking in "public places". In this context "public places" means any place to which the public may have access, rather than the strict legal definition based on who owns the property.

Legally, a public place would be somewhere like the municipal park, council-owned library, a school - or any other place that is owned "in public". It would not include a pub, restaurant, hotel, or office block.

> "It is the passion of all proper people, and he who lives without tobacco has nothing to live for. Not only does it refresh and cleanse men's brains, but it guides their souls in the ways of virtue, and by it one learns to be a man of honour."
> (Moliere, on tobacco, in 'Don Juan')

Policewoman and young smoker.

CURRENT LEGISLATION

London Transport employees and the general public are required by law not to smoke when travelling on the underground or waiting on the platforms at underground stations.

Smoking is prohibited by law in kitchens where foodstuffs are prepared for sale to the public, e.g a restaurant. The prohibition does not apply to the areas where people may consume food. In addition a person working behind a bar is required not to smoke. If, however, they are on the customers' side of the bar, they can.

There is also a legislative requirement for smoking to be prohibited where inflammable chemicals are present.

BRITISH RAIL

When the overland rail network was nationalised, and became British Rail, its governing Board was given the power to pass by-laws without having to seek the approval of Parliament. Some of the regional divisions within British Rail have prohibited smoking on all of their trains. They have their own inspectors, some of whom travel in plain-clothes, to gather evidence on anyone breaking the ban, with a view to prosecution.

The legality of the smoking ban on Network SouthCentral trains (the main division serving the south-east coast of England, and London) is being tested through the British courts, and may even go to the European Court of Human Rights. If this happens, it is unlikely that a decision will be made on the legality of the smoking ban until towards the end of 1997.

SMOKING IN THE WORKPLACE

At the beginning of 1996, a new regulation on smoking in the workplace came into force. This requires that "rest rooms and rest areas shall include suitable arrangements to protect non-smokers from discomfort caused by tobacco smoke". The regulation does not apply to workstations.

VOLUNTARY BANS

Some places have banned smoking even though there is no legal requirement for them so to do. While few take out a private prosecution against a person for breaching the ban, it should be noted that some bus companies have. People are therefore advised to abide by any signs telling them not to smoke.

A British survey on 'Smoking at Work' published in 1996 listed the following disadvantages experienced by the respondent's employees as a result of banning smoking in their place of work:
* the fact that employees had to physically leave their place of work to smoke
* the time smokers spent away from work to have a cigarette
* the bad weather conditions that smokers may have to endure when smoking outside buildings
* the restrictions placed on employees' freedom of choice
* the possibility of disciplinary action being taken against those who breach the policy
* the negative image of smokers congregating outside buildings
* the risk of fire from the poor disposal of illicitly-smoked cigarettes
* a lack of morale and increased stress among smokers when faced with restrictions.
This said, around one-third of all respondents to the survey said that their smoking policy had caused no real difficulties. So what happened to the other two-thirds, ie the majority?

APPENDIX B

Introducing FOREST

In the late 1970s, a man was standing on a platform at Reading Station in Berkshire, quietly smoking in the open air as he waited for his train. Suddenly, he was verbally abused by a young woman incensed by his smoking even though she had the rest of the platform to herself and no need to be anywhere near him.

From this incident grew FOREST, although the smokers' rights group didn't adopt that formal title until 1981. From the outset, it publicly declared a willingness to accept donations from tobacco companies, but has refused to advertise tobacco products through its publications.

FOREST exists to promote equal rights for smokers alongside non-smokers. Whether a person smokes or not is irrelevant. What is important is that those who do should receive the same rights and respect in society as everyone else.

FOREST's objectives are to promote equal rights for smokers, and greater tolerance between smokers and non-smokers; to defend freedom of choice for adults who wish to smoke tobacco, and the rights of those who wish to make provision for smokers on their premises; to oppose discrimination against smokers wherever it may occur; to increase public awareness of the scientific complexities of the smoking debate, and to enable people to put the issue into its proper perspective.

To meet these objectives, FOREST works in three main areas: research, advice, and campaigns.

Examining the various arguments on the different sides of the smoking debate is vital for any organisation promoting equality. Research is fundamental, for the public rarely sees the full report on a study of smoking. Nor is it usually fully informed about its content, methodological failings, or contradictions with other research in a similar field.

Instead it is given distorted facts, half-truths and, all too often, downright lies.

Research is also vital to develop the advisory capacity of FOREST, especially to businesses that want to introduce or revise a smoking policy. Thus, FOREST has researched literature on sick building syndrome, indoor air pollutants, and ventilation.

Finding out where they are welcome, or what to do if they discover they are not, is the kind of practical advice needed by today's smokers.

Campaigning is also an important part of FOREST's work, on its own or with others whose businesses are affected by anti-smoking policies. Persuading others to adopt commonsense policies (such as introducing smoking and non-smoking areas), getting them to show a little more tolerance to those who have different preferences to themselves, and ensuring that everyone has a better understanding of each other's needs, is at the heart of FOREST's work.

Through a growing range of information leaflets, fact sheets, and more detailed analyses of different aspects of the smoking debate, FOREST helps people to find solutions which accommodate, not solutions which discriminate.

If you would like to know more, write to: FOREST, 2 Grosvenor Gardens, London SWIW 0DH. Tel: 0171 823 6550. Fax: 0171 823 4534.

Closed. What a drag.

A Walk Round London's Parks by Hunter Davies (Zenith, 1983)

Britain - A Lonely Planet Travel Survival Kit by Richard Everist, Bryn Thomas and Tony Wheeler (Lonely Planet, April 1995)

Skoob Directory of Secondhand Bookshops in the British Isles (Skoob Books, 6th edition, 1996)

London Is Stranger Than Fiction by Peter Jackson (reprinted from the Evening News, 1951)

London Explorer by Peter Jackson (reprinted from the Evening News, 1953)

Pipesmokers Welcome Guide 1996 (The Pipesmokes' Council)

Down Your Way by Bryan Johnston (Methuen, 1990)

Walking London by Andrew Duncan (New Holland, 1991)

Follies by Gwyn Headley & Wim Meulenkamp (Jonathan Cape, 1986)

Encyclopedia of Britain by Bamber Gascogine (Macmillan, 1994)

The Macmillan Encyclopedia (Macmillan, 1981)

Fodor's London Companion by Louise Nicholson (Fodor, 1987) - an excellent book

The Cambridge Guide to Literature in English by Ian Ousby (Cambridge University Press, 1993)

London Doors by Charles Viney, introduction by Steven Parissien (Oldcastle Books, 1989)

The Black Plaque Guide to London by Felix Barker and Denise Silvester-Carr (Constable, 1987)

The Night Side of London by Robert Machray (John McQueen, 1902)

London by Samantha Hardingham (Ellipsis, 1995)

The Mews of London by Barbara Rosen and Wolfgang Zuckermann (Webb & Bower, 1982)

The Humidor issues 1 and 2 (JJ Fox (St James's Ltd), 1996)

Sir Walter Raleigh by John Winton (Michael Joseph, 1975)

Holy Smoke by G Cabrera Infante (Faber, 1985)

London Statues and Monuments by Margaret Baker (Shire Publications, 4th edition, 1995)

84 Charing Cross Road by Helene Hanff (Warner Books, 1976)

The Blue Plaque Guide to London by Caroline Dakers (Macmillan, 1981)

London As It Might Have Been by Felix Barker and Ralph Hyde (John Murray, 1995)

A Rennaissance of Pleasure by Zino Davidoff (private edition)

The Beatles London by Piet Schreuders, Mark Lewisohn & Adam Smith (Hamlyn, 1994)

The Blue Plaque Guide to London Homes by Martin Hall (Queen Anne Press, 1976)

Crash the Ash some joy for the beleaguered smoker, filtered by Auberon Waugh (Quiller Press, 1994)

Tobaccoland by Carl Avery Werner (Tobacco Leaf Publishing, NY, 1930)

A History of Smoking by Count Corti (George G Harrap, 1931)

List of English Heritage plaques erected since publication of the Blue Plaque Guide (English Heritage press office)

BIBLIOGRAPHY

Smoking and Its Enemies: A Short History of 500 Years of the Use and Prohibition of Tobacco *by Sean Gabb* (FOREST, 1990)

In Search of Dracula *by Ramond T McNally and Radu Florescu* (Robson Books, 1995)

The Sherlock Holmes Encyclopedia *by Matthew E Bunson* (Pavilion Books, 1995)

The London of Sherlock Holmes *by Michael Harrison* (David & Charles, 1972)

Adult Comics, an introduction, *by Roger Sabin* (Routledge, 1993)

Of Mice and Magic: A History of American Animated Cartoons *by Leonard Maltin* (New American Library, 1980)

The Officially Politically Correct Dictionary & Handbook *by Henry Beard and Christopher Cerf* (Grafton, 1992)

The World Encyclopedia of Comics *edited by Maurice Horn* (New English Library, 1976)

The Comic Book *by Paul Sassienie* (Ebury Press, 1994)

Double Take and Fade Way *by Leslie Halliwell* (Grafton, 1987)

The Ultimate Beatles Encyclopedia *by Bill Harry* (Virgin, 1992)

The Annotated Sherlock Holmes *edited with notes by William S Baring-Gould* (Clarkson N Potter, 1967)

The Oxford Dictionary of Quotations (Oxford University Press, 3rd edition, 1979)

My 60s *by Jan Olofsson* (Taschen, 1994)

Brewer's Dictionary of Phrase and Fable (Cassell, 1971, Centenary Edition)

Ready Steady Go! Growing up in the Fifties and Sixties *by Chris Tarrant* (Hamlyn, 1994)

Good Beer Guide 1994 *edited by Jeff Evans* (CAMRA Books, 1994)

Room at the Inn *by Jill Adam* (CAMRA Books, 1996)

Evening Standard London Pub Guide 1995 *by Angus McGill, cartoons by Frank Dickens* (Pavilion Books, 1994)

City Pack London *by Louise Nicholson* (AA Publishing, 1996)

The Cigar Companion, a A Connoisseur's Guide *by Anwer Bati* (Apple Press, 1993)

Smoke Rings and Roundelays *compiled by Wilfed Partington* (John Castle, 1924)

The Face of London *by Harold P Clunn* (Simpkin Marshall, 1935)

Everybody's Historic London *by Jonathan Kiek* (Quiller Press, 1990)

The Connoiseur's Book of the Cigar *by Zino Davidoff* (McGraw-Hill, 1984)

The Daily Mirror Old Codgers Little Black Book No.3 (1977)

Time Out Guide to London (Penguin, 1995)

The Gentle Art of Smoking *by Alfred Dunhill* (G P Putnam, 1954)

A Puff of Smoke *by Ian Scarlet* (Robert Lewis, 1987)

The Guinness Book of Records 1997 (Guinness Publishing 1996)

FURTHER READING:

Free Choice   the bi-monthly newsletter of Britain's smokers' rights group, FOREST. Also, a wide range of other publications on different aspects of the smoking debate. For subscription details and a publications catalogue contact: FOREST, 2 Grosvenor Gardens, London SW1W ODH. Tel: 0171 823 6550. Fax: 0171 823 4534.

Pipesmokers Welcome Guide
- a free, glossy, informative annual publication available from most good tobacconists or by sending a self-addressed, stamped, A5 envelope to The Pipesmokers' Council, 19 Elrington Road, Hackney, London E8 3BJ.

JJ Fox's The Humidor
- a cigar newsletter published three times a year and distributed via the tobacco departments in Harrods and Selfridges. Join the free mailing list by sending your name and address to JJ Fox (St James's) Ltd, 19 St James's Street, London SW1A 1ES.

Thank you for smoking
by Christopher Buckley (Andre Deutsch, 1995), a very funny novel about the chief spokesman for the academy of tobacco studies

The Ultimate Pipe Book
by Richard Carleton Hacker (Andrew Deutsch, 1995) - probably the best guide to the subject currently in print.

The Ultimate Cigar Book
by Richard Carleton Hacker (Autumngold Publishing, Beverley Hills, California, 1993).

Cigar Chic   a woman's perpective by Tomima Edmark (The Summit Publishing Group, Arlington, Texas, 1995) - an entertaining, classy read that fits nicely in the pocket.

The Illustrated History of Cigars
by Bernard Le Roy and Maurice Szafran (Harold Starke, 1993) - sumptious coffee table book.

Pipes and Tobaccos magazine
- published quarterly by Spec-Conmm International, Inc., 3000 Highwoods Boulevard, Suite 300, Raleigh, NC 27604-1029, USA. Foreign subscriptions, $24 a year.

Smoke   by Andrew Jefford, (Evening Standard £4.95). Selection from his informative, amusing weekly column in ES magazine.

last but not least...

Cigar Aficionado magazine,
- probably the most influential publication in the recent history of smoking. Classy, authoritive, enormous and available four times a year for $26.95 in US funds from PO Box 51091, Boulder, Co 80323-1091, USA.

If you are unable to get these publications in your local bookshop, you may find copies on sale at JJ Fox, Harrods or Selfridges, or you may be able to obtain them direct from the publishers.

Sam, Tower Bridge.